# YOU CAN DO IT!

*To Patricia, Elle, Miranda, and Madeline.*
*That's how I know God loves me, because He gave me you!*

# CONTENTS

**CHAPTER ZERO**

"You're a Filipina"      1

**CHAPTER ONE**

History Is Short      19

**CHAPTER TWO**

The Conspiracy Theory of Conspiracy Theories      45

**CHAPTER THREE**

3+2=5; True, but It Could Be Super Racist      65

**CHAPTER FOUR**

Punching Sideways      81

**CHAPTER FIVE**

"I Saw a Sketch on *Saturday Night Live* Last Night..."
—President George Bush      97

**CHAPTER SIX**

"Never Let a Good Crisis Go to Waste"
—Winston Churchill      115

**CHAPTER SEVEN**

"Support the Troops!"      131

**CHAPTER EIGHT**

"There Are Some Things That Are Worse Than Death"
—Robert Kennedy Jr.      137

# CONTENTS

**CHAPTER NINE**

When the Bullied Become the Bullies 151

**CHAPTER TEN**

The Patron Saint of Medicine 169

**CHAPTER ELEVEN**

Global Barbecuing 189

**CHAPTER TWELVE**

Running Out of Actual Terrorists 201

**CHAPTER THIRTEEN**

I Don't Want to Be Lenny Bruce 219

**CHAPTER FOURTEEN**

But There Is More Than Hope 235

*NOTES* 251

# YOU
# CAN
# DO IT!

# CHAPTER ZERO

# "YOU'RE A FILIPINA"

*"If you go to America, all you and your children will ever be is maids."*

Look, I'd like to get to *me* as quickly as possible, as this is *my* book. But I must apologize because before I can do that, I have to supply some needed backstory. Before we make the leap to me and my life and my hopes and dreams and aspirations, we must first wade our way through adultery, a military scandal, and an underage girl.

So here goes. Welcome to my book.

"You're a Filipina. If you go to America, all you and your children will ever be is maids!" This was probably not the most positive or inspiring opining one could hope to hear but it was precisely what my great-grandfather, Lolo Estacio, warned his daughter (my maternal grandmother), Victoria, who was then pregnant with my mother. Heeding her father's advice, Victoria never ventured to her husband's homeland, the United States of America.

Before my mother, Pilar, was born, US Army soldier Stanley Ulysses Monroe had left the Philippines for good. She would have to have a childhood and try to survive World War II without a father.

1

So, how did my mother's father, Stanley, end up in the Philippines anyway? The family rumor, always repeated in hushed tones, was that Stanley was something of a rascal.

Michigan-born Stanley Monroe found a small studio apartment in which to live. The apartment building provided services — a shared bathroom, a shared kitchen, and a shared landlord's wife. Upon discovery by her husband, Stanley, long opposed to facial disfigurement, hightailed it to the nearest Greyhound station where his money took him as far as Texas. After his family declined to help, he decided to *be all he could be* and joined the US Army.

Now in uniform and with basic training completed, Private Monroe reported to his first duty station and was given his first assignment.

As is customary, army privates are given the lowly job of driving the jeeps for their superiors, which is how (and definitely why) most generals die in war...being driven by morons. Private moron Monroe, newly uniformed idiot, was assigned to drive the base captain's wife. So drive the captain's wife he did. Shortly thereafter, he was caught driving her, apparently in a horizontal position while lying on top of her, in his superior officer's bedroom. You see, Stanley Monroe was apparently slightly handsome with a come-hither smile. Obviously, unpleased with Stanley's new and unapproved additional duty, the base captain found a way to remove this embarrassing and compromising overachiever by transferring the soldier to another base. Not just any base would do, but preferably a base in dense jungle where one could die of dengue fever, malaria, or better yet, be killed by native warriors with Kris knives whose blades were infused with scorpion venom, giving their enemies wounds that never heal.

That's how Private Stanley Monroe wound up in the Philippine islands.

Not long after, Private Monroe met my maternal grandmother, Victoria Estacio, and against her family's wishes, she eloped with Stanley at the ripe old age of fifteen. They would have five kids together. The youngest "babe" would be my mother, Pilar. She was still in Victoria's womb when Stanley abandoned the family. Pilar was born February 19, 1929.

Supposedly at first, Stanley wanted to bring his family to the United States — but this was the late 1920s — and his Midwestern Michigan family considered his Filipino family (perhaps because they were short but more likely because they were brown) an unfortunate embarrassment to them. The hopeful side of me would like to think it was because Stanley's family must have worried about how these small brown people, with their small brown toes, could easily get frostbit in the cold winters of Michigan as the reason why they didn't want him to bring the family over. But being a man who used to gamble with Norm Macdonald, I'd wager it was more likely that my great-grandparents were racist old white assholes.

That is when Lolo Estacio uttered his infamous words, "If you go to America, all you and your children will ever be is maids!"

So stay she did. And Stanley never returned to the Philippines.

As is most common in Filipino society, my lola (Tagalog for "grandmother"), Victoria, never spoke ill of Stanley or expressed any bitterness to Pilar or to any of Pilar's four elder siblings. (That's right, they had five kids together, and he still left!) It's the kind of long-suffering common to my people from the Philippines. They would rather suffer inwardly than deal with their problems outwardly. For four hundred years they lived under Spanish rule and all the unimaginable cruelty that that rule entailed. I've yet to hear a story of Spanish rule that had a sweet side to it. It's always "Start speaking our language, believe in our God, take our diseases while smiling, or we'll stomp you with our horses and then impale you."

Even the name, Philippines (the nation archipelago of over four thousand islands, maybe more, nobody knows), has nothing to do with the indigenous island itself. In fact, it was named after King Philip II of Spain, and they have no woke plans to change it anytime soon.

My mother and her two sisters starved but survived the Japanese occupation of the Philippines. She had two brothers, however, who did not.

Pilar's eldest brother, Bill, was drafted in the US Army under a deal with President Franklin D. Roosevelt that allowed non-US-citizen Filipinos to enlist to fight the invading Japanese.

You see, most Americans know that the Japanese attacked Pearl Harbor on December 7, 1941, as President Roosevelt declared. But very few non-Filipinos know that the very next day (just nine hours later, to be exact), December 8, 1941, the Empire of Japan attacked the Philippines. That was *our* day of infamy and our day of getting our asses bombed. The United States Army, led by General Douglas MacArthur in the Pacific theater, was quickly being overrun by Japanese forces. There would be no reinforcements or much needed supplies for MacArthur's besieged battalions. They weren't told to try to defeat the Japanese onslaught by US Army Command. They were simply told to hold out and delay the Japanese Army for as long as possible. MacArthur consolidated all his units on the Bataan Peninsula and the island of Corregidor. This would be their last line of defense.

Like all invading forces over the course of history, the Japanese considered themselves liberators. I don't know for a fact, but I would bet that the Japanese even had some liberty-sounding name for their invasion, like Operation Filipino Freedom!

However named, the battle for the Bataan Peninsula, which started on January 7, 1942, would be one of the most brutal and bloody battles of the entire war. It was a living hell. They held out for over three months, longer than anyone could have imagined, including the Japanese, who didn't take kindly to those trying to limit their ever-expanding empire. Finally, after stalling the Japanese invasion forces long enough for MacArthur to make his getaway, on April 9, 1942, US soldiers surrendered.

The Japanese would take US Army personnel prisoner, even though they considered "surrender" to be a great disgrace worse than death. However, for Filipinos, their fellow Asians, that was another story. They were not granted the same measure of Japanese "kindness" and most were not usually taken prisoner but killed on the spot. Those surviving US and Filipino troops had to walk the infamous Bataan Death March. The Japanese gave instructions for captured US Army personnel to "*KŌSHIN!*" or march! An astounding 75,000 American and Filipino prisoners of war, given no water or food and in the blazing heat of the Philippine jungle, were forced to make the arduous trek on foot. An estimated 500 to 650 Americans died during the march. No one knows how many Filipinos died. Estimates are anywhere from 5,000 to 18,000. If a soldier fell down, from the intense heat or lack of hydration, they would be killed by a Japanese soldier's bayonet.[1]

I'm not 100 percent sure if my uncle Bill was in the war-crime-ridden Battle of Bataan, but it makes sense that he was. Because it was there in Bataan that he was captured and, along with other surviving US soldiers and those brave but unfortunate Filipinos that fought alongside them, took part in the infamous death march.

As rumors and innuendo were the chief forms of information at that time, word was given to the family that my mother's brother survived the death march but died of dysentery in the prison camp. US soldier Bill Monroe was seventeen years old.

Pilar's other brother, John, refused to believe that his older brother, Bill, could possibly be dead. He said he would go find him in the mountains with the other guerrillas who were still resisting the Japanese forces in the dense jungle. Try as she might, Pilar could not convince John not to go. Staying up all night, she argued with him, knowing what would happen to him if he was captured.

John gave her all the money that he had — 100 pesos — and told Pilar to hang on to it for him and made the promise to Pilar that he would come back to get it. He never did. After that early-spring morning, she never saw him again. The Japanese captured John and tortured him. Yet because he knew nothing, he could tell them nothing of the rebels, the resistance, or their locations.

Once again, the rumor mill got word back to the family that John had been captured.

Victoria was told by the Japanese to come get her son John or he would be executed. Victoria had to make her Filipino Sophie's Choice. She knew by what other Filipinos had experienced that if she went to the Japanese, they would torture her in front of her son to make him talk and most likely kill them both. But if she didn't go, her son would surely be killed.

Victoria had three daughters to also care for, so she stayed.

John was beheaded by the Japanese; he was fifteen years old. I was with my mother at her sixtieth high school reunion, held this time in Northern California (the town of Daly City is nicknamed Little Manila). There were only around ten classmates left. One of them knew Pilar's brother John and remembered why the Japanese thought he must have known where the guerrillas were holding out. When John left that morning, he was wearing his older brother's US Army boots.

As a boy I used to ask my mother to tell me her war stories. She liked to tell them and tell them she did. She told me the reason she survived was because she was never afraid, and in fact, she said the war was the most exciting time of her life.

Mom told me how her mother took their worn bedsheets and, along with her sisters, made decorative pajamas out of them to trade with the peasants (farmers) for *kamote* (sweet potatoes). How she walked days to trade those pajamas with the farmers, who knew that the roles had reversed in this strict class system where the highest members of this class in wartime were those lucky Filipinos that had food. How her cousin, Clarice, cut her hair short so she would look like a boy and wrapped her breasts tightly to conceal that she was a girl.

Clarice came and asked Pilar late one afternoon to go on one of those long trips to trade for *kamote* with the farmers, but my mother didn't have a good feeling about it, and Victoria didn't let Pilar go. Clarice was never seen again. I like to think that the reason you are able to read this book is because of Pilar's choice to not accompany her cousin that day.

My mother told me how, after the war, she and her sister found money that the Japanese buried in a cave and took it back home along with what she thought could also be valuable...metal pineapples! Thankfully my mother's Japanese-Filipino brother-in-law Oscar Hamada gently took away the pineapple-shaped hand grenades from my mother and her older sister Rose (yet another reason you're able to read this book).

My grandmother washed the money as best she could and that's how the two young Monroe sisters were able to pay for school. You see, public school ain't free in the Philippines. My mom was a very proud woman and remembered that her other classmates knew that she and her sister used "dirty money" to pay for their school education.

Not unsurprisingly, neither my mother nor anyone else in the family hated the Japanese. I find Filipinos to be the kindest and most forgiving of people. They truly exemplify the spirit of forgiveness that Christ asks His followers to live by.

Somehow my mother did end up meeting her father, Stanley, quite by accident. After she graduated from the University at Santo Tomas in the Philippines, her friend was seeking medical treatment in America, and her friend's family paid for Pilar's trip to accompany her. That's how Pilar made her way to America in the 1950s. Because her father was an American soldier, she was automatically a US citizen. It was always her dream to come to America; she always felt like she was an American even in that faraway island.

My mother loved this country with a passion. She knew how if you were a US citizen, your potential was unlimited. Literally anything was possible if you lived in America. The only thing holding you back would be yourself. Though she was still literally ignorant about almost everything, she was able to leverage her college education and get a job at an insurance company (and also because insurance companies will hire almost anyone — more on that later).

My mother was living in an apartment in downtown San Francisco when a woman knocked at her door one morning. The woman said her name was Lorraine and that she had been receiving my mother's mail. My mother, the most untrusting person imaginable, instantly tried to close the door on Lorraine—but Lorraine was able to put her foot in the door jamb so she could continue talking with her. Lorraine explained that she was pretty sure Pilar was related to her husband…Stanley Monroe. They sure as heck looked a lot alike. Lorraine had been getting Pilar's mail because they shared the same last name—Monroe—and apparently the same Stanley.

When my mother came back from work that day, she found her apartment completely empty. Stanley and Lorraine had moved all her belongings into the small hotel he owned, the Gartland, on Polk Street in San Francisco. My mother then lived in that hotel for several years, despite having never met her father, Stanley, until then.

Thirty-one years later.

I was twelve years old when my aunt Jean (she was the oldest in the family) came to America for the one and only time in 1975. I accompanied her and my mother on a trip to Stanley's apricot orchard near San Jose. We spent a nice afternoon there, and as we were leaving to get back into my dad's 1974 Ford station wagon, my long-suffering aunt finally asked the question she had come all those thousands of miles to ask—"Why did you abandon us? Both of your sons died."

Stanley stumbled, and I don't believe his answer was sufficient for his eldest child. Instead of apologizing, he said he got malaria in the Philippines and lost his memory for a while. It was a regrettable moment and I never felt good about visiting my grandfather after that day. As we got back in my dad's Ford station wagon, I remember my aunt Jean saying, "Now that I have seen my father again, I can die in peace."

Jean died six months later.

* * *

Baguio, in the northern mountainous region of the Philippines, is where my family came from. They are a tribe of indigenous mountain people called Igorots. But don't call my mother that! Whenever I said the word, my mother looked at me with eyes that could and sometimes did bodily harm. Usually this was followed by a "pinch and twist." The pinch would get your attention but it was the twist that followed that made you never want to repeat whatever activity made Mom pinch you in the first place. Being called Igorot (sounds like "ignorant") would put my mother in a mood. I guess she didn't like being referred to as an indigenous person. For my mom, calling her an Igorot was like calling her somewhere between a "hick" and the n-word.

The higher elevation gave this part of the Philippine islands a more temperate climate (not as scorching hot as the jungle below), so much so that it even snowed in some winters. They have very large trees. Baguio is known as "The City of Pines," with plenty of fresh water so there was better rice farming, and the girls were better-looking, too! So of course other tribes wanted to come up there from other regions to enjoy the good indigenous life as well. However, our Igorot tribe had an ingenious way of keeping other tribes away — they were headhunters, and they had a tool just for that purpose, the head ax, which was also used in the household. There would be shrunken heads on sticks and they would line them up along the steep mountain path. Then the road would be lined up with just the sticks.

The intended message to other tribes was obvious: "We got plenty of sticks but we are running out of heads!" These not-very-subtle road signs seemed to do the trick.

Through my experiences I've found that Filipinos are an incredibly kind, gentle, and generous people. When I visited the island as a small boy, my mother's older sister Tita Rose asked me, as was her custom, "Robbie... is there anything I can do for you, my dear?" I looked up at the palm trees in her backyard and said, "I'd like a coconut." There was a slight hesitation in my aunt's eyes and she said, "Okay, Robbie."

I had no idea that this was not the season for coconuts in Manila and that my auntie would now be sending one of her maids (no matter how poor you are in the Philippines you have maids; even maids have maids in an ever-descending level of poverty in the Philippines) to another province that was two days away by bus to get me my coconut. They silently heard my accidentally extravagant request and took it.

At the same time, Filipinos can be very violent and try and do kill each other, mostly with sticks and knives. About ten years ago I performed stand-up in Manila to a mostly quiet but polite and attentive audience. It seemed like they were listening to me like I was their village priest. It turned out they were all completely sober. I found out that I was performing the night before an election. Alcohol cannot be sold the day before an election in the Philippines because the people there get a little crazy with their elections and tempers have risen to the point where people have killed each other for voting for the "wrong party." (Sound familiar?)

On April 21, 1898, the United States declared war against Spain and its holdings in Mexico, Cuba, and the Philippines.² At the time, the Filipino rebels were succeeding in ridding their island of their four-hundred-year Spanish occupiers. Unknown to the Filipino rebels, Spain sold the Philippines to the US for twenty million bucks, basically a big house in Malibu.³ Many Filipinos were grateful and greeted the Americans happily because they thought they were there to help finish off these conquistadors. However, some rebel tribes realized what was really happening: the Americans were supplanting the Spanish with their own imperial ambitions. A violent uprising ensued. Filipinos of the Sulu and Moro tribes attacked American outposts. So ferocious were these Filipino warriors that it forever changed warfare hardware. The Moro would take a concoction of native herbs and jungle drugs that would keep them charging, even after they were bleeding to death from the US Army's Colt .38 revolvers. The US Army decided they didn't like being stabbed by these little warriors after they had already killed them, so they requested a revolver with a much bigger bullet. They wanted a gun powerful enough that it would make a charging Filipino warrior not only stop, but send him back from where he came, and that, dear reader, is how the Colt .45 revolver was introduced to the United States Army. It continued to be very popular as the weapon of choice in World War I all the way up into Clint Eastwood's movies.⁴ (Clint Eastwood's voice: "The Colt .45 revolver, the most powerful handgun in the world!")

Anyways, the other side of my family was less violent and mischievous but they still had their moments. My dad was a very sweet Jewish man from San Francisco, California. Marvin was born in 1931 to Molly and Zigmund Schneider, Ukrainian and Polish Jews, respectfully.

My paternal grandfather, Ziggy, owned a barbershop on Market Street in San Francisco next to the glorious Fox Theater. Unfortunately, the theater along with the barber shop are long gone now. Anytime you see a town in America with a large very old theater that is still standing, just know it's only because the town was once so broke they didn't have enough money to tear it down.

During World War II, Ziggy would cut a sailor's hair, give him a shave, and maybe remove a pimple, while Dad would make a dime shining their shoes.

At the cash register there would be a "Your Chance to Win a Brand-New Schwinn Bike!" sign. It was a picture of the shiny new red bike on a cardboard stand that had places for the lucky patron to put in a dime and peel back the sticker to see if you were the lucky winner! But unfortunately for the patron, Ziggy had already peeled all the stickers off and then glued them back on. So sorry, no lucky winners today! But my dad had a brand-new red Schwinn bike!

My dad's earliest memory was when he was three years old. Between smoking cigars and playing cards, Ziggy and his other Eastern European pals would lift my dad up, put him on the table, and make him recite the Yiddish jokes that Ziggy made him memorize. These were the first live comedic performances in the Schneider family. They would not be the last.

I really admire my dad. He saw the inequity and immorality of treating human beings differently because of their race. Marvin Schneider, a young Realtor in San Francisco, in 1954 was one of the very first to refuse to adhere to race-based zoning codes and rented to African Americans. "*All* people deserve to be treated with dignity by the very virtue of being a human being," I can still hear him say.

I remember one story specifically that my dad got quite a kick out of. In the San Francisco Bay Area, my dad rented a house to a lovely Black family. It was soon discovered that the house next door to them was occupied by a racist Irish family (as if there were any other kind). We'll just call them the O'Learys (maybe that's too close to the *original*). But anyway, let's continue. The O'Learys were less than pleased with their new next-door neighbors. They raised quite an Irish shitstorm, with a never-ending stream of Gaelic complaints. Undeterred, my dad bought the house on the *other* side of the O'Learys and, to my dad's squealing delight, rented it to *another* lovely Black family.

That my dad married an Oriental (which is what my mother was called on my birth certificate, and yes, they were still using the word "Oriental" because that's what it said on the fucking world map — "The Orient" — in the early 1960s) showed that he was an open-minded and forward-thinking individual. In other words, a real liberal. The fact that my dad had just finished reading the book *Suzie Wong* when he met my mother probably helped a little bit as well. The small problem of my dad thinking my mom was Chinese for the first half of their marriage shouldn't detract from his cultural largesse.

I presume I get my rebellious nature and antipathy to authority from my pops. His best friend and chess partner, Archie, was a former high-up official in the IRS. When my dad told Archie about his frequent tax audits, and how he would set up a nice chair and a cup of coffee in a quiet room for the tax man to go over my dad's financial records, Archie suggested a different reception for the IRS official. "First, ask them for their badge number, and then call the office and ask them to confirm it is them. They'll get furiously screamed at by their superiors," Archie said. "Then give the IRS agent a small box to sit on and invite the kids over to run around, chase each other, and scream while he's going through the paperwork." This had a dramatic effect on the duration of the IRS agent's inspection. I can still see my dad smiling while my brother and I were hitting each other in the face. My dad even paid his 1968 tax bill in two separate checks, dated one day apart, just to lure the IRS out to foreclose on his properties, claiming he only paid half. Then my dad produced the two checks and said, "What do you mean? I paid in full!" The joy my dad found seeing the tax man leave sheepishly almost made the 1968 10 percent tax surcharge to fund the Vietnam War worth it.

I decided to start this book off with this background of my family to help give further context of what will follow. My childhood in the San Francisco Bay Area with my parents of mixed-race backgrounds shaped my view of the world. Specifically, that America afforded the greatest opportunity for peoples from all nations and all faiths. Unlike what my great-grandfather said, when my family eventually made it to America, we became more than maids. My Filipino cousins have become doctors, nurses, nurses, nurses, and nurses. (There may be a maid or two in there, those of my relatives with head injuries, but *mostly* nurses!) The last time you were in any hospital in the world, chances are it was a Filipino that found that small vein in your arm. And lucky for you because she usually got it in one prick! That's the problem with diversity. You don't want to force people to do things they're not best equipped for. Phlebotomy is what Filipinos are *maid* for! Small fingers to find a small vein in one go. You don't see Filipinos in the NFL, as quarterbacks or placekickers, and for good reason. We have short arms and short legs — I can kick a football about eight feet on a good day. To risk sounding "antidiversity," you don't want a seven-foot Nigerian dude trying to take blood out of your arm. After fifteen tries, you're gonna say to him, "Dude, this isn't working. Your finger is as big as my dick!" You definitely don't want this guy giving you a prostate exam either. "Sir, please go out in the hall and find somebody half your size of Oriental descent. You know, a Filipino." And speaking of pricks, one of them avoided nursing school long enough to become an internationally famous comedian.

Years later, in 1992, my mother appeared with me on NBC's *Saturday Night Live* on the Mother's Day special along with the other cast members' moms, where she announced to the country that I was, indeed, half Filipino, confirming I was the first person of Asian descent ever on *Saturday Night Live* (and still managing to avoid using the word "Igorot").

Now, as I reflect on the miracle not only of our divine existence, but the success my family tree has blossomed into, I realize the same freedom that empowered my mother to build a new life for me is what I need to fight for.

The United States of America is the greatest experiment of freedom in human history. When I said publicly that I want my children to have the same opportunities to flourish in this freedom experiment, mainstream media tried to ridicule me. When I played characters of different nationalities throughout my career (which I didn't write but was simply cast in), twenty years later, the woke media tried to label me a racist — which is funny, because to me I thought being able to play vastly different people than yourself in movies is what makes you a good actor.

Who is Rob Schneider? Well, most people know me from the movies I've been in with Adam Sandler. Furthermore, it's become clear to me, because of those roles, people think *I am* those characters. I love playing silly, goofy people because that's what makes *me* laugh. Just like when I was a kid watching Peter Sellers in *The Pink Panther* movies when *he* was playing other silly people.

In Netflix's *Real Rob*, I play a fictional version of myself where I am a megalomaniac asshole. Is that who I am, too? I hope this book lends a more nuanced look at who I am as a human being, and not just the "making copies" guy. Imagine that!

Just the same, I realize what the Chinese say is true: "Perceptions, even false, have their consequences." But the lines of political identity are being drawn while they're still being shifted. And today's labeling of people on the Left *and* on the Right doesn't allow for much nuance. You are either placed in the Liberal box or Mussolini's box.

Like I said in my wildly popular streaming comedy special on Fox Nation, *Woke Up in America*, "I am a traditional Liberal, which, apparently, makes me a right-wing fascist now!"[5]

I define my traditional liberalism as standing up for women's rights, gay rights, and civil rights. I believe in free speech, body autonomy, and not judging a person by the color of their skin. These, among other values, have somehow become conservative issues. To quote Ronald Reagan: "I didn't leave the Democratic Party, the Democratic Party left me."[6]

So much has changed so rapidly. I mean, it's only been a couple of years since we've learned that women could have dicks! Now, if you speak your mind in Hollywood, you go from playing the bad guy in *Spider-Man* to "Naked and Afraid: Celebrity Edition"! (Which was a lot of fun, actually. Except for the red ants making a nest around my anus.)

Anyway, I knew I was on the right track when I was attacked after appearing on Glenn Beck's radio show for saying, "I must put God, my family, and my country before my career." All the problems we face today are preordained and they are here for the same reason God put the forbidden fruit in Eden. God wants shit to happen! He wants to test us. All of us. While our government wants us dumbed down, fat, sick, injected with experimental substances, eating toxic foods, and wasting our lives in fear, God wants to test us, to keep us strong in mind, body, and spirit. He wants to challenge us as individuals, as families, as communities, as a nation, and as human beings.

I draw upon the words of Father Chad Ripperger: "Jesus has already won; this is all just a mop-up mission..."[7] This is all His test for us. Unlike other belief systems and religions (say, cancel culture, for example) that call upon their believers to hate and destroy their enemies, our religion calls upon us to love our enemies. To love others as thyself. What a beautiful way to go through life!

In this world where the battle lines of free speech are constantly redrawn, I'm telling my story as a Hollywood comedian turned vocal advocate for open dialogue. In this book, you'll see the enduring power of an individual voice against the backdrop of historical precedents, modern challenges, and the transformative path of our free speech heroes. Together, we will explore the intricate dance between expression and suppression, revealing how understanding our past, confronting our present, and anticipating our future can illuminate the path toward a society where free thought isn't just a privilege but a right for all.

There will be no more long-suffering for this Igorot. And if anybody wants to try to silence or cancel me, they sure as hell picked the wrong Filipino.

You can do it: speak your mind, America.

## CHAPTER ONE

# HISTORY IS SHORT

"You don't find out who's been swimming naked
until the tide goes out."

— Warren Buffett[1]

I voted for Trump in 2016. For some people, that's an issue. We didn't have much of a choice, it was either vote for Trump or vote for a murderer. Just kidding, I'm not saying Hillary Clinton was a murderer. *Anybody* can have forty of their friends and coworkers accidentally die violently in suspicious accidents or commit Jeffrey Epstein.

First of all, I was in California, and I was right on the kitchen counter and I had the ballot, because you know, in California, they mail you a hundred of them. I didn't fill them *all* in (I'm not an asshole), just, you know, three or four of them. Five at the most. Seven tops. Trump, Trump, Trump, Trump, Trump. Because here's the thing, I know the guy. I don't know him well, but I am the only author you're ever going to read that made a movie — *Home Alone 2* — with the forty-fifth president of the United States, Donald Trump. We had to put him in it. It was his hotel. He's a big dude! He was just walking around in front of the camera and we thought. "Maybe if we put him in it, he'll go away." So we did, and he did.

Anyways, I didn't think much about it, so a few years after that, I appeared with him on *The Tonight Show with Jay Leno*. Remember when Trump would threaten to run for president, and didn't do it, before eventually his threat became reality? This was one of the times he was just threatening. So I was on the *Tonight Show* with Trump, he was the first guest, and I'm backstage with Jay. Jay said (in high-pitched Jay Leno voice), "You got any jokes about Donald Trump?" I said, "No! I got one, but I'm not going to say it." "No, you should say it," Jay prodded. "*You're* gonna be out there, *he's* out there, say it! It's a joke, he's going to know it's a joke. You know, we can have some fun with him!" Keep in mind, this was before people realized Donald Trump wasn't as gracious as one would hope he would be when joked about.

Anyyyyyyways, so we're doing the segment and Jay Leno looks at the big clock underneath camera one and sees that we have forty-five more seconds of time. He says, "What was that thing you were saying backstage to me about Trump?" Under my breath, I said, "You fucker," but I'm a whore, so I went for it. I said, "Well, you know what the difference is between me and Donald Trump? When I first got started, my daddy didn't give me forty million dollars." Not a big laugh, but what came after was worse.

I swear to God, Trump looked right at me and said (in Donald Trump voice), "That's not true, you're a liar. Liar. Liar. He's just lied, it's not true."

I didn't think much about it. Several years after that, I went through a divorce, and I was really depressed. I wasn't leaving my house or anything. My publicist was worried about me. "Just get out of your house," she said. "People need to see you. I've got an event for you to go to. Just go to this event, they'll have your name, you'll have fun, it'll be good for you!" So, I got in the car. Next thing I know, I get out and there's this huge event, and there's all these people, and cars, and cameras, and shit. I went up to the place where I was told to go. They had a name tag for me, and it said "Rob Schneider, Judge."

I said, "What is this shit? Judge of what?"

"This is the Miss USA Pageant, now owned by Donald Trump, and you're one of the judges!" You know how rich guys, they get like two homes, and maybe a convertible car for the weekends? If you're really, really, really rich, you get like a sports team. But if you're *between* that, like Donald Trump, who really, *really* wants to be around titties and have an iron-clad excuse to look at fifty bikini-clad young women (not including the ones from Puerto Rico or Guam), owning a beauty pageant could be the street you want to drive down!

So I get my little judge badge and they whisk me into the back room with the other judges, the only one I still remember was the one-legged ex-wife of Paul McCartney. Then Donald Trump comes in and he says, "Hey listen, vote for whoever you want, I'm not going to tell you who to vote for, vote for who you want, I don't care. I'm not going to tell you, you vote for who you want. *BUT*, if you love your country, like I love my country. If you love your country, if you're a patriot, because you want America to win, right? Vote for who you want, not going to tell you who to vote for, but if you want America to win Miss Universe, then vote for *these*." Then he pointed to a picture of a blonde with big tits. "Miss Texas. You want America to win, right? *These* babies are our best chance of winning Miss Universe."

So, I was like, fuck, I'll vote for whoever *you* want. I didn't even know I was going to be here an hour ago. So, then we had to meet the contestants who came in, and we already knew who we were supposed to vote for, and it was all the same shit. "I'm Miss Rhode Island and I believe in global peace and squirrels!" You know, whatever words they could pronounce they said! We weren't dealing with real *thinkers* here. Then this other contestant came in, and she was the *opposite* of the well-endowed blonde from Texas. Opposite, meaning as far away from blonde as you could get, if you get my drift. So she came in and said, "Listen, I didn't even want to be here." And I jumped in and I was like, "Me too! I don't want to be here either!" "But my friends said I'm pretty," she continued, "I should just do it, what the hell, I might get lucky. I only need $100,000 to finish my last year of medical school, and the cash prize is $100,000, so, here I am."

All of the judges kind of agreed, let's just give it to her, you know? That year, and I swear to God, Miss USA was given to the nonblondest contestant possible. You would've done the exact same thing I did. The blonde from Texas is going to be fine, you know, she's going to find a guy like Donald Trump (who she already found). But this girl, who can actually help people in her life, a *doctor*, so we all voted for her and she won Miss USA.

After the pageant, we were told by USA pageant employees that all the judges were required to go back to that same room and that Donald wasn't very happy with the results of the vote. We did, and soon Donald walked in and he was less than enthused with our choice. First words out of his mouth were "You don't love your country. You don't." And then he looked at each judge, and said, "You're a loser, you're a loser, you're a loser," and then he looked right at me and he said, "And you're a loser, and that's why you never made *Animal 2* because you're a loser." All the judges slithered out of the room as quick as possible.

I remember my small Filipino legs being slightly wedged under my chair, which delayed my exit. As I went to leave, he was between me and the doorway, creating an awkward moment between me and beauty pageant owner Donald Trump. I said, "Donald, I'm sorry that you didn't get the girl that you wanted. I can tell that it really meant a lot to you, and I'm sorry." And then, my self-destructive nature reared its ugly head. "Also," unnecessarily restarting the conversation, "I'm sorry for that joke I said about you on *Leno*."

He said, "What joke?"

Realizing my mistake, I said, "It's not important."

"No, I like jokes," he insisted. "What was the joke?" he said, his six-foot-four frame looking down on my five-foot-five frame. "Tell me the joke."

"Well, you didn't like it the first time," I said.

"Tell me the joke!"

"It was just the differences, you know?"

"Of what? What difference?"

"Between you and me!"

"Which is what?"

My voice went up several octaves and I squealed out, "My daddy didn't give me forty million dollars when I got started."

I swear to God, he looked right at me and he said, "I hate you now, I do. I hate you. Seriously, I really hate you. You're a loser."

Whatever…I thought to myself. "It's not like you are ever going to be *president* of the United States!"

★ ★ ★

On July 3, 2020, I got a call from a friend who is a professor of medicine at the University of San Francisco and was working for the National Institutes of Health (NIH). He is quite a brilliant man that, through his five-decade career, is remarkably accomplished. At the university he teaches other doctors *how* to be doctors. He is perhaps the foremost researcher in the world on diabetes. He even worked with NASA on developing an artificial pancreas. By a stroke of luck thirty years ago — when he was still practicing family medicine for diabetes — he was my dad's doctor and extended my dad's life by perhaps a decade.

But first, let's step back a few months, to the early days of the COVID pandemic.

In March of that year, the *New York Times* had attempted to cancel me along with Dr. Drew Pinsky (a real doctor as well, unlike nondoctor and *Times* reporter Jeremy W. Peters) because we, in their words, "scoff at staying home," and we had made the calm and rational observation that "COVID doesn't appear to be a virus more deadly than the common flu."[2] Furthermore, that we should take normal precautions like we would with any flu — that is, protect the elderly and those with immune compromises and continue along with society as normal. So of course, for this perfectly logical and rational and nonfearmongering response, we were attacked by nonphysicians like Peters (who didn't respond to a request for comment despite being an alleged journalist).

This mainstream media attack gave me a glimpse of the government and media's agenda, and like so many other "conspiracy theories" during COVID, six months later, they become fact.

But back to my friend...

In the afternoon of July 3, 2020, my friend at NIH called me. I asked him directly, "What's really going on with COVID?"

Tellingly he said, "Don't quote me, but receptor twenty-six looks a little sticky," which was his way of saying that one of the receptors on the COVID virus looked altered. Altered so it could jump to humans and thus meaning the entire virus could have been manufactured in a lab. This contradicted what America's foremost authority on infectious disease (and highest-paid government worker), Dr. Anthony Fauci, said — that basically it was a zoological virus that made the jump to humans from somebody eating a bat out of a Chinese food truck in Wuhan, China. But the other more telling thing I got from that conversation was that the smartest dude I knew in medicine felt he *couldn't tell anybody* this information because the government had already decided what "the science was."

I was taken aback...the government had created an atmosphere that was silencing real scientists. The best in their field, like my friend, who couldn't say what he (and I am sure others) discovered. The government and their allies had an agenda and finding out what the real truth was wasn't part of it.

That is what happens when there is no firewall between industry and governmental agencies. If my friend spoke out, he would have had his career ruined like the other doctors and scientists that spoke out at the time. He saw what was happening to them, and he decided to be quiet. Silenced doctors and scientists is what you end up with when you don't have scientific debate because some (paid) official has declared that the "science is settled."

We all know what followed after that. The world got shut down. Kids as young as two and in preschool were having masks forced onto their faces at daycare centers. I'll never forget those videos, and unfortunately, those kids will never forget that trauma. Restaurants, businesses, and schools were being closed. Notably, California governor Gavin Newsom kept open strip clubs, weed stores, and liquor stores (which I greatly appreciated),[3] but churches and schools were shuttered. One of the saddest things I remember was children sitting outside of a Starbucks, with their computers, trying to get Wi-Fi because they didn't have Wi-Fi at home. And those were the lucky ones that at least had a parent with a computer.

This is an example of why you should care about free speech. In human history, the ability for humans to have free unfettered speech is remarkably short, rare, and for the very privileged few. Sure, through history there was always the option for one to speak freely, but you risked losing your head over it. Free speech without prompt head removal has only existed in a few places, and periods, throughout history.

It was during the French Revolution (1789–1794) when free speech was declared an inalienable right for man in the Declaration of the Rights of Man and of the Citizen.[4] This experiment in free speech lasted all of five years before the head removal system resumed, this time unabated, which eventually gave rise to Napoleon.

Meanwhile, the United States of America has had free speech since it was put into the US Constitution in 1791. While America has its imperfections, our First Amendment protecting free speech is the beacon of hope the world over. It is the longest-running and greatest experiment of free speech humans have ever had the chance to participate in.

Our democratic republic has inspired several other versions of democracies to create similar free speech protections like Canada, the UK, Australia, and some European countries.

This was particularly evident in the post–World War II era. These nations did not have free speech as a fundamental founding principle to their society as the United States did, and therefore it's more vulnerable to erosion. Outside of these examples, there are few other long-standing periods or places of protected free speech in human history. (By the way...congratulations, you've made it to page 27).

First, let's step back. Back to before we even had civilization. Back before people were confused about which bathrooms they should use. I'm talking way back! Back before we were somehow okay with paying ten times more for shit at the airport just because we're about to get on a plane.

The only reason we've been able to have a divided society of workers and farmers — that became rulers, priests, and armies — is because for most of the last 10,000 years, Earth has been a reasonable and pleasant landlord that gave us a comparatively mild climate (sorry, John Kerry and Al Gore). We've had no civilization-ending supervolcanoes for the last 74,000 years.[5] No end-of-all-human-aspirations asteroid impacts for the last 66 million years. No Snowball Earth era where Earth was a ball of ice like 716 million years ago. As a fortunate result, the planet's most successful tenant has wildly flourished: insects. But the planet's *second* most wildly successful tenant, human beings, has flourished as well, building complex cities, cultures, and languages. They've also built civilization-ending thermonuclear weapons and respiratory pathogens, but that's beside the point I'm making here. (To people reading this in the bookstore, this isn't free, you know! The cash register is behind you — put the pistachios down and buy this, you've already bent the pages!)

Because of mankind's success, and Earth's cooperation, humans have even created the enlightened principle of acknowledging an individual's right to speak his mind with some protection or at least no fear of deadly reprisal.

Now, let's consider protected free speech. Imagine human history is a vast desert, representing long stretches of time and places without free speech. There are a few oases that represent the rare and precious periods and places where free speech flourished. Finding free speech in the desert of human history is as rare as finding an oasis in an actual desert — most of the estimated 108 billion humans ever born spent their lifetime wandering the desert without ever being afforded that unique liberty.[6]

Sadly, we seem to be living in a time when free speech is under attack even in the freest of societies. The question is, could the very long history of human beings having to live a life of fear, void of free speech, be repeating itself again?

Unfortunately, we are not that far removed from a time of head-removing non–free speech societies. In fact, history is quite short. One of the most remarkable things about history is, indeed, how short it actually is. If you shook my hand right now, you would be only seven handshakes away from Napoleon. I am friends with the great director John Landis, and John Landis was friends with legendary American director Orson Welles, and when Welles was a boy, he met Sarah Bernhardt on Broadway, and then when Bernhardt was a child, she was friends with Marie-Anne Walewska, who was married to Alexandre Colonna-Waleski, the illegitimate son of Napoleon and his mistress, Countess Marie Waleska.

That's how short history is.

Even today, free speech is still reserved for a shockingly small number of people. Today, nearly two billion people in China are living without free speech — constantly being checked and evaluated for what they say and do in an ever-increasing camera-policed world. They cannot enter any store, or take any public transportation, without first showing their identity — and if their social credit score is below the state-approved number, they are forbidden.[7] What's Chinese for "Oh no! We suck again!"? This is a hellish dystopia unimaginable even in George Orwell's nightmare. We definitely don't want that in America. But I must inform you, dear reader, that awful dream is the direction in which we are going, not the opposite. I write this book as part warning, part siren call to action. Living in a world where every interaction, communication, and financial transaction is monitored, manipulated, and eventually controlled by government is slavery. And of course, the best slaves are the ones who don't even know they are slaves and who will fight tooth and nail to keep their own enslavement.

We must call this by name: Mao's Marxist Communism redressed and disguised as social justice; diversity, equity, and inclusion; and identity politics.

As my friend Robert Kennedy Jr. said, "There are some things that are worse than death." I think most Americans like me would agree, "Give me freedom or give me death!"

It's a miraculous opportunity that in God's experiment in consciousness (humanity) that we would also get to participate in the experiment of freedom (the United States of America).

Consider what is at stake when we give up these freedoms. What happens when free speech goes away? When you see the erosion of free speech, like we're seeing now, it's a quick and slippery slope to greater repercussions. As my friend Andrew Doyle writes in his book *Free Speech and Why It Matters*, "Free speech is the marrow of democracy. Without it, no other liberties exist. It is detested by tyrants because it empowers their captive subjects. It is mistrusted by puritans because it is the wellspring of subversion. Unless we are able to speak our minds we cannot innovate, or even begin to make sense of the world."[8] (As a matter of fact, if you're still at the bookstore, and weren't already coerced to buy this book, go buy his, it's way better — though I haven't read the whole thing — *but that quote fits in really good right here, maybe I should give him some of my book money.*)

Basically what Mr. Doyle said in his smarty-pants English accent is this: without free speech, we lose all the cultural complexity and creativity that make life worth living.

There seems to be a misconception of free speech by those that want to quantify and eliminate speech that they find unkind (or the overused term, "hate speech").

Real Nazis, the verifiable historical Nazis, not the watered-down usage of the word today as in "you're a 'Nazi' if you have the gall to say there's a direct correlation between morbid obesity and early death." Okay, but I would just like to remind people that you never hear anybody say, "Hey! That eight-hundred-pound man turned one hundred today!" Real-life Nazis were all in favor of free speech, as long as you agreed with *them*. Consider the chief Nazi propagandist and actual historical Nazi Joseph Goebbels. As Noam Chomsky said, "Goebbels was in favor of free speech for views he liked. So was Stalin. If you're really in favor of free speech, then you're in favor of freedom of speech for precisely the views you despise. Otherwise, you're not in favor of free speech."[9]

If free speech is anything, it is protecting the speech that you loathe. If it truly is objectionable and abhorrent speech, it should be obvious to anyone. The silencing of the speech is never going to remove the sentiment behind it. Rather, the suppression may justify its ugliness. Much better to hear these unpopular utterances in the open where they can be exposed and shuttered, not by silencing them, but by the supposition of better views in the open marketplace of ideas.

Free speech and associated freedoms create our societal norms. When free speech is diminished, there is a direct rise in fear; distrust; the death of potentially new, culturally enriching ideas; incarceration; and then leading to, well, actual death and mass murder. When we have free speech, we have a rich and creative society, which enables:

Economic growth and prosperity (free market)

Government accountability and an informed public (free press)

Personal autonomy and self-expression (personal freedoms)

Human rights and social progress (free debate)

Peaceful conflict resolution (freedom to find common ground)

Innovation and creativity (freedom to challenge the status quo)

So, if you don't like money, accountability, transparency, individuality, safety, creativity, or the occasional dirty video on your phone, then by all means oppose free speech. (By the way, the government knows every site you go on, even in safe browser mode — sorry, David Spade!) Your right to express the speech that I vehemently disagree with is something I fight for because it is your right to speak freely. It is, in fact, the terrible and horrible things that need protecting the most. Not because you have to agree with any of the opinions aired, but because of the slippery slope of who exactly would be the one that would get to decide just exactly what abhorrent speech is. Would you be okay if I got to decide for you what you could say? Then the same should go for Facebook's Mark Zuckerberg or Google's Larry Page and Sergey Brin.

As we've witnessed in the last four years, the speech that was restricted and censored from scientists, doctors, and other professionals (like my friend at the NIH) turned out to be demonstrably true. If free speech wasn't suppressed then, the world could have avoided the draconian shutdowns that it went through and all the economic, emotional, and physical suffering that ensued. ("Oh my God, Rob, you're so smart! What was the junior college that you dropped out of again? I want to make sure I never send my kids there.")

For people of a certain political identity that claim to support the poorest in our communities, it was the poor that ended up suffering the most from the pandemic response. After decades of hard work, African American schoolchildren's reading skills had just caught up to their peers', and now after the two years of COVID, 42 percent of their skills have fallen off the cliff of literacy.[10] If you still oppose this idea of free speech, I'll save you some time and let you stop reading this book while you're waiting for your flight in front of the airport bookstore shelf. If you're still not convinced and are afraid of the harms of unfettered free speech, I believe if you keep reading, I can persuade you that the cost of weakening free speech is far more perilous.

Now that those nauseating free speech naysayers are gone (I'm sure I'll hear from them again on CNN anyways — you know, the ones with the purple hair, not the ones naturally born with purple hair, but the Sharpie-pen-factory-explosion survivors), I'm glad we're all on the same page that free speech = societal balance. We can now examine how free speech, and our culture, has evolved through history.

Our culture evolves and devolves much like the tide. Just as the tide ebbs and flows, societal attitudes have their rhythms of progression and regression. ("Oh my God, you're way smarter than your movies!")

Times of intense social change, like the 1960s, '70s, '90s, or the 2010s, are like high tide — new ideas and new voices flood, and reshape, our societal landscape. Periods of conservative backlash or political apathy like the 1950s, '80s, 2000s, and 2020s are like low tide — where society retreats to safer, more traditional grounds. It is a cycle, and what is considered conservative today was something considered quite radical ninety years ago. Yet that radical view has put us in a truly better place now. Contrary to today's cultural critics, it's impossible to say we aren't in a better place as a society in the twenty-first century. Unless you're a race hustler, you'd have to agree that we are in a much better place for men, women, and minorities than we were sixty years ago.

Just like tides, there is often an undercurrent at work in our society, too. Consider the Roaring Twenties, a period where a post–World War I economic boom fueled a high tide of creativity in the Jazz Age and loosened social mores. At the same time of this prevailing high tide of new ideas, Prohibition was an undercurrent working against the tide — prohibiting the manufacture, transportation, and sale of alcohol. The result of the prohibition caused a clashing tide and undercurrent of illegal activity: speakeasies, widespread noncompliance, social resistance, syphilis outbreaks, and the great wealth accumulations of Al Capone[11] and Joseph Kennedy (future ambassador to the UK). This clash led to the Nineteenth Amendment ending Prohibition.

Society will always have friction. This friction is necessary. Putting groups of people together who have disparate views causes a myriad of problems. But it is precisely these problems that open the door for innovation and opportunity. You don't get to a smooth society without the friction between the tides and undercurrents. And you don't get societal friction without free speech.

I foolishly assumed that things would continue to be more open and more liberal (in the classical sense) after the counterculture high tide of the 1960s and '70s. However, if I had paid attention in history class, I would've known that what goes up must come down. "Surely," I thought, "we'll continue to have more free speech, and more openness in society in general! How could we not? We just had Jimmy Carter and now Ronald Reagan is president! What could go wrong?"

I was working at a gas station in 1979 in San Francisco called Chang & Chow 76 (John Chow and Patrick Chang 76 station) during the glory days and splendor of the Carter administration. I remember the long lines of cars of people waiting to get gas, and how pissed off people with an "odd" license plate number were when I informed them they couldn't get gas today because it was an "even" license plate number day. It reminds me of the vitriol in January 2024 Chicago of those that were coerced by the Biden administration to purchase electric vehicles[12] only to realize their car batteries don't charge quickly (or at all) in freezing weather,[13] and they had to wait in the subzero temperatures for hours as I drove past them in my eight-passenger eight-cylinder

Escalade (that only got twelve miles per gallon on the freeway no less, but still worked in the freezing cold unlike you Tesla-driving dipshits!).

But I digress. (And I own three Teslas in the never-freezing state of Arizona.)

In the '80s, the tide went back out to sea, and our culture went through a conservative stifling through the Reagan years. For those of you who don't remember or weren't alive in the '80s, understand that we went through a similar cultural recession in the 2000s after the 9/11 attacks and now again in the 2020s. But by today's standards, the 1980s free speech erosion is extremely modest compared to what we are experiencing today.

In 1988, toward the end of that cultural recession of the Reagan years, there was a famous Supreme Court case. *Hustler* magazine had published a cartoon suggesting that televangelist Jerry Falwell had a sexual escapade with his mother in an outhouse (replete with cartoon depiction). Taking great umbrage at this salacious, incestuous allegation, Falwell sued *Hustler* magazine and its owner Larry Flynt for libel and infliction of emotional distress.

Here's some unnecessary background information about *Hustler* magazine. I remember a box of girlie magazines my dad had that I discovered when I was ten years old. It was clumsily hidden in the closet under the stairs of our house. There were copies of *Playboy*, which showed beautiful naked women that seemed to have an unrealistic perfection to them — not that I cared then, I just couldn't believe I was seeing actual boobies! Then there was the French magazine *Oui* that didn't care or have the money to touch up the photographs, so these girls looked more like real women with their imperfections intact. Then there was *Penthouse*, which specialized in being more daring and explicit than *Playboy*, and audaciously showed women's genital hair.

Mind you, dear reader, this was a few years before *Hustler*, which, in one of its first editions, featured a paparazzi shot of a topless Jacqueline Kennedy Onassis, the widow of former president John F. Kennedy, on a beach in the south of France. I know what you're thinking— "Classy!" *Hustler* opened the doors, and more specifically the legs of women, leaving nothing to the imagination. They showed female genitalia unabashedly, and that particular part of the woman's anatomy was the predominant feature of each photo *spread*. Now, with that knowledge in your head, we will go to the ruling of the Supreme Court.

The Supreme Court ruled in favor of *Hustler*, saying that public figures have a higher threshold for proving libel and emotional distress and cannot recover any damages caused by parodies or characters that any reasonable person would not believe to be factual.[14] ("Any reasonable person" is something we'll come back to later.)

While this was meant to be a humorous piece in the filthiest of all girlie magazines, the Supreme Court wasn't interested in evaluating the humor or the filth of the piece, or whether it was even funny or not. The Court was only interested in whether it could be said at all in a free society.

They found that stifling this free speech, regardless of its vulgarity and offensiveness, was an erosion of the right to speak freely. The protection of Falwell being offended wasn't more important than the protection of society's right to free speech. Not just the ability to speak freely, but also the freedom for others to hear the speech uttered as well. For when you limit free speech, you also deprive the listener's right to hear the free speech. This is a very important point. Because if free speech is derailed, what would be next after that? (Holy shit! This could affect me, Rob Schneider!)

If we did give in to the culture vulture warriors and their kooky demands for "safer speech," who precisely would be the ones deciding what our free speech can be, and just how much free speech are we allowed to have? Whoever is interested in assuming that role can also kindly stop reading this book now.

*So why is Rob Schneider talking to me about free speech?*

Believe me, when I was on *Saturday Night Live* thirty years ago, or making movies for Disney, Sony, Warner Brothers, and Fox, I never thought, "You know what would be even more fun than making millions of dollars traveling around the world making movies with all my friends? Arguing about free speech with thousands of woke twentysomething Gen Zers and about whether 'men' who suck at sports when playing other dudes should be allowed to compete against women in women's sports! And if they *aren't* allowed to compete against women, at the very least, they should be allowed to shower with them?!"

For hundreds of years, the satirists of their times have been the ones most familiar with societal tides. The value we add to society is helping explain society to society in real time.

The very best comedians — the Bill Burrs, the Chris Rocks, the Dave Chappelles, the Sarah Silvermans, and the Adam Sandlers (it is my aim to be in that lauded group as well) — are holding up a mirror to society and saying, "This is what's happening. Let's talk about this a little before we accept it as part of the culture." These days, people go to see comedians not just because they want to get a good laugh, but also because they sincerely want the comedians to make sense of a world that seems to have gone mad, relatively quickly.

An artist must talk about the times in which he lives. The Nobel Prize winner in literature, Italian playwright and satirist Dario Fo, said that "a theatre, a literature, an artistic expression that does not speak for its own time has no relevance." He also said pointedly, "With comedy I can search for the profound."[15]

When I saw the remarkable Dave Chappelle in 2016 on a Wednesday in San Francisco, it was packed, and I couldn't help but notice that there were two shows happening simultaneously. There was Chappelle's actual show that was three hours long, and then there was the other show: the reaction of the people in the audience. The people were looking at Dave for answers. For someone to make sense of their experience in a world that no longer made sense to them. For the audience that night, and for many similar nights since, Chappelle was equal parts comedian and equal parts soothsayer.

This isn't particularly new either. Humans for centuries have relied on plays and comedy shows to make sense of the society around them.

In Ancient Greece, comedies and tragedies used characters to explore moral and ethical questions. For example, Aristophanes' *Lysistrata* (411 BCE) used humor to comment on the political situation of Athens while Sophocles' *Antigone* (441 BCE) presented a conflict between civic duty and familial loyalty, reflecting on the tensions within Athenian democracy. Later, Shakespeare was subtly critiquing social hierarchies, politics, and human nature. Plays like *Richard II* (1595) and *Macbeth* (1606) explored themes of power and legitimacy, indirectly commenting on the current monarchy and societal structures of his time.

The 1700s and 1800s produced satire in literature. Writers like Jonathan Swift with *Gulliver's Travels* (1726) and Charles

Dickens with novels like *Oliver Twist* (1837) and *A Tale of Two Cities* (1859) offered up their works to challenge issues such as class disparity, poverty, and injustice. And I very much look forward to finish reading all of these very soon!

Comedians, or at least the good ones, understand the rhythm and patterns of cultural tides, as well as society's landmines (riptides) which provide and act as fertilizer (shit) for our material. That's what makes stand-up comedians our culture's de facto intellectuals. It's not that we're smarter than everybody else (far from it!), but that we're willing to submerge ourselves into dangerous cultural waters. In fact, I would say it's our job. And unlike doctors, scientists, academics, and bloggers (like *New York Times* blogger and scaredy-cat Jeremy Peters), we are not reliant on research grants, endowments, clicks, tenure, or the super important invitation to their annual (fill in the blank) gala. As long as people are still willing to stand in line to buy a ticket to fill an establishment that sells liquor on a Wednesday — a comedy club or theater — we have job protection.

That is until Pfizer buys every comedy club in America! (Why did I just give them that idea?!)

Comedians are filling a vacuum of cultural necessity. Those in the halls of science, politics, and academia have been effectively neutered, and now those halls are one echo chamber of illiberal liberalism. "Student-facing" academic administrators who identify as liberals outnumber conservatives at a rate of 12:1, but I don't think they fit into traditional liberalism (more on that later).[16] What happens is the intellectuals, the artists, writers, academics, and thinkers have found their livelihoods threatened, coercing them into going along with a hypocritical theology that calls for more of the wokeness religion. Not only can surfing against the tide of societal change soak you, it can kill your career and, at some times in world history, could get you killed outright.

In 1593, the Elizabethan playwright Thomas Kyd (1558–1594) was arrested and tortured under suspicion of treasonable and heretical activity. Which would give one pause to think that couldn't happen again today, yet now there are comedians that have been arrested in the UK, but not for the crime of not being funny, but for upsetting somebody in a tweet.

The story goes that writings denying Jesus Christ were found in Kyd's dwelling. Though they didn't kill him when they captured him in 1593, when he was released, he was unable to find any work and was dead a year later, at thirty-six, deeply in debt.[17]

The famous Spanish poet, playwright, and theater director Federico García Lorca (1898–1936) was executed by Nationalist forces during the Spanish Civil War. This execution is widely believed to be politically motivated as a response to Lorca's works. His liberal views, support for the Republic, and the fact he was gay undoubtedly also played a part in the decision to kill him by firing squad.[18]

Consider the case of Mikhail Bulgakov (1891–1940), a prominent Soviet playwright and author, known for works like *The Master and Margarita*. His career was a roller coaster of artistic struggle under the Soviet regime. One of his notable plays, *The Days of the Turbins* (based on his novel *The White Guard*), though initially popular and even favored by Stalin, eventually faced criticism and censorship. Bulgakov's works often subtly criticized the Soviet government and society, leading to a complex relationship with the authorities. He faced a period where his works were banned, and he couldn't publish or stage his plays. Bulgakov even wrote to the Soviet government, seeking permission to emigrate if his works could not be performed or published. Despite the oppressive censorship, Bulgakov continued writing, and many of his works, including *The Master and Margarita*, had to be published posthumously. Today, Bulgakov is celebrated for his imaginative and allegorical storytelling, which provided a veiled critique of Soviet life.[19]

Then we have the Soviet Nikolai Erdman (1900–1970), whose plays like *The Mandate* and *The Suicide* are now revered as some of the most famous plays of the 1920s. He was arrested while working on a script that would eventually become *Jolly Fellows*, the first Soviet comedy musical. After they arrested him, the Soviets did what they were known to do, and banished Erdman to Siberia. Though they didn't kill him, perhaps he got an even worse fate for a comedian: he had all his works stripped of his name, and a blanket ban on any of his art that prevented the rest of the world from seeing it, until his plays and films made their way to the West in 1969, just before his death. Now his work rests in the US Library of Congress.[20]

So, if you're thinking to yourself, "Well, yeah, sure, Rob, but I mean that's Russia, a civil war in Spain, and 1500s Elizabethan England that you're talking about — that could never happen in the US," guess again, bi-atch! These are simply just historical evidence that cancel culture is nothing new. We are living through an artistic stifling now, just as these artists did.

The unique American art form of stand-up comedy started in the beginning of the twentieth century. There was a writer going around who was famous for his satire and comedic takes on all things Americana: Mark Twain. Twain's first-person narrative style of writing was as unique as it was uproarious. Combined with his southern drawl, Twain's stories would leave his audiences laughing and gasping for air. He would perform these stories in town halls around the country, and people would pay a dollar for the privilege of hearing him. He would tell stories about traveling to faraway exotic lands like Hawaii (if you thought Hawaii is hard to get to now, just imagine how hard it was to get there 130 years ago!). You would have to call Mark Twain our first stand-up comedian. Stand-up comedy, like America's other world cultural enriching art forms — jazz, the blues, and rock and roll — has been exported worldwide, because it was born in the greatest freedom experiment in mankind's history.[21]

From then on, we got more comedy from the likes of Mort Sahl, Lenny Bruce, and George Carlin, each building off the one before them to create the stand-up genre we have today. Not to mention, recently freed prisoner Bill Cosby. By the way, the Coz is going back on tour. The tickets are not that expensive, but there *is* a two-drink wake-up-with-his-dick-in-your-mouth minimum. These comedians, like the author Henry Miller, helped push the boundaries of what our culture found acceptable, or obscene. Miller's book *Tropic of Cancer* was set in France during the late 1920s and early 1930s and was a candid portrayal of the author's decadent life, including explicit sexual content (whoring). Upon its publication in France in 1934, the novel was banned in the United States for its explicit nature (whoring). But it found its way into American culture by college kids sneaking copies back from Europe (after whoring). It wasn't until another Supreme Court case, *Miller v. California* in 1973, that a barometer for obscenity — dubbed the Miller Test — was developed. The Miller Test focused on whether the average and reasonable person (someone who doesn't engage in whoring), "applying contemporary community standards, would find that the work, taken as a whole, appeals to the prurient interest; whether the work depicts or describes, in a patently offensive way, sexual conduct [whoring] specifically defined by applicable state law; and whether the work, taken as a whole, lacks serious literary, artistic, political, or scientific value."[22]

What is it about words, the utterances of which make people so uncomfortable and threatened that courts and judges must be summoned to seek redress?

## CHAPTER TWO

# THE CONSPIRACY THEORY OF CONSPIRACY THEORIES

"I cannot believe I'm that dangerous."

— Mort Sahl[1]

Originally, I wanted to write a book called "You Only Get to Keep the Stories," because in show business, you *only get to keep the stories*. Movies open, movies close, some movies are hits, some movies are misses. As Chris Rock says, "You're on the list of 'who gets to make movies' one day, but they never tell you when they take you *off* the list." So fame goes, houses go, women go, money for sure goes, but the one thing you get to keep . . . is the stories.

I've been very lucky. I've been able to work with some terrific actors. I've made more movies with Adam Sandler than any other actor. Besides Adam, one of my all-time favorite actors to work with was my pal Martin Landau. We made the very last movie for Orion Pictures, *Pinocchio*, the wooden boy, played by *Home Improvement*'s Jonathan Taylor Thomas, who, unfortunately, grew about seven inches by the time we finished filming the movie. We had to literally dig a ditch for him to stand in so the adult actors (me) weren't looking eye to eye with Pinocchio. (Don't believe what you read on the internet — I'm actually five foot five.)

I was excited because I'd be working with the guy who just won the Academy Award for playing the morphine-addicted actor Bela Lugosi in *Ed Wood*, Martin Landau, who also gave incredible performances in *Tucker: The Man and His Dream* and *Crimes and Misdemeanors*. Tim Burton had asked me to be in *Ed Wood* as well, but when I asked permission, I was told I couldn't get out of my day job at *SNL*. That's why when 20th Century Fox wanted me for *Home Alone 2: Lost in New York*, I knew better than to ask for permission. They said, "Would you like to be in this movie *Home Alone: 2*?" and my response was "Well, what time exactly do you plan on shooting this movie? Is it during the day?" Luckily for me, they *did* shoot during the day. So, for the better part of a month, I would shoot *Home Alone 2* during the mornings, and then hustle on over to my night job, writing and performing on a popular late-night TV show at 30 Rock. So basically, I didn't sleep for weeks, but when you're in your twenties, you don't need sleep. That's why people in their thirties and forties, who have families and lives, rarely get hired for *Saturday Night Live*. They want young, hungry talent — kids who are just beginning their careers on the fringes of show business and have an air of desperation about them. That was me. That was Adam Sandler, David Spade, Chris Farley — that was all of us. Am I revealing too much?

On the other side of the spectrum was Martin Landau, an established movie actor with an awe-inspiring pedigree. There were only two actors that were accepted into The Actors Studio in 1953. One was Martin Landau. The other was an actor by the name of James Dean. They became best friends, and you can find wonderful pictures that Dean took of Martin in their Acting Studio days. Martin was in Alfred Hitchcock's *North by Northwest*. After working with Martin for a couple of weeks I felt comfortable enough to ask, "You were in Alfred Hitchcock's greatest picture, *North by Northwest*. How does something like that even happen?" And he said, "Well, Hitchcock came to see me in a play on Broadway." I said, "Man, that's just incredible." Later on that night, after a few Czech beers (that's where Budweiser comes from, by the way), he told me the whole story.

Landau reflected, "So here I am, in one of the greatest movies of all time, doing a scene with one of the most famous movie stars of all time, Cary Grant, with one of the greatest directors of all time, Hitchcock. After we filmed this iconic scene where I stepped on Grant's hand at the top of Mount Rushmore, I finally got the gumption to ask, 'Hey Hitch, what was it about me that you saw on that Broadway play that made you want to hire me to be in this movie opposite Cary Grant, Eva Marie Saint, and James Mason?' Hitch said in his thick Cockney accent, 'Well, I thought you'd make an excellent homosexual.'"

I think we both laughed for about seven minutes. The fact Marty told me that story was very illuminating to what a great guy he was. On one of those beer-drinking nights in the Czech Republic, he said the best thing about acting I'd ever heard. "Write this down!" he said, and I wrote it down on the back of a cardboard beer coaster.

The next morning, he charged into the makeup trailer and came up to me. "What was it that I told you last night? It was the most succinct summation of the acting process I've ever said. What was it?"

I still had the beer coaster in my pocket from the night before. Because I was still wearing the same clothes from the night before. Because I had been drinking the night before.

On the back of the coaster I had written, "Find it. Express it. Suppress it."

That contrast and that dynamic is what creates a memorable performance.

*Find* the idea of what you're trying to get from the other actor. *Express* it in different and interesting ways to get what you want from them. Finally, *suppress* it. Because nobody is ever nakedly honest about what it is they *really* want, so they suppress it. Thus, recreating real human behavior, which reveals the universal truth that everybody can relate to. Which is this: Everyone wants something. "Maybe," Martin said, "*maybe* once in a movie," and he put his hands up over his face, with his fingers interlocked, peeking between. "In real life, nobody shows how nakedly bad they want something. Maybe once, at the most, in a movie it's exposed and the audience can get a glimpse of the character's real desperation."

"Stelllllaaaaaa!"

* * *

It was said during the days of COVID that the difference between a conspiracy theory and the truth was about six months. Anyways, here's a plot for a Hollywood movie:

A secretly viral contagion leaks out of a lab (not so secretly), and the entire world is infected. The globe is shut down. Businesses, schools, and even churches are all closed. Children over two are forced to wear masks. A few strip clubs remain open in California, because you know, why not? Daily life comes to a screeching halt. An experimental (back comes the secret) jab will be made compulsory for all humanity to return to normal life. The evil scientists cover up the origins of this virus with their own story — it came from a bat sandwich. After the shot is given, perfectly healthy people (who don't believe in secret things) all over the globe die suddenly.

The public must not find out the truth, because it would undermine the (secret-y billionaire-y) people that started, funded, and created the medical emergency. So, the powers that be — including the government and pharmaceutical, medical, media, and tech communities — must perpetuate and defend the lie. They attack anyone who dissents or deviates from this (crazy, overblown, secret-as-shit) government narrative.

If that sounds like a shitty sci-fi movie of the early 2000s, you're only *half* right. It was actually a shitty sci-fi event that happened in early 2020, and all of us were in it as unpaid fucking extras!

However, dear reader, it wasn't the first time in the history of the United States a "gangster mentality" was used to keep the story straight.

John F. Kennedy was the bright hope for the nation when he was elected president in 1960. He famously said, "Ask not what your country can do for you, ask what you can do for your country," which was in stark contrast to our current administration's policy that goes something like "We'll just print up a bunch of money and give it to you! You stay home and don't worry or ask questions about how it all gets paid back! Hopefully, we'll be dead by then. Just continue binge-watching Netflix and eating your marijuana gummies."

On November 22, 1963, in Dallas, Texas, Kennedy made a bad life choice and took a regrettable ride in a convertible. A week later, the new president, Lyndon B. Johnson, established the President's Commission on the Assassination of President John F. Kennedy. It would be chaired by Chief Justice Earl Warren, and thus later became known as the Warren Commission. The Warren Commission's primary objective was to investigate the circumstances surrounding President Kennedy's assassination, and the subsequent (and very fortunate) killing of Lee Harvey Oswald, the alleged assassin.

The Warren Commission's report, presented to President Johnson on September 24, 1964, and made public three days later, concluded that President Kennedy and Texas governor John Connally were shot from the sixth-floor window of the Texas School Book Depository by Lee Harvey Oswald. It concluded Oswald acted alone, ignoring an easy kill shot when Kennedy's car faced him, instead waiting until Kennedy's car turned 180 degrees, deciding to take the impossible shot between two trees that, by the way, were quietly removed days later. Notably, as political scientist and social critic Michael Parenti says in his famous speech, "The JFK Assassination and the Gangster Nature of the State," Oswald also used "a rifle whose sights were not even set, an Italian weapon, by the way, which the Italians said was most famous for being a weapon that never killed anyone on purpose."[2]

Oswald was shot two days later and killed by alleged patriot and strip joint owner Jack Ruby — an apparent fearless defender of liberty who must've loved his country so much and felt so horribly for the Kennedys that he stepped away from his titty parlor and took it upon himself to stop any further investigation of the murder of the most powerful man on earth by killing the suspect and potential lead witness of the crime. This was made possible by the Dallas police — who allowed the armed owner of the town's only totally nude drinking establishment into a parking garage just as the accused killer of the president was being transferred — "Nothing to see here! Move it along, people!"

Many didn't, and still don't, buy the Warren Commission's story. Was there a second shooter on the grassy knoll? people wondered. It was the Cold War, so maybe the KGB did Kennedy in? JFK's brother Robert was the attorney general and was fighting a hard and scrappy battle against organized crime, so maybe it was the mob? LBJ was the next in power, maybe he had a hand in it? Or (hold your inquisitive ears) was the CIA behind it? Kennedy did intend to slash the agency's budget following the disaster of the Bay of Pigs invasion of Cuba, where the agency lied and deceived the young commander in chief.

In the Bay of Pigs invasion, the CIA (under the preceding president, Dwight Eisenhower) developed a plan to train Cuban nationals in a revolt against Castro. The neocons (a polite way to describe warmongering demons that favor military intervention regardless of the morality of their actions) of his day bamboozled and cajoled Kennedy into going along with the plan. They were attempting to force Kennedy's hand into escalating the war. After the first of two planned airstrikes went poorly, Kennedy canceled the second wave of air attacks. The Cuban nationals and CIA operatives, who were pinned down in the swampy area with their backs to the sea, were slaughtered (or captured) like, well, pigs, in an embarrassing international fiasco.

Unfortunately, America's neocons would keep repeating lies (and getting themselves and their friends in the war business well paid) while lying the nation into war after war, going around smashing up the world. This strategy, as American historian Dr. Charles A. Beard called it in 1947, was "perpetual war for perpetual peace."[3]

It is, in fact, these neocons themselves who are the real conspiracy theorists. They see opportunities in war and create an illusion of fear to achieve their aims: to deplete America's treasure, maintain their power, and further enrich themselves and their cronies in the same military industrial complex that President Eisenhower warned the American people about in his final address to the nation.[4] While the CIA looked like fools after the Bay of Pigs embarrassment, Kennedy likewise realized he couldn't trust the agency and, as he said, had intended to "splinter the CIA into a thousand pieces and scatter it into the winds."[5] Yet the Warren Commission excluded any evidence or suggestions that put into question their foregone conclusion that the twenty-four-year-old Oswald, a communist recruiter (who in his recruiting career enlisted zero fellow comrades), killed the thirty-fifth president and leader of the free world all by his lonesome — with the shittiest weapon ever made by the shittiest army in World War II, Italy.[6]

After the Warren Report came out, the public was talking (as they are wont to do when their leader has his head blown off), and 46 percent of the public (which is basically half) did not think Oswald acted alone.[7] In a free society, every citizen is entitled to an "agency approved" opinion, so the CIA had to quickly concoct a plan to deal with those Oswald-lone-assassin deniers. Similarly, a Pew Research Center report in June 2020 found that a public opinion poll indicated that 25 percent of the American public thought it either "probably or definitely true" that "powerful people intentionally planned the coronavirus outbreak," which put those "powerful people" in a similar position as the CIA was with Kennedy and their sure-shot Oswald.[8]

If the CIA couldn't come up with a way to convince the people of their preferred conclusion, then they had to at least diminish and drag through the mud any doubters or deniers. In declassified document CIA DOC 1035 960 from 1967 titled "Countering Criticism of the Warren Report," the CIA spells out just exactly how they intended to do so — using (for the first time) the term "conspiracy theory" in a derogatory way as a means to demean and discredit naysayers.[9]

The CIA writes, "This trend of opinion is a matter of concern to the US government, including our organization" ("our organization" translation: professional killers). The dispatch paper continues: "Conspiracy theories," they write with disdain, "have frequently thrown suspicion on our organization [the CIA], for example by falsely alleging that Lee Harvey Oswald worked for us. The aim of this dispatch is to provide material for countering and discrediting the claims of the conspiracy theorists." Here it is, a playbook written by the spooks themselves.[10]

Jumping ahead to show these tactics are still very much at work, in the 2020s, more than fifty former intelligence officials signed a letter saying they believe the Hunter Biden laptop story "had all the earmarks to be intentional Russian disinformation propaganda."[11] The intelligence community provided Hunter's father, Joe Biden, political speech plagiarist, ice cream enthusiast, and forty-sixth president, cover so he did not have to deny it was true but could instead just reference the letter. "Well, fifty other people said it was fake…" Yeah, fifty former intelligence officials — translation, fifty professional *liars* lying.

You only need to look at these declassified documents in all their unredacted glory to see for yourself (and you'd have to agree) that the government's playbook for free speech suppression tactics have been used time and time again.

The document breaks down how to respond to those who dare to question the government's story based on who they are. For the "friendly elite contacts (especially politicians and editors)," they suggest to "urge them to use their influence to discourage unfounded and irresponsible speculation" (that is, avoid your own common sense). It is, in their opinion, irresponsible to question them and the Warren Report. After all, these paid government employees and professional liars should be above reproach, because they have a higher calling than the boring old truth — protecting their own interests by silencing critics.[12]

As the dispatch continues, they encourage propaganda to quell the public's justified inquisitiveness: "employ propaganda assets to answer and refute the attacks of the critics [that is, threaten their livelihoods]. Book reviews and feature articles are particularly appropriate for this purpose." This was the 1967 edition, when people still read books and newspapers, and watched TV on the TV, instead of on their phones. It was literally decades before Facebook's Mark Zuckerberg became a billionaire (and, thereby, ending his involuntary virginity). This is how the CIA used the media half a century ago and not much has changed — except the size of Jeff Bezos's yacht and his testosterone performance enhanced biceps. This is perhaps the sequel to *Revenge of the Nerds* that no one asked for.

The CIA gave us the five ways to discredit "conspiracy theorists": "[we] should point out, as applicable, that the critics are (i) wedded to theories adopted before the evidence was in, (ii) politically interested, (iii) financially interested, (iv) hasty and inaccurate in their research, or (v) infatuated with their own theories." Reading between the lines, they're saying anybody other than the professional liars in the intelligence community is either self-deluded, stupid, seeking money, power, or doesn't have the full story. The motives for finding the truth, in a so-called free society, about the murder of their young president (or why two-year-olds should be forced to wear masks) mustn't be allowed to be openly discussed or debated.[13]

A half century later, Matt Taibbi (a unicorn in journalism), in April 2023, exposed the censorship industrial complex with his published findings that became known as the Twitter Files. In his discoveries, he found that the FBI was working with Twitter (in the pre-Musk days) in systemic suppression. They used, among other tools, shadow banning, which manipulated the algorithm to bury tweets without the tweeter's knowledge. This, of course, is censorship and a violation of the First Amendment. Yet it's rarely discussed openly in the media — they're literally censoring their own censorship.[14]

We can see the obvious similarities in the Kennedy era and the COVID era and realize this idea of controlling the narrative and calling the counternarrators conspiracy theorists is one of the oldest tricks in the book. Through Matt Taibbi, dear reader, you can see the government was telling Twitter and other social media empire executives the same thing: suppress and discredit anything that questions the government's narrative.

Back to Kennedy — those authoring the Warren Report had a conclusion they wanted to prove. Instead of trying to find the truth, the Warren Commission went into the report to support their assertion that Kennedy was shot by a lone gunman. Any other possibility was intentionally excluded.

They used for COVID the same kind of writing-with-the-end-in-mind that they used for the Warren Report. There are many people who could look back at the Warren Commission and go, "Well, that was most likely a government cover-up...but this COVID stuff surely is legit...our government wouldn't lie about something so serious as a flu bug." People who think this way are struggling with confronting an inconvenient principle: governments grab power at the expense of our liberties. That's just the very essence of government.

Cognitive dissonance, the discomfort and pain we get when we hold opposing thoughts in our head, is something we all must get more comfortable with. While we hold the United States and its brilliant system of checks and balances in high regard, is it also possible to think that they would deliberately lie to us? That they could kill a president? That they could also shut down the entire economy because of a virus gone wrong or was that the plan the whole time?

Could they really use the conspiracy theory playbook to silence us for asking any of these questions?[15]

The answer is a simple yes. They have, and they will continue to do so, unless we learn their game, and a great example of how to learn their game just happens to come from another stand-up comedian — the great Mort Sahl.

From his biography, *Last Man Standing: Mort Sahl and the Birth of Modern Comedy* by James Curtis, here is how Mort's rise to fame was described:

"On the evening of December 22, 1953, a slight, diffident man took the stage in a brown suit salvaged from the traveling wardrobe of the Stan Kenton band. The newspaper he held in his hands wasn't merely a prop; his cues, typed out on index cards, were stapled to its inside pages. There is no record of what he said, nor precisely how long he was on, but by all accounts he went over big." Soon, Mort was a sensation known for his political commentary that television host Steve Allen called "the only real political philosopher we have in modern comedy."[16]

He was dubbed revolutionary for his way of using comedy to talk about the real world of politics. Soon, he was traveling the country playing clubs, theaters, and college campuses. He was in TV, film, and even had a one-man Broadway show. He was the first comedian to ever appear on the cover of *Time* magazine. Soon, he was approached by Frank Sinatra to write jokes for him, and then for President Kennedy, for Kennedy to use on the campaign and fundraising trail.

Unfortunately, Mort's routine shifted after Kennedy's Dallas commute.

Mort turned his searing social commentary comedy into an obsession with criticizing the Warren Report. He was one of the people that made the CIA create the playbook on conspiracy theories in the first place. Being the preeminent political comedian going against the government's preferred conclusion made him a target. As he went against the power and influence behind the Warren Report, he was labeled a "conspiracy theorist," discredited, and kook-ified. His popularity waned as did his television appearances, and soon thereafter, so did his career. It's further explained in Mort's biography how his popular show *Mort Sahl* was canceled:

"Mort reflected on the thirty-nine weeks of episodes he had done for the station, and decided that the Kennedy assassination had to be the underlying factor in the pressure on Metromedia to cancel his show. 'Outside sources,' in other words, were banding together to stop him from talking (and more succinctly, from being heard).

"On December 29, Sahl flew back to Los Angeles to give the press his side of the story, which amounted to the station's 'business consideration' being wholly and directly related to his criticism of the Warren Commission Report and his inquiry into the conspiracy to kill the president."[17]

Mort was canceled.

The once revolutionary comedian was silenced.

"I cannot believe I'm that dangerous," Mort told the press after his cancellation. "And I don't think they're turning me off because of that."[18]

Stand-up comedians matter because they have a unique position in society to stand up and speak while other voices remain silent. It is at times like during the Warren Report, or COVID, that those using their First Amendment right of free speech are needed most.

There're still a thousand boxes on Kennedy that the Biden administration has refused to release, citing national security, from something that happened over sixty years ago. Incredibly, in 2023, one of Kennedy's last surviving Secret Servicemen in Dallas that fateful day, Paul Landis, admitted to leaving the magic bullet on the stretcher. WHAAAT?! Which means the theory of the magic bullet must also be laid to rest as well, proving that Oswald could not have acted alone. In fact, in 1979 the Congressional Committee on Assassinations ruled that

Kennedy "was probably assassinated as a result of a conspiracy. The committee is unable to identify the other gunman or the extent of the conspiracy."[19]

Now a scientist can have his research grants dry up because he's not going along with the government narrative. A doctor can have his medical license taken away by his state's medical board. A duly elected president who refuses to go along with the plan can be removed from power. But a comedian, well, he or she can be easily dismissed as a clown. Especially if they're a conspiracy theorist. We are still serving as the court jester. The king will laugh at the jester, who represents the people, until the jester goes too far and gets decapitated. Now, in the present day, you won't lose your head for it, but they'll go after your pocketbook and you might lose your YouTube channel. In Mort Sahl's case, he went from Broadway to telling his jokes at a coffee shop every Thursday. People still showed up to see him even many years later, his newspaper still in his hand, but now Mort would read from his wheelchair. Mort managed to, unlike Bulgakov in Russia, make a living, but his celebrity died in the same 180-degree turn with Kennedy.

Investigative journalism used to be about questioning everything. Now, all they question is the question askers. What are *their* motives? Instead of asking or getting to the bottom or doing any actual investigative journalism, the media will just regurgitate the talking points of what the government tells them. Then, they demean, demonize, and vilify those who go against it. No investigation necessary. The government narrative is now considered fact — it is unquestionable and unmovable.

Anything that deviates from the story will get you relegated to that of an unhirable conspiracy theorist. They didn't even have to tell people not to hire Mort Sahl. They just knew not to hire Mort

Sahl because of his conspiracy theory label. A scarlet letter that he would never shake.

For me, as I got the prestigious title of "conspiracy theorist" during COVID, I learned from Mort and knew I would not be deterred. They went after me to make me unhirable, and they were successful for quite a while during COVID. Yet my duty as a stand-up comedian is to make society laugh and help make sense of the world. So, even during COVID, I would go to any club that would have me (in any part of the country that was still open, that is) and I would play their game of "limited-capacity social distancing." I'd find a way to make sure like-minded people that sensed, as I did, everything wasn't exactly on the up and up with COVID, if they wanted to hear me, could. Instead of doing seven full shows, I would do shows with the capacity limits to make sure I got them *all*. And FYI, the fourteen sold-out shows I did is the record for sold-out shows at the Zanies Comedy Club in Nashville, Tennessee. When California mandated that any venue with over 1,000 tickets sold would require proof of vaccination or a negative COVID test to get in,[20] I instructed the theaters to sell only 999 tickets, unlike other comedians like Patton Oswalt.[21] I wasn't going to be making health decisions for people that wanted to see my shows.

Now, "conspiracy theory" has become an accepted term and is a widely used tactic that we see all the time. I got death threats for some of my tweets during the scamdemic. What I believe were pharmaceutical black ops (spooky, right?) were working to silence me. The media was just one of their tools. Here's a headline the literary wizards at the *Daily Mail* came up with in July 2021:

Selma Blair is "Fine" with Rob Schneider Voicing His "My
Body My Choice" Stance on the COVID- 19 Vaccine and
"Understands the Concern"...after Comedian Goes on
Twitter Rant Urging People to "Just Say No" to the Jab.[22]

First off, the use of the word "rant" seems a little harsh, but I'm
glad their thesaurus works. Anyways, I said, "my body, my choice,"
when I was referring to the vaccine mandates, which is what liberals used to use when arguing for abortion rights — you see, it's
only "your body and your choice" until the liberals tell you that it's
not "your body, your choice." Liberals be like, "Just take the same
shot that we all were questioning when Trump was president." Of
course, no one in media dared call those Democrat vaccine skeptics
antivaxxers like soon-to-be vice president and antivaxxer-while-
Trump-is-president, Kamala Harris. On Twitter, formerly known
as Twitter, I said, "Just say no!" borrowing from drug expert and
former first lady Nancy Reagan's successful campaign — you know
how teenagers always listen to seventy-year-olds!

A *TMZ* reporter (they're known to be world-class thought
provokers) asked the always lovely and talented actress Selma Blair
her opinion of *my* opinion. Selma was relevant here because at the
time she was immunocompromised herself and in remission following a battle with the very tough illness multiple sclerosis (MS).
The media was essentially looking for Ms. Blair to give them an
"alley-oop pile on" to call me a grandma-killing conspiracy theorist so other media outlets could further bury me. You can already
tell from the context that they wanted her to say something like
*"Rob is selfishly putting my life at risk by not taking the jab."*

Thankfully, Selma didn't take the bait.

Instead, she surprised this poor excuse for a journalist and said, "I don't mind what he says at all. But at the same time, you know, it's hard when everyone is hurting from something that's very oppressive — you know these shutdowns, and businesses, and health and I understand…" Then she added, "My son had a vaccine injury when he was very young. I understand the concern that people have."[23]

The last part of the video about her son having a vaccine injury was not splashed all over the media. In fact, it wasn't mentioned in ANY OF THE ARTICLES that ran with the story.

Why, you may ask, would they exclude what seems to be such a significant part of the story? Here's the answer: What Selma said goes against the narrative — that there may be a problem with the saintly group of drugs, vaccines — and what goes against the narrative is off limits. The media has sold its soul to pharma. They would rather protect pharma's bottom line (and their continuing ad revenue) than the nation's children.

Main-steaming-pile media wanted to make me dangerous. They wanted to make me irresponsible. And here's a new approved pejorative to add to the list: "unhinged." Like I'm a fucking door or something. They wanted to make me all of those things the CIA playbook outlined: self-deluded, stupid, money hungry, and power thirsty. They wanted to make me a conspiracy theorist.

Just like Mort, I, too, refuse to believe I'm dangerous. The opposite is true — it's dangerous to *not* question the narrative. It's dangerous to *not* exercise your free speech. It's on us to move the conversation forward and stop the story from being written without our voices included.

However, our voices can't and won't be included if we censor ourselves…

As I said at the beginning of the chapter, it just takes six months for a "conspiracy theory" to become truth. But actually, I apologize and stand corrected. Sometimes it can take three years — AstraZeneca globally withdrew their COVID vaccine on May 7, 2024, citing a decline in demand after mounting pressure (lawsuits) for blood clot–causing side effects.[24]

# 3+2=5; TRUE,

# BUT IT COULD BE

# SUPER RACIST

Hello again. Same book, different chapter. In this chapter, we're going to focus on frontal nudity, and the difference between a Brazilian wax and a Portuguese breakfast. Sorry, that's what I made movies about in the early 2000s. This chapter is about the c-word, the original c-word, "censorship," and if there's time, "cunt." But the first cunt, censorship.

The most dangerous form of censorship is self-censorship. Writer Jonathan Day says self-censorship is "a void, into which steps the government or its allies with spin and propaganda to reinvent truth."[1] Most people would consider this objectionable, if not downright potentially dangerous, to let that void be filled by those with conflicted interests or a particular agenda.

When society loses its rational footing, it's important to have well-reasoned and sensible people counter the loose-thinking dim-wits and, at the very least, bring society back to a place of reality. When we censor ourselves, we remove ourselves from the communal debate and we let the potentially flawed ideas from whoever is guiding the conversation take hold.

The first example that comes to mind is 3+2=5. That was the first thing taught in philosophy by Dr. Palmer from Oxford University, where I was lucky enough to be in his class while he was academically slumming at College of Marin in 1983. To quote Dr. Palmer specifically, he said, "Three plus two equals five, whether the universe ever existed or not." In other words, there are some things that are beyond debate. If we are to make sense of the world, there must first be a logical foundation on which to build our house of knowledge.

Now you can close the book. I hope I proved my point. If that point of logic eludes you, maybe you should find something else to read, like something by race hustler Ibram X. Kendi — real name Ibram Henry Rogers, which isn't as cool a name, obviously. You know, Rogers, like *Mr. Rogers' Neighborhood*, is way cooler with the X, especially if you take out the Rogers completely. I'm thinking about adding a consonant to my name, too. Might help me sell more books or come up with more academic papers than Rogers accomplished while leading the Center for Antiracist Research at Boston University. We, or Boston University even, don't know exactly what was produced with the $43 million funding his department.[2]

As Douglas Murray says in his new book, *The War on the West*, Western society is under attack. "Things like race, which has never been better, are presented like things [that] have never been worse."[3] While the West is fair game, China seems to be immune from racial criticism, even though they are currently imprisoning over a million Uyghurs, but if my community college doesn't have at least one gay Peruvian professor in the philosophy department, then I'm the bad guy. The monumental civil rights achievements and accomplishments, exemplified by the great American Dr. Martin Luther King's dream, that a person should "not be judged by the color of their skin, but by the content of their character," forever made the world a better place.

However, sometime in the first quarter of the twenty-first century, an exception has been found in this skin pigmentation "dream": Whitey. Good old Whitey! "Whitey, *you* can be judged by the color of *your* skin." If you happen to be born *white*, by no choice of your own, not only are you automatically racist, but you are also the benefactor, and oppressor, in the system of white supremacy. I consider myself half white and half Asian, so now I find myself stuck trying to figure out which half of me is oppressing the other. I'm pretty sure my dick is Asian, but my balls look pretty white! I think my balls are oppressing my dick. "Hey! You're making us look bad up there!"

It was the race hustlers who challenged the most basic knowledge that we have in the universe — math! In the race hustler's world, anything is up for debate. Their theory goes "3+2 could equal 4" depending on your cultural background, and if the school district you're in doesn't want you to succeed in life or want you to be able to hold a job at Target!

According to this new math logic, even numbers can be racist. Why was Six afraid of Seven? Because Seven said the n-word and Six didn't want to lose his tenure at Harvard University; because Six had a nice office and a parking space close to the library. So, Six stayed quiet. Six also didn't report on the black university president's obvious plagiarism in over forty academic instances — because that would be systemic racism! As we have all learned, pointing out plagiarism is right-wing propaganda and a racist bludgeon used to destroy the lives of black academics who, being in a white society of systemic oppression, are way too busy and under too much pressure to cite, reference, do their own research, or write their own academic papers.

Don't worry. Claudine Gay, the former Harvard president, has been punished by the university for her plagiarism and scholarly crimes of laziness by still being allowed to teach at Harvard as a professor in the political sciences department, earning a salary of $900,000 a year — plus an office and parking space right by the library. Oh, to be a diversity hire in academic circles in the 2020s — making up their own math rules and surfing the wave of progress and plagiarism all the way to the office of diversity, equity, inclusion, and the bank.[4]

My good friend John Cleese told me of an episode of self-censorship he experienced himself. I must admit it wasn't a case of pure self-censorship, it was a mix of comedy censorship and self-preservation. Self-preservation, specifically someone not screaming something about how awesome God is while painfully killing you, is *completely* understandable and, I might add, comedically forgivable. It was a sketch that Cleese was working on for the last great major work of the comedy troupe Monty Python, *The Meaning of Life*. For those that appreciate (know) comedy,

Monty Python was the highwater mark of comedy of the twentieth century — it's unarguable. Python aficionados, like myself, are religious devotees to the British troupe. They were really The Beatles of comedy. The series was monumentally influential, changing comedy forever. Python raised absurdist progression to the level of literature. But even good literature doesn't make you howl with delight like the joyful silly comedy of Monty Python. Aside from the series, their cinematic effort, *Life of Brian*, has been consistently voted the greatest British comedy film of all time.

*The Meaning of Life* (which, to my understanding, was mostly written on holiday in the Bahamas) was, for this Python nutball, a first-day, first-showing event! It was in San Francisco on Polk Street before noon on a Friday. There were only two attendees for that first showing. In the front, as close to the screen as possible, was me. In the very back row was the cackling laugh that I had heard so many times before at the famous Holy City Zoo comedy club on Clement Street, and it was none other than the one and only Robin Williams. Both of us were howling and barking at every joke in *The Meaning of Life*. From the beginning scene of the Catholicism-inspired dance musical number "Every Sperm Is Sacred" to death visiting a group of holiday goers in a cabin who all died from eating salmon mousse. As death leads their ghostly apparitions out of the cabin, Michael Palin famously ad-libbed, "But I didn't even *have* any of the mousse!" Cut to many years later, Cleese told me about his episode of comedic self-censorship/self-preservation. He had a sketch about the Iranian Islamic leader, the ayatollah, who had just supplanted the US-backed shah. In the sketch, the ayatollah was discussing his disdain for the West. John (not me, I have nothing to do with this, this is all *John*! John Cleese. Spelled C-L-E-E-S-E, British!), in the ayatollah's voice, says, "You degenerate Westerners, with your decadent toilet paper, plumbing, sanitation, and running water. Your wicked habit of washing your hands before you eat [etc.]," and that's as far as John could remember. For anybody who thinks he shouldn't have censored himself, let me remind you. You can make fun of Jesus all day long. As a matter of fact, in the '90s there was a videotape going around (back when there was such a thing) by the South Park boys called *Jesus vs Frosty*, where after the South Park kids accidentally build a murderous snowman, they seek a baby Jesus from a nativity scene who decapitates the snowman with His halo. While disrespectful to Christianity, it got them a show on Comedy Central, currently on its fourth decade.

I don't think they would've had the same success with a cartoon about Islam and a baby Muhammad. They might have had a different result, and instead of being given a TV show, they could've been given a *fatwa*. Just ask *The Satanic Verses* author, Salman Rushdie, who was issued a fatwa in 1989 by the ayatollah, and thirty-three years later was stabbed more than a dozen times.[5] The doctrine of Jesus Christ is one of forgiveness and love. Islam? Not so much.

So, I understand why a sketch with that subject matter was not enthusiastically embraced by the other members of Python.

Staying quiet is the most basic form of self-censorship. When you know something to be true, or something to be knowingly false, and don't say anything about it, you help perpetuate a falsehood, like my friend who stayed silent at the NIH. It also makes you a welcomed Stephen Colbert audience member. So, 3+2=5 in whatever culture you grew up with. To wind back on academic standards, teach incorrect math, and ask less of students is to cheat the student. Trying to find a cultural excuse for ignorance, or teaching ignorance, helps no one and makes society dumber.

Pulling people out of poverty must be done through giving people a useful education. An education that challenges people's minds and helps them think critically so they can make sense of the world. It is not done by dumbing down the education out of fear of exposing the flaws in our public school system. We see this with the self-proclaimed "progressive" mayor of Chicago, Brandon Johnson, on his own personal crusade of creating equity among students, dismantling Chicago's high-achieving selective-enrollment high schools. So, instead of finding an innovative way to raise the bar for the lower-performing students, Johnson says, "Let's just lower the bar and penalize the high performers!" God help us all. Mr. WIZARDDDD![6]

Self-censorship, meanwhile, usually happens when somebody is afraid for their job, their reputation, or being accused of some recently made-up cultural phenomenon like "you're a huge transphobe." Out of this fear, they remain quiet, which, left unchecked, eventually leads to being confused on which swim team you should join.

Accommodating some narcissistic mediocre male athlete's desire to finally step up onto the victor's podium cannot come at the risk of putting women in jeopardy. Nor can having dudes inhabit girl's traditional safe spaces like bathrooms, locker rooms, and the boxing ring.

Rather than commenting on this misogynistic assault on women, most media personalities have chosen to self-censor by staying silent. Like when many stayed quiet while two trans cyclists took gold and silver at the 2023 women's Chicago Cyclocross Cup, with a biological female cyclist taking the bronze.

When you self-censor, you may keep your tech job at Amazon but quietly watch as the athletic scholarship and achievement opportunities for biological women diminish.[7]

Not every prominent voice has stayed silent, though.

There was one contributor to the Harry Potter franchise glaringly absent from the Harry Potter twenty-year reunion HBO documentary, *Harry Potter 20th Anniversary: Return to Hogwarts*. One might even say *the* most prominent figure: the author herself, J. K. Rowling. I admit Emma Watson and Daniel Radcliffe made important contributions to bringing the classic children's series to life, but dear reader, may I proffer for your kind consideration that perhaps the most important person was, I'm no Wizard but, the one who actually sat down and fucking wrote it?!

Albeit, for thirty generous seconds, the creator and inventor of the characters, events, and language in the eleven-movie and seven-book saga worth $25 billion[8] that spawned theme parks, Halloween costumes, and a professional sport (for nerds who think they're wizards) was glimpsed (if you didn't blink) through archival footage. Not too bad for a single divorced mother once living on public assistance.

You would think this unlikely female hero would be lifted up and heralded as a champion by feminists and left-leaning ideologues, but you couldn't be more wrong. I'm sorry to inform you, these pseudofemale champions have fallen under a spell, not from Voldemort, but by absolute biological buffoonery — that through no wizardry whatsoever, men can magically be women, just by *saying they are.*

For daring to speak out loud (until very recently) about what has been the most basic anatomical human understanding (that

XY chromosomes = man, and XX chromosomes = woman), J. K. Rowling became known as *she who must not be invited.*

It would be understandable if Rowling was a bit buggered by this codswallop. Graciously, she's not even looking for an apology from all the stars that abandoned her over this "opinion." She tweeted, "Celebs who cosied up to a movement intent on eroding women's hard-won rights and who used their platforms to cheer on the transitioning of minors can save their apologies for traumatised detransitioners and vulnerable women reliant on single sex spaces."[9]

So here we have the most commercially successful author of all time excluded from her own creation's celebration.

It would be hard to fathom Leonardo da Vinci painting the mural of *The Last Supper* and thinking, "Maybe we don't need this Jesus guy. What did *He* contribute anyways?"

I am not immune to the societal pressure of self-censorship myself.

I had a comedy routine that I removed from one of my comedy specials. It was at a very heightened time in society. The exhibitor had concerns about the routine, and I agreed, because it was sensitive and culturally volatile subject matter at that time, and still is. I decided to remove it because it's important to work with people who are willing to pay you for your comedy specials, and to continue my fond habit of keeping my family eating and sleeping indoors.

I took out (what I thought) was a really funny joke — in fact, it was my final closing bit that got roars of laughter from the audience. I agreed the joke was offensive, but it got huge laughs, and as a professional laugh whore myself, the joke's overt offensiveness was part of its shocking charm! Here's the deal: when people go see a horror film, they know what they're getting into. There is an agreed-upon arrangement between theatergoer and fright inducer. You pay money and we scare the shit out of you in a make-believe scenario that we all know isn't really happening. It's a movie, dummy! In this movie, the agreed-upon intention is to frighten you, in as many clever ways as possible, including but not limited to: surprise stabbings, loud screeching music cuts, a Japanese girl with long hair in her face appearing out of nowhere, and the occasional tit thrown in just for "added entertainment value." After witnessing this cinematic experience, nobody complains to the eighteen-year-old manager at the box office, *"That was scary! Way too scary! I did not consent to being this scared! I'm outraged and offended by the amount of fright that this movie incurred..."*

However, for some still-mystifying reason, stand-up comedy is held to a higher standard. Comedians are held more culpable for their spoken words and ideas than for images that show specifically what they're saying, on the big screen no less. For example, Quentin Tarantino can write and then Leonardo DiCaprio can say the n-word repeatedly and they aren't judged as racists as they did in their movie *Django Unchained*. That's because the audience has agreed to the traditional separation of movie character from actual human being. Movies, in this way, are an acceptable art form whereupon we recognize and separate the person from their craft.

However, stand-up comedians are not given the same artistic courtesy. Things a comedian says are taken at face value and judged accordingly, or better yet, somebody else repeats them in a tweet out of context and the pile on by the woke mob's imposed new code of morality — including accusations of racism, sexism, transphobia, or climate change denying (as Greta Thunberg said,

*"How dare you!"*) — ensues. Usually, the accused capitulates just as in the Salem witch trials.

Stand-up comedians are held accountable for not just everything they say, but for other people's interpretations of what they said. Most of whom weren't even there the night of the "offending" performance! If comedians are here to help the culture reflect on some very new and questionable ideas, shouldn't their material get the same benefit of the doubt as Chucky, Freddy, Michael Myers, or Howie Mandel gets? (Hi, Howie, just checking in to see how you're enjoying the book. I know you're reading it with gloves on.)

Sometimes, as a comedian, you have to ask yourself, "How much am I *getting* by doing this bit and how much am I *giving* up?" It's always a judgment call. No matter how hard you're laughing at a bit you just came up with. While self-censorship is editing something you know is funny but could have some career or societal (including marital) consequences, comedic judgment could mean that you're laughing your ass off but you run the risk of laughing *alone*. It truly is a delicate dance. Another brilliant *SNL* comedy writer Rob Smigel was the head writer on Dana Carvey's sketch show on ABC in 1996, *The Dana Carvey Show*. They debuted with a sketch where Carvey was dressed as Bill Clinton explaining how he was going to "nurture the country during his next term," explaining he got estrogen treatments that allowed him to breast-feed.[10] Carvey (Clinton) promptly opened his shirt to reveal eight nipples and he proceeded to nurse a baby doll, several kittens, and a puppy.

Hilarious? Absolutely. But this was airing on ABC, in prime-time (not when *SNL* airs), right after the number-one-rated show on television at the time, *Home Improvement*.[11] As funny as this was, it was a bridge and a joke too far, and they canceled the show after eight episodes.

Now, since you bought this book (or you're still mooching off the bookstore you're in), let me show you my dance of self-censorship and comedic judgment, and I'll tell the joke I cut from my special. For the first time since it was self-censored by me on a streaming service that paid my mortgage for nine months, here is the original ending of my comedy special from several years ago:

*I'm homophobic. Not in the way that the term is used today. I don't hate gay people, I love gay people. I'm homophobic in its original definition when that term was coined in the 1960s. Homophobia, simply meaning: afraid of being gay yourself. I'm afraid I might be a little gay. I don't know. I'm worried one day I might see a dick and say, "OK, put it in a bag, and I'll take it to go! I don't want to eat it here in front of all you people."*

*Let's do an experiment. Let's say Scarlett Johansson had one of those procedures where they took her beautiful vagina — I'm just assuming it's a good one — and they turned it into a penis. I would suck her dick, and I wouldn't feel 100 percent gay doing it. More like 85 percent, tops.*

*"Where do they put the clit on this thing? I'll start there, and I'll do the whole thing, but I just want to know where to start. I'll go up, down, and around — the whole thing, I promise!"*

*But if you really don't wanna be homophobic, then you have to go the other way with this experiment. Let's say they took the Rock, and they took his beautiful penis — I'm just assuming it's a good one. Can you imagine if the Rock didn't have a good dick? "Awwwww! All those hours at the gym for THAT? What a waste!"*

*Let's say they took the Rock's beautiful penis, and they turned it into this massive vagina. I would feel more gay eating the Rock's pussy than sucking Scarlett Johansson's dick.*

While the closing joke that I cut got big laughs, I understood why they would be uncomfortable airing it. I'm presuming it was something they thought they would get backlash for, and they didn't "need" the backlash. The imagined mob influenced them and influenced me, which led to me censoring myself.

No one taking offense would ever care about the specifics of the joke — it was the subject matter alone that was objectionable. To censorship advocates, there are some topics that are off limits. While a rational person would say, "If you don't want to watch it, just turn it off!" That is not enough for these soldiers of cultural protection. They want it silenced, removed, edited, and the offending party must be brought to heel, fired, forced to apologize, and pay a price for their crime of thought.

It was irksome to me that I was supposedly not allowed to make jokes about a topic that was and is currently in the public discourse. The obvious intention of this joke was not hate, or to attack any group, it was an absurd progression of silliness. I wanted to show the extremes of a topical situation and make myself the butt of the joke. Scarlett Johansson doesn't have a penis, the Rock doesn't have a massive vagina, and I've never ordered a dick in a bag to go. That's just me, doing the lord's work. However, the specifics and intentions don't count in the culture wars. All that matters is gaining an advantage and silencing any of those that you consider your enemies. Or, better yet, getting them to silence themselves like I did. Consider yourself victorious in that battle, culture warriors. Culture Warriors 1, Rob Schneider 0.

It was never my intention for me to be on the news for anything other than a movie opening, or a new comedy routine on a streaming service, or a television show where I'm *Behaving Badly*. Yet my opinions on social platforms are now considered worthy of denouncement by the modern mainstream media: a gang of parent basement dwellers that find time to blog for *Newsweek* in between asking Mommy to make sandwiches. Yes, *Newsweek* still exists, relegated to an embarrassing blogger form — on life support, barely clinging to life, on the fumes of cultural insignificance with a readership in the tens of people. They're writing catchy click-baity headlines of an article entirely regurgitating a tweet of mine with the same journalistic standards of a former Harvard University president. Modern mainstream media, which has devolved into a bunch of entitled nonsense written by spoiled, upper-class malcontents, is something we will discuss later.

As de facto intellectuals, comedians are the cultural rearview mirrors. Our jokes reflect the essence of a particular time, place, and attitude, to remind us of the context of where we just came from. We are the golf equivalent of the wedge club. Getting people out of the sand trap or thick rough just off the fairway. You know, like CNN, not focusing on the invasion of the southern border, or the thousands of people dead by fentanyl, but instead hyping up the charisma of the electrifying Joe Biden. *"His age is his superpower!"* Countering the narrative that Biden is a corpse attached to a car battery.

Protecting free speech, and being that comedic rearview mirror, is how comedians give a gut check to society as it ebbs and flows. When things get out of touch, comedians get people to consider whether we've gone too far on an issue — from the sexual liberation of the '60s, the antiwar protests of the '70s, or today's debate of young pubescent girls being allowed to choose their gender, even though it was just twenty-four months ago they still believed in Santa Claus.

We don't give this gut check to piss people off—we do it to make people laugh and, on a deeper level, to validate collective experiences and provoke thought and discussion. We're hopefully bringing people to a consensus when the culture has gone a little mad. After all, because even though I'm a grown man who's half-Filipino, if I decide to identify as Kuon X Chung, a young Korean elementary schoolgirl, and I wanted to use the little girls' bathroom, it would be nice if somebody called me on it.

## CHAPTER FOUR

# PUNCHING SIDEWAYS

All I ever wanted to be was a character actor like Peter Lorre from *The Maltese Falcon*, or Peter Sellers from *The Pink Panther*, or Alec Guinness from *The Ladykillers*. The only person who ever really gave me the opportunity these last thirty years was Adam Sandler. Adam knew I could do any voice or any character, and basically with my blurred ethnicity, it didn't take much makeup to convince the audience I was either a Far-East-Russian-sounding Kazakhstani food delivery worker (*Big Daddy*), or an Asian minister (*I Now Pronounce You Chuck & Larry*), or Middle Eastern prince Habeeboo (*Click*). But perhaps the biggest laughs I ever got was getting beaten with a baseball bat by Drew Barrymore in *50 First Dates*, where I played a milky-eyed Hawaiian sea-life amusement park dolphin handler named Ula!

I basically spent almost every summer of my life growing up in Hawaii, because my grandfather lived there, and because my oldest brother, Stanley, was stationed at the Schofield Barracks in the army in Oahu. (Not a bad place to be stationed in the late '70s, under the

Carter administration.) If you grew up in the cold New England area, like Adam Sandler, you were a chillbilly and your Hawaii was Florida. These were the warm-weather places our parents would take us to when they had the money for a vacation.

Years later, Adam Sandler and I escaped his superstardom for a week by sneaking off to Hawaii in the middle of the night. We went from his crazy fame to the very dark and isolated Paul Mitchell estate on the other side of the extinct volcano, Diamond Head, on the Hawaiian island of Oahu.

We were there by ourselves for about ninety minutes in this secluded island mansion on a dark, moonless night, when we realized if we got murdered, nobody would find our bodies for *days*. Shortly after midnight, we spotted somebody working in the large garden area on the ocean side of the estate. We thought, "Maybe this guy could protect us." So we walked out toward him, and based on his outfit, I immediately recognized him as being someone who lived mostly in the Honolulu/Ala Moana area. He had brown corduroy short-shorts and a faded tie-dye tank top, which is your basic uniform in most jobs for the locals on this most isolated group of islands in the world.

As we approached him gingerly, Adam said, "What's up?"

He turned around to face us revealing that he had one milky eye. Adam Sandler immediately turned to me and said, "You're going to play him in a movie." I knew Adam Sandler long enough to know he was completely serious. Sure enough, twelve months later I would be dressed up as Ula, opposite Drew Barrymore and Adam Sandler, in Sony Picture's monster hit *50 First Dates*, where I ad-libbed, pointing to the milky thing on my face, "And this one's my *good* eye!"

By the way, Ula lost his eye in a fight, and not just any fight, a machete fight, so we made sure to get his complete approval for me to play him in the movie. Ula, as it turned out, was one of the baddest fighters in all the islands. Thankfully, his machete fighting days were well behind him.

A couple of years before *50 First Dates*, I was in Hong Kong making a film with martial arts film star Jean-Claude Van Damme, and we were scouting for scenes in the Portuguese protectorate of Macao (before the Portuguese handed the island back to China in 1999). There was a Triad gang war happening at the time. In America, we've all heard of rival gangs and their "drive-by *shootings*." But in Macao, the preferred form of gang warfare was "drive-by *choppings*," where a rival gang member would drive by on a moped with a passenger on the back, wielding a machete. One would drive, while the passenger on the back would be responsible for the "chopping."

Needless to say, we did not end up filming in the Portuguese protectorate.

(God, those days were fun. I miss those days.)

Cut to: Drew Barrymore beating me with a baseball bat.

In the script, there was just one hit. When I got to the set in Oahu where we were filming that morning, it looked really familiar to me. I thought to myself, "I *know* this place, I've seen it before."

I asked the producer Barry Bernardi, "Why does this location look so familiar?" and he said, "Well, this is where Spielberg filmed the running-of-the-dinosaurs scene in *Jurassic Park*." I said, "*No way!*" and I was psyched. I didn't know how yet, but I knew before the Hawaiian sunset that day, I would be running like the stampeding Gallimimus pack of dinosaurs in *Jurassic Park*.

The plot of the movie was Drew Barrymore's character had a memory problem and was forced to relive the same day over and over again. So Adam Sandler had to find new and inventive ways of meeting her each day. The scene that day was Drew Barrymore finds someone getting beat up on the side of the road (Adam Sandler), and being the Good Samaritan that she is, she gets out to stop the attack.

The first problem was that Drew Barrymore was driving. The second problem was the art directors on movies are always trying to outdo all their art director friends by finding the coolest shit to put in their movies. In this case, the car that Barrymore would be driving was a very cool-looking but sluggishly slow 1970s Volkswagen Thing convertible. As opposed to the dinosaurs running rapidly downhill, for some reason unknown to this day, the topographically challenged director Pete Segal had Drew driving the listless Thing *uphill*. This created a vacuum of time that needed to be filled by some ad-libbing from Adam and me as we waited for Drew's long-anticipated arrival.

As Adam lay on the ground, I ad-libbed (in a Hawaiian pidgin accent) while kicking him, "You come over here, eat our pineapple, make my sister clean your hotel room," with Adam responding, "What does that have to do with anything?" and then Drew Barrymore, as scripted, hits me on my back with a baseball bat.

Scene.

After several takes, the stunt coordinator saw that I was getting a few welts on my back and said, "Do you want me to ask Drew to lighten up a bit?" And I said, "No. She seems to be enjoying herself." Which she was. I saw her practicing her swing between takes.

Once the first setup was complete, we redid the scene from a wider angle, and after this new hit from Drew, I just started running in the direction where the dinosaurs had run. The very clever and instinctive Drew Barrymore followed my lead in hot pursuit, chasing and beating me with the baseball bat. The camera operators quickly picked up and moved their cameras to capture the moment, of Drew chasing and beating me, which led to perhaps the most screamingly funny scene in the movie.

\* \* \*

The audience of a comedy show doesn't lie. In fact, I think stand-up is one of the last true frontiers of meritocracy — where those that are good rise to the top based on their merit, instead of other factors. However, I have noticed in the last seven years, particularly ever since Trump was elected, comedy show audiences seem to be very uncomfortable if there's too much light in the room, and people can see what they're *really* laughing at, and if they're laughing too hard. I go out of my way at my theater shows to make sure that it's dark enough, where people can laugh in anonymity, without feeling that they could be judged and shamed at any laugh — as if they're being videotaped, and the tape can be shown the next day at work.

"Larry, in row twenty-three, laughed at Biden being a corpse attached to a car battery, and now we're not sure if Larry should be selling our kitchen appliances."

Now Larry has to spend the next four weekends in ageism sensitivity training.

Speaking of videotaping, this is exactly why my friend Chris Rock doesn't allow it at his shows. He doesn't allow phones, and they must be locked up in little green expensive pouches. The reason he prohibits videotaping is because he doesn't want to be taken out of context and open himself up to the cancel culture mafia. Especially when he's just working out ideas that are not fully fledged.

A few years ago, a hilarious comedian and fellow *Saturday Night Live* alum, Tracy Morgan, was doing a bit that was to some very offensive, and to others (who were actually there in attendance) very funny. I don't remember exactly, but I'm sure it was about how awkward it was to have sex with a woman in a wheelchair. I know, quite the unique comedy premise. When I listened to the tape, the audience was dying laughing. However, the person in the audience that recorded it shared it out of context, and then in printed form, and non–audience members feigned outrage, defending the fictional girl in the fictional wheelchair in a sexual escapade that never actually happened.

For the sake of argument, let's substitute the comedy routine about a girl having sex in a wheelchair with a horror film where instead of having awkward sex, the audience gets to see and hear a girl in a wheelchair getting slashed repeatedly by a guy in a hockey mask. There would be no cause for complaints and no social shaming. Especially if this was toward the *beginning* of the movie. Two Legs Up!

But for some reason, if a "comedian" tells an anecdote about a romantic romp he may or may not have had in a physically challenged mobile seating apparatus, that's just too far! It's beyond the pale. See, in today's culture battles, comedy does something else to people. If you don't find something funny, or if it offends your sensibilities, it needs to not only remain *unlaughed* at, it needs to be rebuked, shamed, and the offending comedian boycotted.

What is this saying about us?

How we see the world is filtered through the lens of our foundational thinking and our belief system. While people would have no problems questioning things that they don't have strong opinions or feelings about, something that we feel is more essentially core to our intelligence, like humor, can create uproar. Going back to our horror analogy, some will feel totally comfortable admitting "that movie scared (or didn't scare) me," because it doesn't bring into question somebody's value system or their perceived intelligence. However, a sense of humor is a bellwether of their values, sensibilities, and their intellect. You'll rarely hear somebody admit "I don't have a good sense of humor" or "I'm not able to see irony" or "I'm not able to recognize absurd progression scenarios," so instead they stand offended.

When we begin to deconstruct someone's belief system, or question how they view the world, they can become quite hostile.

As my dear friend John Cleese said, "Those who are most easily offended should not be the ones deciding what everyone else gets to watch or listen to." There is a certain elitist tendency of thinking you're protecting someone, while not acknowledging that what you're *really* doing is thinking, "Those people are *far* too feeble to defend themselves. Thank God we were here to defend these feckless weasels. Especially that girl having awkward sex in the wheelchair."

These protectors can feel good about themselves and their millions of dollars and the house by the beach with their army of servants, drivers, and private planes. This is where the term "punching down" comes from. The proposition in "punching down" is that there are somehow people below other people. A rather new premise, I might add. My friend Judd Apatow, our Mel Brooks and the most successful comedy director of our generation and a genuinely great guy (but here it comes anyway...), complained about Louis CK's leaked set where Louis CK made jokes about Parkland shooting survivors, expecting more healing, wondering why comedians have to *punch down*, and calling Louis a "man who mocks our most vulnerable."[1]

Let's discuss this idea of "punching down." Now, there are people that are less powerful and have less money than other people. There are people that are less famous and have smaller houses than other people. There are people that don't live in the Los Angeles area with a good view of the beach that is inaccessible to pedestrians (#poorpeople). But since all people are created equal, there are certainly no people that are below other people. That idea is very illuminating of how media figures like Apatow view other people and his assumption that they need protecting.

After all, it must feel good to reach wayyyy down from the perch of pure goodness with your superior intellect and overflowing empathy to prevent these inferior weaklings from getting their feelings hurt by a comedian who tells dirty jokes in front of consenting adults in drinking establishments. They probably wouldn't have even known their lowly position in life and that somebody is punching down on them if it weren't for Apatow's whining reminders and insistence.

Returning to Tracy Morgan (as if that matters at this point), he had quite the shitstorm to deal with from the shining Apatowian punch-down-prevention warriors. Morgan's routine was something that if you printed it out, and read it, it would sound outrageous. But with the context of the comedy club, the atmosphere, and the audience's overwhelming laughter and consent — the routine is hysterically funny.

All of this harkens back to when I had to appear in front of the ratings board of the Motion Picture Association of America to argue that my film *The Hot Chick* from Disney Studios should be rated PG-13 instead of being labeled with the audience-averse R rating.

Though I won the appeal, ten votes to one, what struck me most was that movie ratings are more lenient toward scenes of violence than they are to scenes of gentle intimacy. For instance, if a woman has her breasts touched, even clothed, it is automatically given an R rating. But in a horror film, a woman could be stabbed in her breasts and they could get the more conciliatory PG-13 rating.

* * *

I appreciate people who compliment me on something I've done that made them laugh. Whether I am between flights at an airport, or having a cup of coffee somewhere, it's nice to see the smile on their face at something they remember. But every once in a great while there is a compliment from someone that brings me back to when I was a kid just hoping to get into show business.

Legendary *Saturday Night Live* writer Michael O'Donoghue loved one of the sketches that I wrote, and I was bowled over that he even saw it. O'Donoghue was the original head writer of *Saturday Night Live*. He wrote and performed in the first sketch ever on *SNL* with John Belushi, "The Wolverines," where Belushi played an immigrant learning English and was taught by O'Donoghue, who hilariously made Belushi use the word "wolverines" in his sentences as he learned the language.

I had an idea for a sketch about a guy with a huge open wound on his head, like someone or something just tried to cave his head in and practically did. So, I went over to Adam Sandler's apartment and together we wrote "Massive Head Wound Harry."

Dana Carvey played the unfortunate man with the gasp-inducing wound masterfully. The idea was a guy who has a bloody exposed head injury (almost like a gunshot wound or failed suicide attempt) shows up at a party. He acts like everything is absolutely fine, but everyone at the party is understandably concerned and horrified. Dana says, "I'm kinda dizzy, I think I just need some food, I lost a lot of blood on the way over here," causing Chris Farley to spit out food.

The sketch had the loudest laugh I'd ever heard on *Saturday Night Live*.

After Dana "accidentally" put his head in the shrimp bowl, he lay down on the white couch. But it wasn't another actor that created the biggest roar, it was a dog. We strategically planted chicken liver in the wound on Dana Carvey's head, and during rehearsals and dress rehearsal, the dog eventually learned where he could get his "treat." By 11:35 p.m., when it was time for the live show, the dog, who had not been fed all day, was understandably famished. So, as Dana lay down, rubbing his head wound on the clean white couch, the dog trainer released the dog, who immediately lunged for Dana's head. Like the Lionel Messi of sketch players, Dana stood his ground as the dog was literally biting and pulling on the prosthetic piece just four inches away from Dana's eyeball. Whereas most actors would be more worried about their self-preservation, Dana reached back and, from the other side, held on to the wig and head wound appliance as the dog pulled violently. Dana almost had to scream out his final line (that *SNL* writer Tom Davis came up with) over the deafening laughter from the audience: "He probably smells my dog!"

One of the joys of being on *Saturday Night Live* was you literally never knew who was going to walk in. One week, one of my favorite actors ever walked in. In fact, his name was practically "Walk In": Christopher Walken.

My first day of work ever on 8H (the NBC studio home of *SNL*) was kind of chaotic and emblematic of what my life would be like for the next five years. First off, nobody tells you what to do. You just kind of have to do what needs to get done, and I didn't know what to do. Somebody, I don't remember who, told me, "Well, write the ten-second promo where the host is introduced for that week's show." And I thought to myself, "Oh, that'll be awesome! I can't believe someone is giving me this all-important duty!" I soon discovered this was the lowest possible writing job and that it was the *SNL* writing equivalent of prison duty. The host that week was a female actress, and I walked into her dressing room and she was in the corner crying, being consoled by Lorne Michaels. Through her tears, she said something like, "I can't believe you talked me into doing this!" And Lorne (in Lorne voice) was saying, "You'll be fine, it'll be fine. We support you one hundred percent. We do this every week. We will be there for you, and you're going to be wonderful, I promise."

I thought to myself, "Does this happen *every week*?!"

I was still easily starstruck, so being in the same room with Christopher Walken and seeing his dirty-blond hair coiffed at a perfect ninety-degree angle (who does that?) was like being a kid actor in an acting candy store. Nobody talked like Walken. He was from New York, but no one in New York talked like him either. His style of speech and the way he would hit words were distinctly his own. But it was more than just that. Walken had his own unique timing. A kind of start-and-stop syncopation that made everything he said sound more interesting. You would find yourself leaning in to hear what he was going to say next, 'cause I don't think he knew either. "Everything... he said... sounded... funny... and you never... knew... when he was... *done*!" He would later tell me that the first thing he would do whenever he got a new script was take out all the punctuation. "I want to be... the one who decides... when, or if, I... *stop*. That should be up to me, the *actor*, not the *writer*! He already did his job... Now I gotta do *mine*!"

One of my ideas for a sketch was a parody of Stephen King's famous horror thriller *The Dead Zone*, where in that movie Walken's character could look into the future or into the past of people he was physically touching and see these monumental events, like the Holocaust or somebody's house on fire that kills a child, etc. You know, the usual awesome Stephen King shit that stays in your brain forever.

Anyway, I thought it would be funny to have a guy who was able to touch somebody and look into their past or future, but he didn't see *anything important*, just inconsequential shit. So, I wrote that sketch with the extremely funny comedy writer, and all-around awesome guy, Ian Maxtone-Graham (who later would go on to write for *The Simpsons*. That's how good this guy is!).

The sketch went like this: (Walken voice) "You have a *daughter*." "Yes, what is it?" "She's at home... with the housekeeper." "Yes." "The housekeeper just waxed the kitchen *floor*. Your daughter is running on the wet kitchen floor!" "And?!" "She's leaving footprints... the housekeeper is annoyed... she has to do that part of the floor over..." The sketch was full of stuff like that. And it murdered! There are very few better feelings in life than having your sketch kill with the host, especially with an Academy Award winner and an acting legend like Christopher Walken.

The best part was I got to put myself in the sketch so I could act with Walken myself.

In the *Dead Zone* sketch, Christopher shakes my hand and says, "Tomorrow, on the way to work, you're going to buy a cup of coffee. Then you're going to get a cab."

"Yeah?!" I said. "Does the cab crash?!" (Worried)

"No...but you're going to forget the coffee in the cab."

(Less worried) "Okayyy..." I said. "I guess I'll have to get another cup when I get here."

"Look, you don't get it, do ya? You're WASTING COFFEE!"

One of the coolest things at *SNL* was that, early in the week, the guest host would go to the different writers' offices, and you'd get to talk to them and have some time to discuss ideas. Just you and *them*! You had ideas, and maybe they had some ideas, and if they liked it, your sketch would probably have a higher chance of getting on the show! Which meant you stayed in show business for at least another week!

But instead of talking about sketch ideas (I already had that killer *Dead Zone* idea), what I *really* wanted to do when I got Christopher in my office was to ask him about the acting methods he used. At that time, I was really submerged in method acting. As a young actor, you are just trying to make it. So you think you have to have *this* agent, you have to have *that* kind of method, you have to be in the *right* acting school. I was very fortunate to be a newbie talent repped by the Bernie Brillstein management company. Literally every star on *SNL*, past and present, was represented by Bernie, including the big boss, Lorne Michaels himself! One of the other comedians repped at Bernie's company was Garry Shandling. Garry recommended an acting class taught by legendary acting teacher and coach, Roy London. That's where and how I met David Spade! David and I became instant inseparable pals. London's class had some students who would go on to do amazing things: Brad Pitt, Jeff Goldblum, Sharon Stone, Elisabeth Shue, Pamela Anderson, David and me. (After Roy's unfortunate death, his school was taken over by the equally brilliant acting-coach genius, Ivana Chubbuck.)

But back to my hopes and my acting needs. In my NBC *SNL* office with the door safely Matt Lauer'd, I asked Christopher, "So *you* do the Stanislavsky method? You know, the whole sense memory technique?" (Which I always found confusing but everyone else was using it or *said* they were using it.) He looked at me and he said in his Christopher Walken way, "*No!*"

I was shocked.

I said, "You don't? I thought all the New York Actors Studio [Lee Strasberg's] actors used sense memory."

"No, I don't!"

"Well, what do you do?"

Walken said, "I don't do anything."

He saw the look of shock on my face from all the acting-lesson money I had been wasting for the last five years. My whole acting foundation, and everything I'd ever thought about acting, and what I hoped and thought I needed, suddenly crashed to the floor.

He reached out and touched my knee reassuringly. Gently, Christopher said, "I just *play*…The phone *rings* at four in the morning. *All* the things that go through your mind before you answer the phone…'Did my father *die*? Was there a plane *crash*? Is the building on *fire*?' It's all *as if*…I just *play*."

I threw the method acting out the window after that, and I've never had more fun acting ever since. I just *play*.

I'll always be grateful to Christopher Walken for how generous he was to give a young actor that priceless jewel of advice.

Now, if *you're* a young actor, go directly to the kiosk at the airport that you're in and pay for this book.

## CHAPTER FIVE

# "I SAW A SKETCH ON SATURDAY NIGHT LIVE LAST NIGHT..."

— President George Bush

It was the nineties. I got into a fight with my girlfriend, and I don't remember quite how it happened, but I got locked out of the apartment. This was after being on *Saturday Night Live* for a while, so unlike the first couple of years, I had money to live in a very nice place. Late-night network TV didn't pay anything like prime time. Whereas it was common for stars at the eight or nine o'clock hour to make a hundred thousand dollars an episode, sleepy shows on Saturday nights paid less than a tenth of that. I know, still pretty good. But that was if you had been on the show for several years and were a hit. Luckily, that was the sweet spot I found myself. My third season I was making $9,500 a week. But there were usually only two shows a month, three at the most. Still, I was able to afford to live in a fancy place on Stuyvesant Square Park, one of these old commercial buildings converted into expensive apartments. I knew I finally had money because I actually had a tree in my backyard. Fuck yeah! No one gets a tree in their backyard in New York City. I had one, bi-atch! I was also able to afford another luxury item: a girlfriend.

Now that I think about it, I should have been in round-the-clock therapy, not on national television working hundred-hour weeks.

Anyhoo, I left the apartment and found myself locked out. This was on a Friday night, and the next day, Saturday, was show night. Luckily (and unluckily), Chris Farley lived in the same building as me. So, I went up to Farley's apartment and knocked on his door. He opened it with a large smile that was honestly alarming. After three years of working with Chris, I was used to it. There was always an air of danger around Farley. Sometimes he would come into work with a wound on his arm sporting forty new stiches that looked like he was just in a war zone.

"Oh, what a nice surprise!" he greeted me.

First time I had ever heard about Farley was in the office of Bob Odenkirk of 30 Rock. Odenkirk was a writer for the show, decades before his *Breaking Bad* fame. Bob has proven to be one of the most talented and greatest actors that have ever come out of *SNL*. Luckily for Bob, as a sometime performer, he never hit it big on *SNL*, avoiding the "comedian" typecasting that yours truly and so many other *SNL* stars would be labeled with. Spade and I had been hired as writers for the last four episodes of the 1989 season, and as Odenkirk talked, I couldn't help but notice that he had an office with a view of the Empire State Building. I thought to myself, "Holy shit, how cool is that?" As he spoke, I could barely pay attention to what he was saying. My peripheral vision kept going toward that incredible view his office had. Odenkirk said, "We got a really funny guy coming in next year." Then the next line Bob delivered was more cold than anything I had heard before in my life. "He's really, *really* funny, but he's not going to live very long." I'd never heard anybody introduced with that description before, or since, and it caused me to stop looking at the Empire State Building. Unfortunately, and sadly, Bob's description turned out to be all too true. "His name is Chris Farley, and he's the funniest guy I've ever seen." Bob would go on to write Farley's famous "Living in a Van Down by the River" sketch.

I couldn't get over Odenkirk's statement, and I still remember to this day how bluntly and emotionlessly it was delivered. Almost like a surgeon coming out of the emergency operating room and shouting to the relatives, "DEAD!" and just continuing walking.

In retrospect, Chris Farley should have been in therapy, too. I worked with the great addiction-expert doctor, psychologist, and author Dr. Gabor Maté, who helped me realize there was such a thing as generational trauma. I had been gifted with my mother's and father's trauma, though I was deeply unconscious of it at the time. Anyhow, I didn't like Bob for saying that, true or not. It just wasn't nice. Filipinos rarely say anything that is unkind. I'm one of the rare exceptions.

Chris welcomed me into his two-story apartment, which was surprisingly clean and elegant. I told him what happened, and being a lovely Midwestern gentleman, he allowed me to stay.

Farley was soon laughing at my predicament. (Farley voice) "Got into a fight with the little lady, I see. All right, Robbie, looks like it's just us bachelors tonight."

We watched TV in his upstairs bedroom. Chris flipped the channels, and at that time, there was a channel on New York's cable TV called Channel J. Only in New York City in the nineties would there be (or would anyone want) a public access channel that featured full frontal nudity, talk shows with naked hosts and guests, and production values in the $40 to $60 range (Jon Lovitz played one of these naked talk-show hosts on *SNL* in a very funny sketch). This channel was specifically for Manhattan perverts of every sexuality. Back then there was basically two: straight or gay. I remember an unintentionally hilarious advertisement for a gay bar called the Dungeon, where the commercial ended with "Let every fantasy of yours go wild…the Dungeon…let's… *go down.*"

While Chris and I were laughing and he was flipping the channels, we came to Channel J, which was blocked. I said, "Why did they block your Channel J?" And he just said (in his Midwestern Farley voice), "Oh, Robbie, Robbie, let me tell ya, I'd never get any sleep. I'll be honest with you, I gotta work to make a living. So, Channel J became a problem for the old Farles. So I had the nice people at the cable company, who understood the problem *completely*, block Channel J for me."

Because he lived alone, having to block it for himself was something.

Anyway, so after about an hour or so watching *Matlock* in his room, Chris announced it was time to "hit the hay!" Chris was very proud of his upscale apartment. It had a long stairway where he led me to the lower floor. You could tell he had a good mom and a good upbringing, because he set up a bed for me on the couch downstairs, complete with (clean) pillow, sheets, and a nicely folded blanket.

Chris said, "Okay, good night, Robbie! If you need anything, you know where to find me." I said, "Thank you, I really appreciate this." And I did. Then he added, "If you need anything, *anything* at all, I'm just right at the top of the stairs."

"I'm good. Thanks."

"...Anything."

The lights were turned off.

Moments later, as I'm trying to fall asleep, I hear an unmistakable creaking noise, soon followed by another. And then another. In the darkened apartment, I looked up to see a completely naked three-hundred-pound man, slowly walking down the stairs. With a seductive finger in his mouth, Chris made his way to the bottom step, saying, "Do you see anything you *like?*"

We both found ourselves silly with laughter. Farley had a unique way of eliciting a kind of laugh that was funny but also alarming. So, obviously, we were up again. We started watching TV on the *downstairs* TV. This time *I* was the one flipping the channels. As I was searching for something that would keep our short attention spans, the remote turned to Channel J. The *unblocked* Channel J was on downstairs. I looked at Chris and said, "I thought you said you *blocked* it?"

Chris said, "Well, yeah, I blocked it in the *bedroom.* But I got to *live.* After enough hours of abusing myself, eventually I get tired and go upstairs and go to bed."

That was the plan. The plan a crazy person makes.

Boy, what I would give for more crazy times with Farley. But when Sandler, Spade, and I are together, there's always this wonderfully weird buzz of a feeling like we used to get when Chris Farley would bounce in the room...

Usually with something hidden up his ass.

Chris would be having a serious conversation with you, where you knew something was up but you couldn't quite get a handle on what it was. Then after talking with you, Chris would turn around, start laughing, and sure enough, some unspecific bottle of booze would be wedged in his butt cheeks.

* * *

A few years earlier, in 1991, I was in between apartments in midtown Manhattan, staying in a hotel. I was rushing to get to work, my job as a writer and performer on *Saturday Night Live*. I turned on the TV because we were just about to start a war with a country that had the third-biggest army in the world. It was a war against a military that was supposedly so powerful they didn't feel the necessity to have an air force. Of course I'm talking about Iraq. Background information... Iraq didn't even know it was living in a place called Iraq until the British, as they are wont to do, drew a map around several traditional warring tribes that hated each other in the early twentieth century and said, "Okay, you guys. You are now Iraq!"

As I watched the TV, I saw a slightly befuddled American lieutenant colonel at a press conference getting grilled by reporters and saw that the raw gathering of news, in its initial collecting phase, is very messy. The reporters seemed to be asking questions that could be deleterious to our troops, who are now about to start fighting a war on foreign soil. I knew that this would be the cold opening and I ran as fast as my little Filipino legs would take me to 30 Rock, floor seventeen. Out of breath, I ran toward the office of the head writer and producer, Jim Downey, and saw Jim talking to the bulky presence of the longest-running feature player in *Saturday Night Live*'s history, and future ex-senator, Al Franken. (Al was later forced to resign from the Senate for phantom grabbing a woman's boobs — who would've seen that coming?)

I said, "Jim, I've got the cold open! It's how messy these press conferences are, and the reporters asking inappropriate questions that could harm our troops!"

And Al Franken yelled out, "I had that idea!"

I didn't say what I was thinking, which was "Well, if you did, we'd be writing it by now," and that was exactly what we did.

Now, when I said "we wrote," that was an exaggeration. Most of the brilliant sketches on *Saturday Night Live*, like "Jane you ignorant slut," Change Bank, and Norm Macdonald's *Weekend Update* (to name just a few), and without exception every astute political sketch, were written by the real genius of *Saturday Night Live*, Jim Downey. Jim wrote for thirty seasons of *Saturday Night Live*, and no disrespect to Lorne Michaels, his real genius was finding talent and more importantly keeping the network away, so we didn't have to deal with any of their "notes." We were in a cocoon of comedy where we could pretty much do whatever with few exceptions during my time there (pre–social media). We were able to do what *we* wanted — things that would make *us* and our *friends* laugh (which is what *Saturday Night Live* does at its best) — with little or no network interference (censorship). As this was my first real job in show business, I didn't realize how rare it was, and how lucky we were, to have a protective gorilla like Lorne that the NBC suits were so scared of. Lorne's prestige and the decades of comedy that he had presided over managed to keep the network at bay. Long before I was hired on *Saturday Night Live*, Lorne stayed above the fray of writing comedy and was the chief decider of what sketches aired that weekend and gave notes accordingly.

I would learn later how uniquely democratic this process was. Unlike other television shows, everything written by the writers got read by the very talented performers in front of a room filled to the brim with people. Truthfully, as the biggest department, most of the people in the room were wardrobe people, which did tilt the odds in favor of musical and Broadway-flavored sketches. But just to get the opportunity to have your sketch read, and your ideas aired out loud, was and still is a rare commodity in show business. Chances were, if you got big laughs on something you wrote, you got your shit on that Saturday, including if you had a good idea for a political sketch that week. Especially if you had a genius like Jim Downey around at *SNL*.

Lorne called Jim Downey "the best political humorist alive."[1] Jim wrote the best political comedy sketches (so far) of the twenty-first century. I remember one where the reporters are falling all over themselves and favoring Obama over Hillary in the 2008 presidential campaign. I remember it went something like "Senator Clinton, in your two-state solution for Israel and Palestine, how can you exclude Hamas from the peace talks when they are the duly elected representatives of the Palestinian people in Gaza?" Then, the question for Obama: "Senator Obama, who's your favorite basketball team?"

In comedy writing circles, whether in the *Simpsons* writers' room, or David Letterman's writing staff (Downey was the head writer at the inception of the groundbreaking *David Letterman Show*), or the *Seinfeld* writers' room, Jim is revered nonpareil. He's one of the three legendary writers that came out of the *Harvard*

*Lampoon* in the early 1970s — where he graduated with a degree in Russian literature — the other two being John Hughes (*Home Alone, Breakfast Club, Ferris Bueller's Day Off, National Lampoon's Vacation*, and *Planes, Trains and Automobiles*) and Douglas Kenney, who wrote the groundbreaking and generationally influential movies *Animal House* and *Caddyshack*.

"We wrote" meant Al Franken and I listened and marveled as Jim Downey wrote, acted out, and played every character of the sketch that would become that week's cold open, titled "Desert Storm Press Briefing" — it was played brilliantly by Kevin Nealon and the late Phil Hartman. I laughed and tried to write down every hilarious utterance and word Jim was saying. I could barely breathe as the progression of absurdity for each reporter's question built to a hilarious climax. Truthfully, the sketch didn't change much from his initial creative outburst that morning. I don't really know if Al and I contributed a thing besides our uproarious laughter of approval.

This sketch reminds us that *Saturday Night Live* was, is, and still can be a way to capture and accentuate the nation's mood. The president of the most powerful country in the history of the world would talk about a sketch on a late-night TV show, in the moments leading up to a major ground offensive. Twelve hours after the sketch aired, there was the president referencing it and using it as his administration's rational excuse to delay disseminating information about the oncoming war to the press.[2] Now, because of that roughly three-minute sketch on Saturday night at 11:35 p.m. eastern time, the press would have to wait to get information until whenever the government decided to give it.

The sketch featured Phil Hartman as Cheney, Kevin Nealon as Lt. Col. William Pierson, and Mike Myers, Dana Carvey, Julia Sweeney, Tom Davis, Jan Hooks, Conan O'Brien, Tim Meadows,

Chris Farley, and me as the reporters. This is basically how the sketch went, brilliantly played by Kevin Nealon and Phil Hartman:

> [Open on press conference discussing the Gulf War]
> Cast member opens with saying that there are certain sensitive areas that he's just not going to get into. Particularly, information that might be useful to the enemy.
>
> First question: "What date are we going to start the ground attack?"
>
> "That would be something that I cannot discuss here."
>
> Second question: "Where would you say our forces are most vulnerable to attack?"
>
> "Again, that goes into the category of things I cannot divulge."
>
> Third question: "A two-part question. Are we planning an amphibious invasion of Kuwait, and if so, where exactly will that be?"
>
> Kevin tries to explain again why this is an inappropriate question.
>
> Fourth question: "I understand there are passwords that our troops are using on the front lines. What are some of those?"
>
> [Audience laughs uproariously.]

And then finally, the last question is from me, in the last row of the press corps, dressed in obvious Arab headgear speaking in a nondescript Middle Eastern accent (foreshadowing all the different nationalities I would play in twenty-seven different Adam Sandler movies): "Yes, Farud Hashami, *Baghdad Times*. Where are your troops, and can I go there and count them?"

The sketch was a smash success and accomplished what *Saturday Night Live* can do at its best: say the thing we're all thinking but haven't said, or ridicule a part of the establishment — in this case the messy reporting of the press — that *needs* ridiculing. Later that night, we enjoyed the weekly party that Lorne Michaels was kind enough to throw for the host and the cast after every show — before the advent of camera phones — where the cast could relax, be ourselves, carouse, and drink.

Monday morning, still slightly hungover, I got what I thought was a crank call from fellow *SNL* writer, the lovely Christine Zander. "Hey! The president just talked about your sketch on the news last night!"

*"Whaaat?!"*

Still not believing, I threw on my clothes and I ran back over to the seventeenth floor of 30 Rock and put a VHS tape into the video player where I watched Sunday Night's *NBC Nightly News*. Sure enough, there was the forty-first president of the United States, George H. W. Bush, between functions talking to a reporter and (I paraphrase) said, "I saw a sketch on *Saturday Night Live*" (which, according to the *New York Times*, was rushed to the president by the White House chief of staff John Sununu) "where the press was asking inappropriate questions..."[3]

My naïve twenty-seven-year-old self said, "Well, that was cool!" Here's what I now know is less cool: handing the government an excuse to delay and decide when and what to tell the fourth estate, the press — the people's champion.

At *Saturday Night Live*, besides having to cover my naked ass during the Italian waiter sketch per our show censor begging me, "Please don't show your ass or I'll get fired," really the only thing that we had to worry about was swear words and things that were considered... obscene.

Obscene? Hmm. What is obscene? And exactly *who* gets to decide what's obscene? Believe it or not, before you could get real estate lady porn on your phone (David Spade's favorite, by the way), there used to be laws of what was obscene and what you could or couldn't say. Dirty words themselves used to be enough to put somebody in jail, somebody like a comedian.

*Wait a minute, I'm a comedian! This could affect me! What about my life? My hopes, my dreams, and my aspirations??*

Leonard Alfred Schneider, better known as Lenny Bruce (1925–1966), became a monstrously successful stand-up comedian, compulsively selling out his venues, and, when deemed appropriate by the executives, appearing on major national television like the pre–Johnny Carson *Tonight Show*–type programs.

In 2017, *Rolling Stone* named Lenny Bruce number three of the top fifty stand-up comics of all time behind Richard Pryor and George Carlin.[4] Truth be told, there might not have been a Richard Pryor or a George Carlin if it weren't for Lenny. Or a Chris Rock or a Dave Chappelle, for that matter.

Lenny was one of the guys who broke the obscenity rules for comedians — but he paid a price for it with his own life; he died of an "accidental" drug overdose at the age of forty, after being deemed unhirable and blacklisted by nearly every club in the United States. Unlike how Mort Sahl was unhirable because of his "conspiracy theorist" label, Lenny was unhirable because of his "obscenity" label.

First, Bruce was charged (and acquitted) for breaking obscenity laws for using the word "cocksucker," at the 1961 San Francisco Jazz Workshop. As Lenny said, "The word, 'cocksucker,' is not obscene, it's something nice that somebody does for another person. The word 'war' is obscene." One time, the police just went into a club in Los Angeles where Lenny was "allowed" to play and smashed all the toilets so Lenny couldn't play there that night. Can't have a bar going with no toilets...[5]

In 1962, he was arrested again for a show at the Troubadour in West Hollywood, and the jury for that trial ended up deadlocked. Just two weeks after he was arrested for the Troubadour show he was arrested after a performance at the Gate of Horn in Chicago. For the Chicago case, he was convicted and sentenced to a year in prison. *A year in prison.*[6]

Retreating to New York, which he thought was his last safe haven for his stand-up comedy, Lenny found a gig making $3,500 a week (which would be $35,000 today — you can find a way to live on that) at Howard and Elly Solomon's Cafe Au Go Go in Greenwich Village.

Over three hundred people came to see him every night.

In the audience was Herbert Ruhe, a former CIA agent and, if I may say so myself, a rather large cocksucker. Ruhe wrote down what he could of Lenny's set and handed it over to the police. The next night, undercover cops recorded his set and transcribed it. The night after that, Bruce was arrested for a "violation of Penal Code 1140-A, which prohibited 'obscene, indecent, immoral, and impure dram, play, exhibition, and entertainment...which would tend to the corruption of the morals of youth and others.'" You know, real estate lady porn.

He was dealt three charges, each with a maximum punishment of three years in prison. *Three years in prison for each charge.*[7]

Lenny got out on bail and promptly performed another show the next night at Cafe Au Go Go.[8]

I guess Lenny was trying to live his quote, when he famously said, "If you can't say 'fuck,' you can't say 'fuck the government.'"[9]

A long, arduous trial followed that inevitably ended in Lenny's conviction and sentencing to "four months in the workhouse." Just like with Tracy Morgan, Lenny's stuff was read aloud in a court of law during his trial. He didn't get the benefit of a talented comedian performing his material in the darkened consenting comedy club. Instead, it was unperformed and read aloud word for word in the sterile setting of the brightly lit courtroom. This rendition of Lenny's act would "eat it" in the courtroom, and he would just seem obscene because of the words he was using. As any self-respecting comedian would, Lenny took great umbrage at someone else botching *his* material.

Lenny never saw his appeal as he died of a "morphine overdose" in his left arm eight months later — curious because he was a left-handed heroin addict. Lenny was found naked, and the police allowed the press in to take photos of his naked body before the coroners were allowed to take his body away. Lamenting his death, one of his New York prosecutors, Assistant District Attorney Vincent Cuccia, expressed regret over his role:

I feel terrible about [Lenny] Bruce. We drove him into poverty and bankruptcy and then murdered him. I watched him gradually fall apart. It's the only thing I did in Hogan's office that I'm really ashamed of. We all knew what we were doing. We used the law to kill him.[10]

During Lenny's life and trials, the power of obscenity laws to destroy America's brightest and bravest comedian (and somebody of such cultural significance) scared many into silence.

After Lenny's pointless death, prosecutors shied away from going after comedians. For the cancel culture warriors of the day, Lenny Bruce's lifeless corpse was enough. Lenny died because his guaranteed First Amendment right of free speech was denied to him. You see, the Bill of Rights is just a piece of paper. It requires the people to stand up and insist it be not just an eighteenth-century paper but breathed aloud by its citizenry.

Because of Lenny's sacrifice, we are better off from what he did for comedy and more importantly for society. Lenny built the sidewalk that Dick Gregory, George Carlin, Richard Pryor, all the way up to today's brilliant comedians — Chris Rock, Dave Chappelle, Bill Burr, Louis CK, Sebastian Maniscalco, Daniel Tosh, Sarah Silverman, Whitney Cummings, David Spade, and Adam Sandler — walk on.

Now, history doesn't seem that short when something like this happened to a comedian, in the United States, during the 1960s. I was alive at the time! Lenny was a groundbreaking performer whose material seems mild by today's standards, though it may not seem as fresh anymore, because today's comedians have built on the foundation that he set. He was a really, *really* great comedian, but he was destroyed by his denial of free speech. I remember as a small boy laughing hysterically with my parents in a movie theatre at his animated short, *Thank You Mask Man*. Really funny.

Even though it's decades later, we don't find ourselves moving forward to more unfettered free speech, but regrettably backward to "fettered" speech and toward the trials and tribulations of the late Lenny Bruce. Today, comedians are hectored, canceled, and once again their words are taken out of context and repeated by nonperformers. They're losing their incomes, and in some places in the world today, comedians have found themselves in jail for jokes. Bassem Youssef had to flee Egypt because he had a warrant issued for his arrest by the president of Egypt for "spreading false news with the aim of disrupting public order."[11]

Indian comedian Munawar Iqbal Faruqui was deemed to have "intent" to offend, and as *Time* magazine notes, he was arrested *for a joke he didn't even tell* and was given *four years* in prison.[12] While in the UK, Mark Meechan, a YouTuber who goes by the screen name Count Dankula (and has over one million subscribers), was convicted of a hate crime for a joke that was deemed "grossly offensive" — a video he posted to his YouTube channel where his dog gives a Nazi salute as a simple trick.[13] Even today and in nations we'd think are "freer," comedians are still getting arrested for jokes.

Just like the best of *Saturday Night Live*, Lenny and the comedians that followed him are a way to capture and accentuate the nation's mood. Once again, the question comes back sixty years later: What is obscene and who gets to decide? Because if you can decide what's obscene — in today's parlance, "hate speech"—then you get to decide what is allowed to be said. (That sounded soooooo smart just then. My junior college would be soooooooo proud of me!)

In the foreword to *How to Talk Dirty and Influence People*, Lenny Bruce's autobiography, Kenneth Tynan described Lenny as the pearl in the oyster. "Constant, abrasive irritation produces the pearl: it is a disease of the oyster..."[14]

The oyster is our nation, and for every new problem our nation produces, there is the opportunity for great artists to add another layer of luster over our collective pearl, making something beautiful. But the pearl is an irritant and, in fact, is killing the oyster. In the same way great art — whether films, poetry, painting, music, or stand-up comedy — can expose a part of our society that needs excising. Censorship, and the feckless twats who propagate it, is removing valuable pearls that could enrich, illuminate, and help liberate our society. Jewels like comedian Lenny Bruce.

The best comedians, like my friend Chris Rock, one of today's preeminent comedians and social critics, expose the problems that society would prefer to ignore. Chris Rock can subvert us to his point of view by his brilliant use of absurd rationality. During the George Floyd riots, Rock commented: "I know it's hard being a cop. I know it's hard. I know that shit's dangerous. But some jobs can't *have* bad apples. Some jobs, everybody gotta be good. Like, pilots. American Airlines can't be like, 'You know, most of our pilots like to land. We just got a *few* bad apples.'"[15] Not very reassuring!

One of my favorite Lenny Bruce bits had nothing to do with social commentary. It was about the quick turn a waiter could have at your favorite Chinese restaurant.

Chinese waiter (in a thick Chinese accent): "Where is your beautiful wife?"

Lenny: "We got divorced."

Chinese waiter: "Oh, you better off!"

## CHAPTER SIX

# "NEVER LET A GOOD CRISIS GO TO WASTE"

— Winston Churchill[1]

I know the scamdemic was pretty scary in 2020. We all had access to constant and immediate news on our phone for the first time in history. You can only watch so much real estate lady porn before you get sick of it and say to yourself, "I better see what's on the news." Then we saw scary COVID news updates like, "Wait a minute, this guy's parachute didn't open and *he* died of COVID!"

We now all know that they exaggerated the scamdemic in the beginning. It was scary because you saw they tried the same shit they tried during the swine flu, but after dozens of people were burdened with Guillain-Barré syndrome after getting the swine flu shots, they stopped giving people the shots.[2] This was before the revolving door of the pharmaceutical industry controlled the regulatory agencies like they do now. They couldn't get enough people scared during the swine flu nonepidemic. We weren't quite as lucky this time. Now the people are as influenced by their phones as they were in Nazi Germany in the late 1930s.

Hitler's propaganda minister, Joseph Goebbels, knew that they had all other political parties outlawed, in jail, or Jeffrey Epstein-ed. Likewise, they controlled the newspapers, radio, and movies, where the German citizens were besieged by Nazi propaganda newsreels in theaters before every film. Yet Goebbels knew that the people could avoid the movie theaters, turn off the radio, and choose not to read the newspapers. But there was one thing that every citizen in Germany couldn't avoid: *billboards*. Patriotic, omnipresent billboards on every street glorified and reinforced the Nazi Party line.[3] Soon, they turned the people into cult-like followers who could be led to their own destruction. Now, in the present, instead of billboards we have push notifications on our phones from news apps, social media, or, if deemed necessary, directly from the government "emergency" alert service itself. During COVID, besides the "mask up" signs on freeways, they had something more effective: compliant two-legged walking mask-wearing billboards on every street and in every Target, Walmart, and grocery store. You know, the stores that were allowed to be open, not like one of those small stores that you owned, but the big stores where the virus gave everybody a free pass knowing that everybody needed to get their toilet paper.

We are all addicted to some degree or another to our phones. We are influenced by the daily barrage of information at our disposal. Our brains are overloaded. Our susceptibility to being swept up and mentally herded into the pen of our own political self-identification has never been higher. ("Oh my God, you're soooo smart!")

They called us COVID deniers and vaccine-hesitant refuse-niks. So what do we call these people who don't see any problems happening? You know, the modern media that seems willfully and blissfully unaware that any problems had occurred. After all, to them, the rate of athlete fatality was just a coinkydink. (Even a study published by the Cold Spring Harbor Laboratory Press downplaying any links acknowledged that of their 1,653 respon-dents, "in 63 [3.8% of cases], including 9 fatal events, there was a plausible association with COVID-19 vaccination.")[4]

Anybody who sees people collapse live on TV is just falling to a frequency illusion bias, although you've never seen it before in your entire life or on YouTube, and neither has anyone else, only "because you want to see it so that's what you're looking for." Now you're noticing something that neither you, nor your friends, nor anybody else who's lived has ever seen before. Luckily, unlike most people these days, I watch CNN, so my syndrome is way better. I have liberal "no problem at all with the shots" syndrome, which just like the other three remaining CNN viewers (who stopped going on Twitter and would neeeeeeever listen to Joe Rogan), I don't notice all the extra heart attacks in the healthiest people alive playing professional soccer, people in their thirties needing pacemakers, or reporters on TV passing out on live television. What a QAnon waste of time.

Unlike the liberal attitudes of the late 1960s and '70s — question everything — the new liberal intelligentsia has a differ-ent slogan: Question nothing! Ever! Swallow whole everything the government tells you and regurgitate the liberal talking points on social media ad nauseam. I admit, it's a clunky bumper sticker — you have to get really close to the back of their vehicle to see it all — but if you get close enough, you'll notice one thing for sure: the lone driver is wearing a mask.

Your fellow liberals pleaded with you, as my friend the great Jimmy Dore did, "Don't do your own research, or God forbid reeeeead. Doing your own research became a terrible thing during Covid…'I'm gonna go buy a car.' 'Don't look into it!' 'Well, how will I know which car to get?' 'Ask the salesman, he's the expert! What are you, Henry Ford?'"[5]

Thankfully, we as a society have learned a few things. Unlike the 1970s, liberals who dare ask any inconvenient questions of the 2020s government must therefore *all* be right-wing extremist Trump supporters, even if they claim to be lifelong Democrat voters. Especially if they're Hispanic or Black (you know, their own race traitors like Clarence Thomas or Thomas Sowell). Or, blasphemy of blasphemies, they have the gall to listen to Tucker Carlson, who, on February 8, 2024, the *New York Times* referred to as a "diminished figure in the United States since leaving *Fox News*, where he averaged an audience of 3 million a night."[6] I guess math is racist after all at the *New York Times*, because Tucker's audience "diminished" from 3 million to 35 million viewers on his first episode of *Tucker on X*.[7] Somehow, these questioners are the fascists because, after all, you know, words don't mean the same thing anymore. We already talked about how the word "Nazis" has been watered down from people who murdered 6 million Jews to its new usage: someone who doesn't clear their table at Starbucks or takes up two parking spaces (like I do), or if you don't think a thirteen-year-old girl should be allowed to decide to cut off her own breasts. You know how thirteen-year-olds aren't allowed to get tattoos, drive a car, buy a gun, join the army, vote, or drink alcohol? It's because we know they're not good decision makers. I mean, listen to the shitty music they like — that's a sign right there. Those restrictions are in place because we as a society know that these young, very impressionable *children* don't have fully developed brains and shouldn't make such life-altering decisions at such a tender age. Decisions that could prevent them from breastfeeding their own child one day, or that could even cause them to become infertile. Hey, people, you can't even rent a car in America if you're under twenty-five! What do Hertz, Avis, and Enterprise know that our medical establishment seems so blissfully unaware of?

This is a big leap from what the liberal intelligentsia condemned not so very long ago. Remember how awful gay conversion therapy was? You know, where somebody could supposedly get talked out of being gay? What was that conversation like?

Gay conversion therapist: "Hey! Stop watching so many Broadway musicals and get that dick out of your mouth, you're straight!"

Former gay person: "Okay, I'm sold! I found this session to be the most helpful."

We've made quite a jump to *surgical* conversions, where the medical profession is carving up little boys and girls, which has to be at least ten thousand times worse than conversion therapy. A Dutch teen died from complications of a vaginoplasty in 2016.[8] I'm sure his parents take solace in the fact that at least no one tried to talk him out of being gay in those terrible gay conversion therapies.

I remember being in Chicago during the pandemic, where I had to wear my fake mask.

That's right. I wore a fake mask during the whole pandemic,

proudly. (They sold those fake masks, by the way!) While it looked like a mask, it was in actuality dark panty hose material doubled up, and unless the flight attendant was really looking, I usually got away with it. Of course, you could take your mask off if you were eating or drinking, because like any good lethal virus that has any integrity or morality at all, COVID-19 would give a generous pause in its lethality to allow you to sip your Bloody Mary at 37,000 feet. You know, like diplomatic immunity, the virus gave you temporary viral immunity — especially if you were pretending to look out the window and take half the flight nursing your drink like I usually was.

If you didn't question Governor Gavin Newsom's dictate around Thanksgiving 2020 to quote "keep your mask on in between bites"[9] — while he went maskless at the most expensive restaurant in California, Napa County's French Laundry[10] (not that great, actually, and $1,500 a plate) — then you really are a mindless governmental drone and shouldn't be allowed to drive, vote, or chew food without being monitored "between bites." Because if the government told you to bite your cheek and finish the rest of it, you'd probably do it and start on the next one.

By the way, like most politicians, Newsom only apologized because there was mobile phone photographic evidence of him maskless, taunting the virus, defiantly not masking up between bites, just rereading his own tweets on his phone. During his perfunctory press conference apology, Gavin (who never held a real job in his life) stood behind the podium with the seal of the (formerly) great state of California behind him (before the Newsom regime unabashedly ushered in the human-feces-covered streets of San Francisco). And in his

California air-heady-surfer-colloquialism-speak said, "I gotta own this." Own this?! You mean like the people had to "own" losing their businesses and restaurants?

To his credit, in twenty-four hours Gavin Newsom cleaned up all the homeless poop when his political hero, Xi Jinping, president of China, came to town.[11] Newsom can instantly clean it up when he wants to for people he admires — like communist dictators — but not for the people who live there, pay taxes, and have to walk on those streets, albeit very carefully.

You can hourly track the morphine-assisted homeless "gifts" at the Human Waste Map on Sfgov.org.[12]

By the way, politicians lie for a reason. When the truth accidentally slips out between their lips, people get angry. Remember when they ran Mitt Romney as the Republican sacrificial lamb against Obama (they knew they were going to lose, but you gotta run somebody to make it seem like it's fair; otherwise, people will catch on pretty quickly that it's all bullshit)? Anyways, this was back in 2012, dear reader, before everyone was videotaping everything, everywhere they went. You know how when you go to a concert, nobody is actually watching it, everyone is just standing there recording it? We're no longer human beings experiencing life as it happens; we're our own videographers not experiencing life as it happens and then never bothering to watch the thing we just taped. Anyways, back to the Max Headroom–looking Mormon with great hair: Mitt was at a fundraiser in 2012 where no one reminded people to not videotape on their phones, and security was a bit lapse, because everyone in the room knew he was going to lose to Obama. Mitt was given the mic and he made the great error of blurting out something actually truthful to this two-thirds-full room of conservative Americans. He made the shamelessly obvious claim that he was going to have a hard time winning the election because "47% of Americans don't pay taxes."[13] Another *outrageous* conservative Republican smear on the taxpayer. Hey Mitt, it's not 47 percent that pay no federal income tax, it's 40.1 percent that pay no federal income tax, you asshole![14] You're exaggerating by almost 7 percent! As Greta Thunberg would say, "How dare you!"

Of course, Mitt had to apologize, not for his slightly off numbers, but for telling Americans an ugly truth. You see, it's not polite to say out loud that over 40 percent of Americans pay little to zero taxes and that the burden falls on the 59 percent that do. Apology accepted. Curiously, while journalists were up in arms defending those 40 percent of Americans, none of them seemed curious why they don't pay any fucking taxes. That would've been clickbait I would've clicked! Are you paying attention, you *Newsweek* basement bloggers?

Anywaaaaaaaays, I only got called on the fake mask once. On United flight 2185, Phoenix to Chicago, the flight attendant said, "Sir, you need to put on a real mask. You're wearing a fake mask," and then I said to myself, "Fuck, that guy knows because I guarantee he bought one himself, or for his mom, from a different website." You see, the fake mask companies had to keep moving and changing their websites because they kept getting thrown off the internet, YouTube, and Amazon (because, you know, we used to live in a free society before COVID).

They were clever at least, with sites like fakemasks.com, MaskFake.com, Fakefakemask.com, Maskfakefakefake.com, Thisisntafakemask.com, etc. God bless them and their not-buying-into-all-the-mainstream-media-bullshit hearts.

This is what America does best, be creative and make money in any situation. If there're customers who aren't being serviced, fill the void. In my case, I don't want to be told to wear a mask, but I need to fly to Chicago for a gig. That meant for my friend Tony Baldino's club, the Chicago Improv, I had to do twice as many shows because they were socially distanced and we were only allowed to sell 50 percent capacity according to health guru and three-hundred-pound Democratic governor J. B. Pritzker. Yeah, I want to get health advice from this guy!

Seeing the Illinois governor's jowls vibrate at a press conference as he gives his COVID advice is hard to take at extra-large face value. Dear governor, please don't tell me about what you clearly don't know — health! Tell me what you obviously *do* know. What's the best diabetes medication to take? How do you keep your heart from exploding? Where is the best all-you-can-eat deep-dish pizza joint in Chicago, where on your way back to the car you won't get robbed or shot while sneaking extra slices in your jacket pocket?

The positive subversive nature of our capitalist society is why (as we'll talk about later with the great James Lindsay) the workers' revolution didn't take hold in a capitalist society. It's because if you find a need (customers) that isn't being serviced, and work your ass off, you can get ahead. Like the genius and conveniently morally divorced entrepreneur that, in March 2020, bought and hoarded every mask, glove, and hand sanitizer in a five-state area (you know, when masks still had their magical abilities to prevent viral infections) to make a profit.[15] I know, you may say it's immoral, unethical, wrong, and really disgusting, but the only thing more disgusting is I wish I would've thought of it first, been slightly less greedy, and sold them under an assumed name like David Spade or Nick Swardson. "Hey everybody! Look what I found: 200,000 lifesaving wipes, masks, and gloves, and you can have them at a discount! Love, Nick."

So I wore the fake masks and had everyone I knew wear them because I knew in my gut it was all bullshit. Remember how the flu all but disappeared in 2020 and 2021?[16] The same people that believe in the virus hysteria will look you right in the face and say, "Nobody died of the flu because people were wearing masks," and if you say, "What about all the people that got COVID?" they'll say "Well, that's because masks don't really work. You're just a COVID denier."

A lot of people also sensed pretty early that this COVID hysteria had all the earmarks of bullshit and smelled like a street in San Francisco (which made you want to heave), but like Stanley Milgram's 1961 Yale University experiment exemplified, over 65 percent of people will just go along with whatever the fuck the government says...always. For those readers unfamiliar with Milgram's study, related in his book *Obedience to Authority*, people's willingness to do something they were instructed to do by an authority figure was put to the test, even if it conflicted with their conscience. The subjects of the experiment were told (by professional-looking men in white lab coats) that they were teachers "helping" learners (we're all in this together!), and they were instructed to give the "learner," sitting visibly to the subject in an adjacent room, an electric shock for every wrong answer. The subjects were told — and witnessed for themselves — that the intensity of the shocks increased with each wrong answer and caused obvious pain and eventually agony in the "learner" (an actor who was in on it). Shockingly, 65 percent of the subjects, when instructed by the calm official-looking man over their shoulder, continued shocking the learner, astonishingly to the point of (fake) death...all just because an authority told them to do it.[17]

That's right, folks...65 percent.

Point being, how many brave people does it take to stand up to authority? In his 1815 writings, John Adams suspected that a third of the colonists supported the war, a third were indifferent, and a third supported the British. At no point in the Revolutionary War did more than 45 percent of the colonists support the war, and as far as those that actively fought in the war, it was just 9 percent.[18] However, there is a magic number, discovered by Erica Chenoweth, that any time a revolution gained at least 3.5 percent of the population, it never failed to bring change.[19] When it gets to a figure where enough people can get behind it, like 30 percent, that is when great change can happen in society. It takes a smaller number of courageous people to stand up than we think to have society take heed of their warning, prompt people to take action, fight a war against tyranny, or stand up against their own government.

To Milgram's detractors I would say that while some of the big leaps in his study — like using it as a basis of why Nazis were complicit in genocide — have been discounted, the basis of his findings is unarguable. People do what they're fucking told. If it's an authority figure that tells them to do it, ordinary citizens are capable of committing or facilitating monstrous acts, atrocities, and allowing tyranny to foster and continue. Though hard to believe, the Milgram study pales in comparison to government experiments, where instead of using fake subjects, they used real unknowing everyday American citizens.

Operation MKUltra was an abhorrent and illegal CIA operation that was discovered through Congress and President Gerald

Ford's investigation of the CIA called the Rockefeller Commission. They found that the CIA built a program based off a Nazi initiative to find a truth serum to use in interrogations,[20] an idea that was the brainchild of numerous Nazis (not the ones who cut in front of you in Target or misgendered you but real leftover Hitler-in-person-saluting World War II Nazis). These Nazis were supplied by the top-secret program aptly named Operation Paperclip. Paperclip, you know, the thing you use to fashion anti-Semitic fascist gypsy haters together? Operation Paperclip was used to secretly smuggle more than sixteen hundred German scientists, technicians, engineers, and otherwise cheerful, willing coconspirators to the single biggest mass murder in human history into the United States where they were able to continue and improve upon their homegrown Nazi skillset.[21] Instead of using their dastardly deeds for the Gestapo, they'd be working for the historically well-intentioned and kindhearted United States Central Intelligence Agency, who were more than happy to have them (and not the Russians).

You know how some liquor companies import full-bodied French wines? Well, our spooks imported well-aged untried Nazi war criminals.

Allow me, dear reader, to introduce to you Dr. Erich Traub, a Nazi that worked directly under Reichsführer-SS Heinrich Himmler. That's right, Himmler! Dr. Traub was on the other side of the Iron Curtain when the war ended, and the Russians had captured him and had him working on their biological warfare programs. Dr. Traub was considered the foremost expert on viruses and their weaponization. He and his family escaped Russia for West Berlin, and then in 1949, Traub applied for Operation Paperclip employment "affirm[ing] he wanted to 'do scientific work in the USA, become an American citizen, and be protected from Russian reprisals.'"[22] Yeah, that's right, there was an *application* process! Say what you want about Nazi war criminals and their crimes against humanity, but at *least* they came into this country legally.

Traub was working on tick research at the secret army base on Plum Island located just off Long Island in New York while he worked for the US government. Ticks were selected because they were the best covert warriors to spread their blood-borne diseases to humans. If you're thinking to yourself, "This sounds like a terrible idea," well, I would have to agree with you on that one, reader. Sure enough, a tick bit a power plant employee, who then, after going home to their family in Lyme, Connecticut, found a new breeding ground for a new disease named after the town that it first destroyed in 1975: Lyme disease.

This disease was discovered only three years *after* the beyond shameful Tuskegee Experiment (formally known as the "Tuskegee Study of Untreated Syphilis in the Negro Male") ended its secret forty-year run.[23] In that breach of human rights, the US government told 600 Black men that they were testing them for "bad blood," while they were secretly infecting 399 of them with syphilis. In exchange for their participation in the study (which again, they didn't know they were agreeing to get fucking syphilis injected into them), they received (according to the CDC itself) "free medical exams, free meals, and burial insurance."[24] Uh, free *burial* insurance? Whenever I'm offered free burial insurance, I know that not everything is on the up and up, especially after I just gave my wife syphilis when I'm almost certain I didn't cheat on her.

Over decades of the Tuskegee study, scientists watched more

than 100 men die from their untreated syphilis, despite having a functioning treatment for the disease developed ten years into the forty-year "study."

Yes, it was wrong, and it was an outrage. But do you think that stopped them?

Anyways, cut back to the 1970s where the Tuskegee Experiment just ended and (thanks to our Nazi bug enthusiasts) we have Lyme disease mysteriously giving school children rheumatoid arthritis.

Through President Ford's Commission on CIA Activities within the United States (also known as the Rockefeller Commission and, later, the Freedom of Information Act) it was revealed that under Operation MKUltra, the CIA (our Nazi-importing supposed good guys) illegally experimented on unknowing human subjects — American citizens, you and me — to find substances and tactics to use in interrogation. For twenty years, MKUltra used hospitals, prisons, academic institutions, and pharmaceutical companies as fronts to test the effectiveness of psychoactive drugs like LSD on unwitting people to see if they could get closer to the Nazi dream of a truth serum. Here's a direct excerpt from the Joint Hearing Before the Select Committee on Intelligence that said:

Some 2 years ago, the Senate Health Subcommittee heard chilling testimony about the human experimentation activities of the Central Intelligence Agency. The Deputy Director of the CIA revelated that over 30 universities and institutions were involved in "extensive testing and experimentation" programs which included covert drug tests on unwitting citizens "at all social levels, high and low, native Americans and foreign." Several of these tests involved the administration of LSD to "unwitting subjects in social situations." At least one death, that of Dr. Olsen, resulted from these activities.[25]

Overall, the CIA spent twenty years and $87.5 million (in today's dollars) studying how they could drug American citizens in an attempt to learn more about how to interrogate the human mind. Likely, that meant there was an unknown number of CIA operatives doing what their superiors instructed, even if it conflicted with their conscience, but it wasn't just them — the navy conducted their own nonconsensual human experimentation.

Operation Sea-Spray was the secret 1950s experiment on the *entire* population of the city of San Francisco (where I was born) to see how a city of like size would hold up against a bioweapon attack. To do this, the United States Navy sprayed two different nonlethal bacteria — *Serratia marcescens* and *Bacillus globigii* — at a rate that would be lethal if the substance was anthrax. Within two weeks of the experiment, eleven people were hospitalized for very rare and serious urinary tract infections, and one person died because of their UTI, which they didn't even get from anything fun.[26]

With just these examples, we can clearly see that the government seems to have no qualms or conscience experimenting on its own people without its citizens' knowledge or consent.

If these aren't examples of sociopathic behavior, then I would ask, dear reader, what is?

# CHAPTER SEVEN

# "SUPPORT THE TROOPS!"

The attraction that draws so many people to our shores is the promise of a better life. A new start, a chance of living your dreams, not just for yourself, but for your children. America still provides that hope, and nobody understands that hope more than recent immigrants who came here from totalitarian regimes, like Yeonmi Park, who escaped the hellhole of North Korea.[1] High-level North Korean students, the few that there are, are told in school that Korean is the world's most common and popular language. They are only half right... the most popular boy bands are Korean boy bands.

While many of us take our freedom for granted, these new Americans know how precious and rare this commodity truly is. Freedom. And the cornerstone of freedom is free speech.

Under the same First Amendment is freedom of the press. These two are put together not by accident. Free speech and a free press are entwined and inseparable. We cannot have real free speech if we do not have freedom of the press, where individuals can express themselves through publication and dissemination of information, ideas, and opinions without interference, constraint, or prosecution by the government. I believe this is now more challenging than at any other point in my lifetime.

In the waning days of the former Soviet Union, people knew that the "press," *Pravda* and TASS, were nothing more than government mouthpieces, and people had to rely on word of mouth to really know what was actually happening.[2] That's what makes propaganda so much more insidious in so-called free societies because here, many people still believe the *New York Times, Washington Post*, and the Google search engine. However, if you're reading this book, you have woken up to the bullshit parade and I'm sure you rely moron (sorry, more on) word of mouth and don't just swallow the tidal wave of corporate and government propaganda.

Back when Google was just googol and only meant ten to the power of one hundred, the idea of the internet at its inception was the potentiality for the broadening of freedom of ideas. The democratization of information and knowledge was now accessible for all, and an encyclopedia of ideas was at your fingertips. But just as we've seen that the news media has been consolidated, so has the internet been consolidated from the power of the masses into the hands of a few big corporations. A few tech companies — Google, Facebook, and X (Twitter) — rule the internet and the information on it. Robert Epstein, renowned psychologist, explained the search engine manipulation effect (SEME) and how powerful search engines are, based on what they show us and how they manipulate search results. In his study, a whopping 39 percent of participants shifted their voting preferences as a result of the SEME. He wrote that SEME was a "serious threat to the democratic system of government."[3] (I just googled that shit, so apparently some of this shit is still working.) Known as the Google

Whistleblower, he has been largely ignored. He also had a mathematical model that would've stopped COVID without a vaccine, but more on that later. First, let's focus on my required page count.

These corporate motherfuckers use ranking suppression to decide what you can and cannot see. Through this undemocratic suppression, they can influence what you think and what you think you're seeing. This handful of companies can help shape the reality of their choosing. The ideological bend of these tech conglomerates is undeniably left, and as a result, our internet, news, media, and late-night comedy shows have been ideologically captured.

At this point you're probably asking me, "Rob, is David Spade still reading the book?" I don't know if David's gotten to page 133 of *any* book in his life. I haven't! Anyway, that's a question for David Spade, not me.

You're also probably asking me, "Rob, has anything like what's happening now occurred before in America?"

Well, thank you for your question!

While not a completely accurate comparison, I would make the junior college–dropout argument that President Woodrow Wilson was the Joe Biden of the early twentieth century. He was elected in 1912 (not too far removed from Joe Biden's birthday) and ran kind of like a Joe Biden unifier. Reelected in 1916, in the middle of World War I (1914–1918), Wilson's reelection campaign ran on the promise of not getting America into a foreign war. Isolationism was the respectable form of foreign policy at the time. This is especially true in 1916, when America was primarily an agrarian society and upwards of a third of Americans were farmers.[4] You know, Americans with hogs, cows, skinny chickens, and before pesticides. They didn't eat the chickens back then; they just ate the eggs. Around five a day, and somehow these farmers and their families stayed thin and all that high cholesterol didn't cause heart disease.

Wilson was elected because the idea of any problems happening in Europe, like war, was *"way* over *there."* This was before international air travel, before we weighed flight attendants, or hired pilots based not on their experience but on the new hiring hierarchy of diversity. Even Wilson's campaign slogan was "He kept us out of war."[5]

So, Wilson gets reelected and then first thing he does is enter us into war. His new slogan — "He kept us out of war until now" — was more accurate but less effective. He and Biden both have this wonderful quality of going back on their promises — the Poynter Institute has been tracking Biden's ninety-nine most prominent campaign promises and he has kept 27 percent of them.[6]

Wilson tried to combat the low public opinion he had for betraying his constituency — or what I would call lying. He created the Committee on Public Information, which was a legalized and systemic pro-war propaganda machine, where they came up with, for the first time in American history, propaganda that was legislated and approved.[7]

Propaganda was now law, and America would never be the same. America would now be besieged with banal sloganeering like "support the troops," with the inference being, who wouldn't support the troops? Who's this asshole not supporting the troops? That mild vague statement is wanting. It doesn't ask you a question, it just insists on a blanket approval. You might call this slogan a half slogan because the semi-intelligent person (junior college dropout of the day) in 1917 might ask, "Support the troops doing *what*? Support the troops staying home and protecting our borders? Yes! I'm okay with that. Support the troops being sent overseas in a war that has nothing to do with America? No! I'll take a pass on that..."

Wilson took his abuse of power a step further when he created the Sedition Act of 1918, which he used to arrest and imprison an estimated two thousand antiwar activists, socialists, and government critics.[8] Most of these Americans were simply Wilson's political opponents, labor leaders, and pacifists. In other words, a bunch of pussies that weren't supporting the troops!

The Sedition Act was one of the most egregious examples of our government infringing on free speech and freedom of the press in United States history. To imprison the dissenting just because they voiced their opinion is an unthinkable crime against, you know, our nation's founding principles. Wilson used this tactic, along with the administration-sanctioned propaganda machine, to rile Americans up with more direct sloganeering. "The Hun are ripping apart Belgian babies!" That was enough for American farmers to leave their hogs with Uncle Norm, exchange their sheep-shit-covered overalls for a rifle and a map of Verdun, ship off to that faraway place (after they voted for that guy who assured them they wouldn't have to), and stop whoever these Hun were from ripping apart babies, from a country they only thought was a type of waffle they ate with their fifth egg. You know, these were farmers, good people but ignorant as all get out.

Cut to six weeks later: shell shock, trench foot, Belgian prostitutes, and gonorrhea. Hey, *support the troops!*

Wilson also brought in the income tax through the newly created Internal Revenue Service, which was promised to be a very temporary measure and is now a permanent part of the government's money grab.[9] In another striking similarity to Biden, and what was mostly hidden from the American public, Wilson was mentally incapacitated after a stroke, but I would wager he still took more questions from the press than Joe Biden does. It was, in fact, Wilson's wife, Edith, that was the unacknowledged acting president. While Biden hasn't had a stroke, his obvious cognitive deterioration, like not remembering something so unimportant as when he was vice president, or if Egypt is next to Mexico, has been explained away by Democrats as just "another Republican smear."[10] You know, with the other conservative smears against Biden, like plagiarism, being caught lying, and selling influence to foreign countries.

The slow creep of the illiberal left has moved into a trot, capturing the media, academia, science, and technology companies unabated. Instead of sedition acts, they have new sloganeering like "hate speech" (any speech they disagree with), "antiracism" (hard to rally the troops against that), and the all-encompassing Trojan horse term "social justice" (you could literally fit any white-hating antiwoman antigay initiatives under that umbrella and still feel safe from attack).

We shall see how fear is the most used and most effective technique to whip us all into a frenzy against our own self-interests. They exacerbate the division between the left and the right to silence those who try to blur the lines.

But where are the comedians that are supposed to make fun of all this?

## CHAPTER EIGHT

# "THERE ARE SOME THINGS THAT ARE WORSE THAN DEATH"

— Robert Kennedy Jr.

I'm convinced that if Norm Macdonald hadn't been a comedic genius, he could've been a criminal genius. His brain worked quite differently than everyone else's.

The morning I found out Norm Macdonald died, I was in Los Angeles, and I was literally calling him as I'd been doing for months. I was trying to get Norm to appear in my newest movie, *Daddy Daughter Trip*. I had put Norm in every one of my movies, from *Deuce Bigalow* to my Netflix TV series *Real Rob*. Sometimes he would answer a text or briefly pick up the phone, which I found odd, even for my aloof, brilliant comic friend. I remember I had tex-ted him something an actor told me years ago: "Norm, you never know when it's going to be your last movie . . . and I want your last movie to be mine." Then Norm texted me back "WHAAAAT?!"

Like everybody else, I didn't know how sick he was. I knew there was something up with him, but that was thirty years ago. So, first thing in the morning I'm calling him, and leaving a mes-sage on his machine saying, "Hey, listen, you can just do a *voice over*. I just want you to be a part of this!"

Somebody called me while I was on the phone leaving a mes-sage with him, saying, "I'm so sorry about your friend." And I'm like, "What friend?" Then there was a long pause. "I just assumed you already knew. Norm Macdonald passed away this morning." "What?" I said. "I'm leaving a message for him on the other line!"

Norm was a real special talent and a verifiable genius. I put him in everything I ever did. That way not only would I get to have the hilarious Norm Macdonald in my movie, I'd also be guaran-teed to be able to hang out with him while we were filming. And Norm always delivered a crazy-funny performance. I remember one time Norm had a funny idea for a sketch about a gay marriage counselor. I told him to write it up. But this was years after *SNL* so I'm sure he figured, "What's the point?" But I thought it was hilar-ious, so I wrote it up, even though there was no point. A couple of weeks later I presented it to him and in famous Norm fashion, he said, "What's this?" And I said, "It's the gay marriage counselor sketch idea of yours."

"What?" Norm asked me.

I said, "You know, the gay marriage counselor — that was your idea."

"What are you talking about? I never had that idea!!"

That was the thing about Norm, a lot of times he was lying. But you weren't 100 percent sure if he was lying. Maybe 80. Or if he was indeed lying, you didn't know the depth of the lie, and you didn't know for sure if *he knew* he was lying! That was a lot of the charm of Norm. He would tell crazy stories and you had to figure out what part, if any, was the truth. Or whether the whole thing was just another of his elaborate inventions. One of my favorite jokes of Norm's was quite self-revealing. (Norm voice) "Do you ever find yourself in the middle of a *lie* and you realize, wait a minute, there's no possible way I could *benefit* from this lie. Why am I *lying*? 'Hey, did you see that new *Star Wars* movie?'

"'Yeah…'"

That's basically the joke.

I said to Norm once, "If you weren't a comedian, you could be a sociopathic thief or murderer," and he didn't take kindly to that. He didn't respond verbally; I think it was too close to the bone.

During the pandemic, Norm said, "Do you know what I stopped eating? Bat! You know what's made it so much easier? The Impossible Bat!"

Norm's illness wasn't the only thing he concealed. He also attempted to hide his love and hope for all humanity. He hated, with a passion, *comedians* wanting to be taken "seriously." But there were times he didn't shy away from saying serious things himself.

My favorite thing that Norm ever did wasn't comedy at all. It was an exchange with the pompous windbag and astrophysicist Neil deGrasse Tyson. Tyson tweeted another of his obnoxious, atheistic, in-your-face tweets on the morning of April 3, 2019, which said, "The Universe is blind to our sorrows and indifferent to our pains. Have a nice day!"[1]

Nice and uplifting, right?

Norm's retort was beautiful in its poetic imagery. In a very Zen Alan Watts–like way, Norm replied, "Neil, there is a logic flaw in your little aphorism that seems quite telling. Since you and I are part of the Universe, then we would also be indifferent and uncaring. Perhaps you forgot, Neil, that we are not superior to the Universe but merely a fraction of it. Nice day, indeed."[2]

I often return to his quote. Thank you, Norm.

After Norm died, I decided to put the fifteen-year-old extremely vulgar and crude sketch, "The Gay Marriage Counselor," on my Instagram account because I knew Norm would've wanted me to.

So, I posted the sketch, and I was happy that people got to discover this gem of a performance by Norm Macdonald and my buddy, Buddy Lewis. I never read the comments on social media because of all the assholes, but I really wanted to share in other people's appreciation and condolences for our pal Norm. So I read a few, which were very touching and funny.

And I said, "I'll just read one more."

It read, "Why did it have to be Norm Macdonald? Why couldn't it have been Rob Schneider?"

\* \* \*

We have an overstimulated population, overstimulating our already sleep-deprived overstimulated minds. Our cell phones sit next to our beds — with the twenty-four-hour-a-day news cycle awaiting us, the endorphins and dopamine rush from checking our social media accounts reinforcing our political echo chamber, and just a few clicks away, every vile form of pornography available to further poison our minds. Is there nothing sacred anymore?

(This is where David Spade closes the book — you made it this far, David, I'm proud of you!)

Today's news from my political echo chamber reinforces my political thoughts (and my new form of twenty-first-century caffeine, a dopamine rush) that crime is rampant and there appear to be no consequences: four migrants beat police and got released without having to pay a cash bail in New York City in January 2024.[3] The truth being crime isn't rampant, it happened *there*. But it isn't about the truth, it's about creating the perception to keep people addicted and engaged. In reality, crime is not happening in most places, but that doesn't achieve the desired effect of making people nervous and drawing them in. That's where statistics can come in to manipulate us further. When they give a made-up statistic that a particular crime, like mass shootings, are up 33 percent, that could just mean it went from nine incidents to twelve. Meanwhile, I have to get a guard dog now. But nine to twelve doesn't sound as dangerous or as sexy as mass shootings are up 33 percent. Of course, we're also not allowed to ask any inconvenient questions like "Is there any connection between these mass shooters and the SSRIs they're on?" Next!

*Click* (endorphin rush). Over a dozen cities and smaller jurisdictions allow noncitizens to vote.[4] So my political echo chamber is reinforced; not only is there rampant crime, these fuckers can now *vote*!

When I was at a major network's broadcasting headquarters recently, waiting to go on different talk shows to promote my movie *Daddy Daughter Trip*, they had televisions up with constant looped footage of young people looting a Nordstrom in Topanga Canyon, California. I said, "Wait a minute, that's where my wife used to take my kids to an indoor carousel!" In between shows during the downtime, I asked one of the producers quietly, "What do you show when there's no 'news'?" She looked at me, confused. I continued, "I mean, what do you talk about when Trump is *not* getting arrested?" The producer said to me, "Luckily he's been getting arrested a lot recently." Foolishly, I continued the conversation.

"But what do you show when Trump is *not* getting arrested?"

"Ohhh…" It clicked. "We show crime! That's our go-to. Because," she said, "there's always crime."

There is always crime; however, in a country of 330 million people, that shouldn't be surprising or unusual. But wherever it's happening, it can and is being used as news. News, meaning something unusual or out of the ordinary. But they never express it in those terms. It's always to make the viewer not turn the channel. Because it's human nature, when you see crime, to go, "Wait a minute, is this shit happening near *me*? How concerned should *I* be? Do I need to move? Oh good, it's just happening in Los Angeles…Detroit…New York…Chicago, or (fill in whatever Democratic-run city you want)." Thankfully, usually not in the red state that we just moved to, Arizona. Like a lot of people, we escaped Chinafornia, I mean California.

Today's other societal mind traps locking us in our own prejudice and landing in our own ideological laps are, luckily for us, a potpourri of different and, dare I say, new societal ills, maladies, and mental problems that no one saw coming even a short ten years ago. (David Spade re-opens the book.) Social media manipulates the susceptible and naïve minds of young children that are going through the confusing years of puberty and telling them they are born in the wrong body. Who's the Svengali that saw that coming? These changes are coming in faster than a Guatemalan family at Eagle Pass, Texas. Fortunately, the feds haven't removed all the razor wire placed by Texas Rangers yet.

Perhaps what started to allow this was a change in our educational system. Back in the '80s, public schools took civics out of the curriculum, so none of us have to be bothered with how our government actually works or operates or what anybody can do to change things.

We just need to take a breath, relax, go to the sink, and fill a glass of water that has been laden with industrial waste fluoride — which, of course, has been scientifically proven to lower our intelligence even more. (David Spade spits out his tap water and yells at his personal assistant, "Where is my spring water in a glass?")

We can't help but notice the definitions of words have been stretched beyond what we knew them to mean. Like "news," which used to mean "an unusual occurrence that is in the public interest" but now can just mean "Taylor Swift's boyfriend screams at his coach!" Attention spans have dropped even lower from YouTube snippets and Instagram clips to where now it's an achievement to hold your audience for eight seconds on TikTok.

People have become anesthetized (#numb) by this cerebral overload. ("You're soooo smart!")

There is a speeding-up process in our culture that has only been exacerbated in the twenty-first century. How much information can our brains take in, assimilate or reject, and sort through in such a short amount of time? For example, my friend John Cleese told me that his mom was born in 1900, in the days of the horse and buggy. By the time she turned sixty-nine, human beings were walking on the moon. Quite a leap, or as one might say, "That's one small step for man, one giant leap for mankind…" Not to be a grammar Nazi (but I will be an actual 1940s Nazi on grammar here), Neil Armstrong technically left out the indefinite article "a" before "man" and should've said, "That's one small step for a man, one giant leap for mankind," but I wasn't the one sucking on oxygen 238,900 miles away from Earth on a sphere with 83.4 percent less gravity.[5]

One of my earliest school memories is the moon landing, when we watched, on a black-and-white TV that was rolled into the classroom, a man in a space suit hopping off a short ladder onto the dusty surface of our closest celestial body. To the other kindergarteners and me, it was almost normal. It wasn't a giant leap for us like it was for Mrs. Cleese (though her real name was Cheese, but that's another story) because we had nothing to compare it to. Like today's kids who now have no recollection of life without social media and their ubiquitous phones — and all the pressure that comes with it.

When I was a kid, no matter what happened at school, like when everyone was rushing to the last remaining civics class (this was 1980) and some kid on the football team pantsed me, and some of my female classmates got a glimpse of my surprisingly large bush, at least when I got home nobody knew about it, and the school shaming took a respite for the night. Now, thanks to your phone, there's no such break, your bush continues to frighten and confuse others and it continues to shame you when you get home!

During the societal turbulence of the 1960s civil rights, we had comedians like Dick Gregory. It was an honor to be his friend, the Jackie Robinson of comedy and the first black comedian to play white clubs, who helped the nation process this transition on late-night TV on *Tonight Starring Jack Paar*.[6] This was an era where we still had separate bathrooms and drinking fountains that had nothing to do with your gender but everything to do with the color of your skin. One of my favorite Dick Gregory jokes is "For years we were protesting to be able to sit at a diner just like anyone else. By the time I was finally allowed to sit down they didn't have anything I wanted to eat."

This is why we need (good) comedians who must risk themselves to be provocative and question what is accepted and use humor to nudge society hopefully into a better place. Through our laughter we would realize how ignorant something is — in this case, in the '60s, to judge somebody by the color of their skin and not "the content of their character."[7] (This is where presidents of Ivy League schools need to properly attribute a quote, like I'm doing, to Dr. King from 1963.)

Today's struggles, while unique and different (and, may I add, crazy), offer up the same opportunities to comedians (again, the good ones) as social critics to help point out today's hypocrisies and outright lunacies.

A comedian's job, as social critics subtly navigating extremely new ideas that have been adopted very quickly (while still unproven), is a delicate dance. The people and forces pushing these ideas are not just asking but demanding that society accept them under the threat of social shaming, name calling, cancellations, and just yelling in general, if you don't go along with this new dogma. While a delicate two-step, it's vital to examine these presuppositions before their instant integration permanently changes our society.

(I admit it. I've been wasting your time up until now. My publisher had a page count — which, although it seemed insane due to my lack of attention span and my desperate need to get back onto social media for my endorphin rush, it nonetheless was an obligation I needed to fulfill.)

The normal speed bumps that slow the integration of consequential changes in our culture have been flattened. These normal speed bumps — our academicians, scientists, physicians, intellectuals, elected officials, and our judicial system — have been compromised through campaigns of fear. It is of utmost importance to protect the same freedoms that gave us our opportunities for success in our chosen careers in the hopes of passing these on to our children.

To accomplish this, we need *new* speed bumps. For better or worse, these newly built replacement speed bumps are outside of academia and the sciences and are in the form of nontraditional media, like podcasts with comedians and recently canceled academics. They are there to fill the void and speak up when these traditional societal checkpoints have been removed.

It's telling that podcaster Joe Rogan is the Walter Cronkite of our age. Walter Cronkite was the most consequential news anchor of the 1960s. When President Johnson felt he had lost Cronkite over the never-ending Vietnam War, he knew he had lost the faith of the American people. On March 31, 1968, Johnson announced that he would not seek reelection. Joe Rogan didn't set out to be a newsman — he is a very funny state championship wrestler from Rhode Island to whom all his friends said, "You're hilarious; you should be a comedian," and he became one. Not to speak for Joe (but I will because this is my fucking book — let him write his own book), but he didn't set out to be the largest independent voice in all media — the *Joe Rogan Experience* on Spotify.

But his $250 million new contract extension with Spotify (which won't be exclusive to the platform this time) speaks to his new cultural importance and the enormous void of opposing viewpoints he helps fill.[8] Without a doubt, comedian Joe Rogan is the most consequential man in social media in the 2020s.

See, in our society, it has fallen to both comedians and podcasters to fill the void created by the successful attack on our intellectuals and academics. The goal for these podcasters and comedians, at their best, is to remind us, dear reader, that if there's something hidden from you, there's something wrong with it.

We saw under the COVID tyranny the rapid removal of constitutionally guaranteed rights. Not incidentally, there is nothing in the Constitution or the Bill of Rights that says, "Yes, you have the right to free speech, the right to free press, and the right to petition the government for redress of grievances, *but*...if there is a really, really bad flu, you don't get them anymore. Sorry!" So, how were our freedoms, almost overnight, taken away from us? Have there been any safeguards put in place to prevent a reoccurrence? What are the signs to look for when the government tries to do this again? By the way, I still suffer from post-traumatic having-to-wear-a-mask syndrome and the ringing in my ears from liberals saying, "What's wrong, you sissy? You have a problem wearing a little mask?" One thing I have learned in my almost two hours of research that I did for this book is that in every instance where authorities took away freedoms from the people, they used the same excuse — declaring a state of emergency.

When I was at the Reichstag Building in West Berlin, smack in the middle of East Germany in 1984, they had all the laws that occurred in Nazi Germany translated into different languages to help people understand what happened in that society, which affected the whole world. Starting in 1934, it listed the laws that were enacted that took away German citizens' freedoms, the first one being the outlawing of other political parties, up until the Nazi government didn't feel it was even necessary to make any more laws, because all the freedoms were already gone, and there was nobody left to fight for them.

Liberties must be taken away incrementally over time. Even in the authoritarian society of Nazi Germany, they had limits on their liberty grab and what the government could get away with. For example, in 1941 the German public protested the Nazis' systematic killing of people with disabilities, forcing the Nazis to continue their plan in secret.[9] Also, there was a years-long gap between when German Jews were stripped of their German citizenship and when German society was eased into the idea of systematically removing them from society and then murdering them. The book *Hitler's Willing Executioners* explains that the architects of Hitler's final solution to the Jewish question found that there would be more support for execution camps if they put them in a place where they hated Jews even more than Germany — in Poland.[10]

Unfortunately, and not infrequently, rights taken away can and do lead to genocide. It's important that we see where the "incremental" taking away of rights leads to.

Here's a leap of questionable connection: in Hollywood, they won't ask you to give up all your integrity in one go — they just take a little at a time. "Just do this movie for the money." "Just do this one meeting with Harvey Weinstein." "The head of CBS Les Moonves wants to meet you in his office...*alone*." "Just do this one Pfizer commercial." "Nicole, just do this one promotion normalizing people eating bugs. It's good for the planet!" Continue down that road, and one day you'll wake up and you're John Oliver.

The most valuable commodity you can have as a human being is your freedom. What else do you got? Your health? Family? Job? Income? Faith? I thought about this during COVID, and I wholeheartedly agree with what my friend Robert Kennedy Jr. said, that "there are some things that are worse than death" — giving up your freedoms and living in a totalitarian system are high on that list. I mean, it's up there with watching *The View*.

That's why people will do anything, literally anything, to get to America. They'll swim ninety miles from Cuba (whereas nobody from Florida is swimming ninety miles to get to Cuba — not even fish). They'll wade waist deep in the Rio Grande to be confronted by razor wire, and that is still not a sufficient deterrent. Chinese nationals, who managed to escape from mainland China, will fly to Mexico, get to Tijuana, and make the unfortunately not-so-arduous trek across the border to get to California.

The one group that is consistently never mentioned in critical race theory and the belief of systemic white oppression is the minority that is doing better than anyone else, including their supposed white oppressors...Asians. Filipinos, Japanese, and Chinese Americans have the highest real median household income of all races in America.[11] This also includes the very new addition to this racial classification, East Indians. I don't know how they feel about being called Asians, but they don't worry about racial classification; they have other worries, like having their stores robbed for less than $950 (because you can't get a felony for stealing less than $950 in California). Asian Americans don't worry about the politics of oppression because they're too busy kicking ass, making money, and trying to keep their status as the highest-earning racial group under wraps.

You ever notice how you never see homeless Asian people in America? It's because we Asian people do not like camping in general, but *especially* camping in urban areas. I think I speak for all Asians when I say we prefer eating and sleeping indoors, and we really like toilets. Preferably smart toilets with heated seats and a button that sprays water up our ass (with amazing accuracy) to give us that oh-so-fresh Asian feeling.

Asian Americans seem to be immune from this white system of oppression, but this doesn't play into the woke narrative, so woke protagonists pretend it is not happening. Still, Asians are the most economically successful racial group in America. Yes, it is a minority, not Whitey, the mother of all oppressors. But this does not support what the race hustlers like X. Kendi and Robin DiAngelo are peddling, so this inconvenient truth must be ignored.

I would prefer, as I'm sure you would, that these new immigrants would legally immigrate here. There must be something about this country, however imperfect, that offers opportunities to all its people, that make it the most desirable place to live in the world. The flames of freedom cannot be extinguished, and I hope that all of what we are currently experiencing is just an opportunity to recalibrate and recharge the batteries of the foundational liberties on which our country was built, and to breathe new life into them. We will discuss these challenges in the next few chapters.

This is me, Farley, Sandler, and Spade in our *SNL* sketch "The Gap Girls," where I play the Donut Hut slut. It was total typecasting. (*Author's personal collection*)

As explosively funny as Farley was, he was equally as sweet. He was even nice when he was really high, and that can't be said of a lot of people. We all miss him. (*Author's personal collection*)

I had a dream of being on *Saturday Night Live*, and that dream came true. (*Author's personal collection*)

Whoo! Yeah! Getting my own office at *Saturday Night Live* was a thrill. All we were trying to do was make our friends laugh and keep the lights on for the next generation, and I guess we did it. *(Author's personal collection)*

David Spade is a true friend and brilliant comic. If you want to have the funniest dinner of your life with one *Saturday Night Live* veteran, pick David Spade. *(Author's personal collection)*

It's about passion. If you find something you're passionate about, and you do it when you're young enough, eventually, you'll find success. If I can go back in time and tell this young man something, I'd say, "Less vintage jeans, more Apple stock." *(Author's personal collection)*

My notes from *Late Night with David Letterman*, and thanks to Dennis Miller for getting me on. After my set, Dennis said, "Now you're in show business." Making Letterman laugh behind me, and having enough stage experience to give him the space so that the audience could hear him laugh, was my comedic survival instincts kicking in, which you get only after several thousand performances. Jay Leno's advice was the best: "If you don't have five minutes that kills every time, everywhere, you don't have anything." *(Author's personal collection)*

Boy, were *we* on TV at the right time. The 1990s and early 2000s, before it got all crazy. Jay Leno was the best comic of his generation, and there was no nicer late-night TV host. When I opened for him in 1986, he drove onto the stage on a motorcycle, and at the end of the show, he waved me over to ride on back, and we rode off the stage together. What a lovely gesture.
*(Photo by Margaret Norton / © August 11, 1997, NBCUniversal/ Getty Images)*

Jerry Seinfeld is a master joke writer and storyteller, and he made stand-up look easy by telling jokes that were seamless with a perfect absurdist progression. We were all in awe of Jerry. *(Author's personal collection)*

There are no accolades that suffice for Paul McCartney. He changed music. He changed pop culture. He invented hard rock music. He raised the level of rock and roll to an operatic art form that has still been unsurpassed. He is our Schubert, our Mozart, our Beethoven. He is the greatest entertainer who ever lived. Pictured here with his wife Linda McCartney, as lovely a person as you could ever meet. Also, Bill Murray. *(Author's personal collection)*

That was a really special birthday party for Adam, because he was able to celebrate with his whole family, his mom, his dad, and his buddies like me and Chris Rock. *(Author's personal collection)*

Adam and me with *SNL* comedy legend Jim Downey. And Adam's first bulldog, Meatball. Adam prefers bulldogs, and even though they snore and keep him up, he never says a word. *(Author's personal collection)*

Not a lot of guys can continue to thrive for five decades in show business, especially in comedy, but Bill Maher is one of those rare birds. *(Author's personal collection)*

Rodney Dangerfield didn't make it big until he was in his fifties. How cool is that? Everybody loved Rodney, and I mean everybody. He had all our "respect." He was our stand-up hero. *(Author's personal collection)*

Working out in between takes on *The Hot Chick*. When you're in a movie, you have to stay in shape. When you're playing a girl in a movie, that's another level...of lunacy. *(Author's personal collection)*

A lot of actors have a star on the Hollywood Walk of Fame, but very few have of them have ever put their hands and feet in the concrete of the Hollywood hallowed ground of Grauman's Chinese Theater. And here I am with two of them, Adam Sandler and Jack Nicholson! *(Photo by SGranitz/WireImage)*

On the set of *Around the World in 80 Days*, where I play another crazy person. Nobody's ever made me laugh harder than the great John Cleese. Monty Python is the high watermark of comedy in the twentieth century, and it is an honor to be his friend. *(Author's personal collection)*

You never know which countries are going to go bananas for your movies, and I'm just thankful that Taiwan picked mine. *(Author's personal collection)*

*50 First Dates* was the first time I realized I was working on a really big Hollywood movie. When I walked onto the set and saw Adam Sandler and Drew Barrymore together in the diner scene, I went, "Wow, this is a big movie." Working with these young, handsome stars at the peak of their power was my greatest experience in cinema. I forgot what he said, but here, once again, Adam is making Drew and me laugh. *(Author's personal collection)*

You can learn more about acting from watching Martin Landau than you can from ten years of acting school. *(Author's personal collection)*

I don't know if it was a compliment, but Stallone said, "Joe Pesci wanted $5 million, and you're cheaper." Thank you Sly. I had a blast on that movie. *(Author's personal collection)*

The Rock and I tried to make a movie together in the early 2000s, and, unfortunately for me, I got busy, and he got busy becoming the biggest action star in Hollywood. Every year at Christmas, I have to look at a meme online that's a picture of the Rock, and they say, "Front of the tree," and then there's a picture of me dressed up as Ula in *50 First Dates* where they say, "Back of the tree." *(Author's personal collection)*

*Home Alone 2* was the only movie I was in that I knew for sure was going to be a hit. I stole a lot of moves from the great character actor Tim Curry. *(Author's personal collection)*

Willie Mays was the first hero I ever had. When I had his phone number in my phone, sometimes I would just stare at it. I can't believe I get to talk to the greatest baseball player of all time, Willie Mays. He would call me when I was in Europe, and it was three o'clock in the morning my time, but I would never tell him. I just wanted to hear him tell his stories, like the catch he made in the 1954 World Series off the bat of Vic Wertz. I didn't think anybody talked like Willie Mays until I went to Alabama and realized everybody in Alabama talks like Willie Mays. *(Photo by Tom Hauck/ Getty Images)*

The Quentin Tarantino roast was one of my best nights ever in show business. I murdered that night. Tarantino was one of the few people to talk to me after *The Hot Chick* didn't open as big as I wanted it to. He said, "I saw it on Christmas. It was my Christmas present to myself. I laughed my ass off." And then he said, "Just get working on the next one. Don't worry about box office. It will have a life, I promise you." And he was right. That movie has gone on to be the movie that girls love and that I'm remembered for most. Pictured here, right before she became a breakout star, the brilliant comedian Whitney Cummings and the love of my life, Patricia. *(Author's personal collection)*

Robin Williams came and saw my last practice before I shot my first comedy special for Netflix. My closing bit, which always murdered and I *thought* I had perfected, after the show I went backstage and watched Robin perform it ten times funnier than I ever could. Man, there's no better comic performer ever than Robin.

Richard Lewis had a very unique voice in show business and was the most wonderfully lovable, neurotic person you'd ever meet. He raised being neurotic to an art form. *(Author's personal collection)*

One of my only regrets was that we never got to make that movie *My dinner with Norm*. I just couldn't get him to do it. He didn't want people to know he was sick. Norm was one of the greatest comedians that ever lived, and I put him in every show I ever made. I miss him. *(Author's personal collection)*

I'm very proud of my Netflix show, *Real Rob*. I loved writing, performing, and acting with my real wife, Patricia, who was wonderful and brilliant in the series. We plan on making season three of *Real Rob*. (But seasons one and two are still available!) *(Author's personal collection)*

It took decades, but it finally happened. Howard Stern, the greatest interviewer there is, got Adam Sandler to sit down with him. Very few people could single handedly reinvent their whole industry. Howard Stern is one of them. (*Author's personal collection*)

Me and Macaulay Culkin, thirty years later. We look exactly the same. Fame, especially super stardom, is extremely difficult. I can only imagine the pressures that he must've gone through when he was only eleven years old. (*Author's personal collection*)

I've known Bobby Kennedy for more than thirty years. Bobby's humanity and compassion for his fellow human beings are what separates him from everyone else who wants to run for high office. It's an honor to be his friend and support him. My mom and dad loved his father very much. (*Author's personal collection*)

Performing live in arenas with Adam Sandler is just a blast, and performing by myself in theaters all over the world has been an awakening to what I really love most about show business—the live interaction with an audience, and trying to make them laugh until they can't breathe. You can do more with a microphone, words, and acting out a bit sometimes than you can do with an entire cast and an entire movie. I love it. Stand-up was my first love, and I'm having a renaissance with it now. *(Photo by Scott Yamano)*

No one can relate to what Elvis Presley went through. But here I am dressed up as Elvis for Adam Sandler's new comedy special, and in this picture, I feel a sense of weariness either from five decades in show business or five hours in makeup. *(Author's personal collection)*

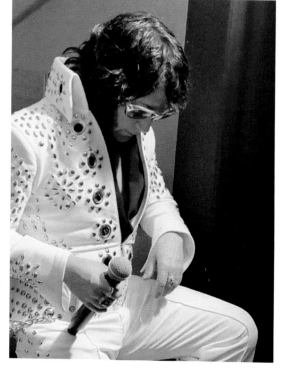

Here's the Filipino mafia—my mom and the rest of my family of Filipinos. Filipinos happen to be the highest per capita wage earners in America. Here, you're looking at nurses, engineers, professors of education, and one junior college dropout comedian. *(Author's personal collection)*

Of all the things I admire about my mom, she never had a sense of bitterness toward the Japanese, who killed her brothers, and she said, "The only reason I survived that war is because I was never afraid. I never felt fear." *(Author's personal collection)*

Sometimes dreams come true outside of show business. The single greatest thing that ever happened to me is that beautiful smile of Patricia Schneider's, and the gorgeous kids she gave me— Miranda and Madeline. *(Author's personal collection)*

Pretty darn good *SNL* cast. *(AP Photo/Justin Sutcliffe)*

# CHAPTER NINE

# WHEN THE BULLIED

# BECOME THE BULLIES

"DEATH TO AMERICA! BUT FIRST...pay my student loans!"

I am paraphrasing the Seth Dillon satirical news outlet, the brilliant *Babylon Bee*, and heir apparent to the *National Lampoon*. What the headline actually reads is "Columbia Protestors Clarify They Only Want Death to America After America Is Done Paying Their Student Loans."[1] This snapshot perfectly illuminates how delusional our citizenry has become by the attack of the woke movement.

I don't seem to remember in my childhood a president letting in 8 million undocumented people. Don't use the word "illegal" — we are supposed to use something nicer. Instead of "illegal," they want us to use the word "undocumented," which I'm sure is still considered mean by people who have previously misplaced their documents and are now undocumented. "Not legal" sounds like I'm calling them deplorables. "Not legal yet" sounds either like some pervy perp entrapment or a tad judgmental and makes them sound lazy, which brings up all sorts of stereotypes, like "you lazy not-legal-yet (insert racial epithet here)." You can almost see them weeping. Albeit in a super lazy way, with their super pervy perp lazy tears.

It's obviously no fault of their own that they're here. So how about we just call these people "accidental border jaywalkers." There, fixed it for you! These accidental border jaywalkers went out for a stroll and lost complete track of which country they were in and the next thing they knew, they were put on a plane and found themselves sleeping in a closed airport terminal in Chicago,[2] or on the floor of a high school gymnasium in Manhattan,[3] before embarking on a career in the wonderful world of sex trafficking.

I sincerely believe, or as sincerely as I *can* be sincere, that if any president in the 1960s, '70s, or '80s let in 8 million accidental border jaywalkers, they would have been impeached by Congress and tried for treason. In the '70s after President Ford, America *did* let in thousands of Vietnamese immigrants, which led to an explosion of nail salons. And later some of those nail salons branched out into waxing and other hair-removal activities. Later, still in that same decade, like Wilson, Jimmy Carter, the other president resembling the current mumbler in chief (Biden), allowed Cubans to flow in by the tens of thousands, Cubans that Castro was kind enough to bequeath to us from his higher places of learning — you know, Cuban doctors, scientists, and professors. Just kidding. Castro opened up his prisons and dumped his rapists, drug dealers, and murderers here with the Mariel boatlift mass emigration. It was 125,000 of them[4] (my book researcher funds have all been used up, so look up your own stats), basically what our current emperor with no frontal lobe gives us on any given weekend on our southern border. This mass immigration not only ushered in the extremely violent Scarface cocaine smuggling era in Miami, but also an explosion of salsa, rumba, cha-cha, and other Latin-themed dances that focused mostly on people grinding each other, causing extreme havoc on the disco movement so soon after *Saturday Night Fever*. Many white platform shoes were trampled and marked up by inexpensive Cuban dance shoes and occasional brain splatter. The brains were easily washed off. Cubano scuff marks, not so much. Thereby ending the era of the wild arm waving dance style of John Travolta impersonators.

I asked Dr. James Lindsay, my good friend, author, mathematician, and political commentator, to help explain the multifaceted attack of this woke religion on our culture, and more importantly, do we stand a chance to defeat the brown shirts and goons of the social justice movement? I should mention that James has written multiple books covering topics like religion, the philosophy of science, and postmodern theory, and he has appeared on Joe Rogan's podcast multiple times, too.

"I don't know if it'll win, but it's doing a pretty good job..." Lindsay said.

Let's say somebody just dropped into modern-day America from the 1950s or 1970s. How do we explain to them what's happening with this woke religious cult that seems to be causing so much social upheaval in America today?

"You know," James said as he laughed, "that's been basically the challenge of my life for the last two or three years...It's best if I describe something that has happened in the past to make sense of the present."

Specifically in this case, we can look at how Mao organized his political revolutions. For a quick historical background on

Mao, a lot of people in America don't know anything about this because we don't learn about it in school (I interject — they won't even tell us our *own* country's history because it's very racist-y), but Mao Zedong actually took power *twice*. The first time was an old-school military coup. You know, the good old strategy in 1949 where he whipped up the peasants, he built up an army, and he waged war on the existing nationalist government and over-threw it and took power. He defeated General Chiang Kai-Shek in the Chinese civil war and pushed his army into the sea (and today's Taiwan). Mao took complete control of mainland China and proclaimed the establishment of the People's Republic of China (PRC). His theories and strategies and general nonsense are referred to as Maoism.[5]

I interject again — how could this somehow lead to young girls being confused about their gender and considering going on puberty blockers? How terrible is that? On puberty blockers, the boys end up getting a micro-penis because the pills mess with their hormones. Micro-penis... That sounds like the smallest of small dicks. You don't shower with the football players when you have a micro-penis, never, *ever*! "No shower, I'm fine, thank you! I'll just stay dirty."

Anyways, Mao took power, lost power, then he took it back. The Cultural Revolution was the second time he claimed his power.

It's funny how bad people say they're going to do something, and then they do exactly what they said they were going to do, and then everybody acts surprised. "If only we would have known! Nobody could have possibly seen this godless communist dictator-ship coming!" Mao *told* us what he was going to do and he *did* it.

Mao very famously put out a speech/essay entitled "On the

Correct Handling of the Contradictions Among the People." Mao did this at the very height of his power in 1957, and what he said was that they had a *formula* that they used to transform China. The first layer of that formula is that you separate the population into two categories, which James refers to as "politics of compliance." The two categories are (1) *the people* and (2) *the enemies of the people.*[6] Basically, this gives you "the goods" and "the bads." You know, like Democrats and Republicans? Yeah!

"The goods" are defined as the people that are going along with what the power says.

Depending on the topic, if it's COVID, those that go along with whatever public health authorities say are "the goods." If it's identity politics, whether it's sexuality or gender or race or whatever, it's those that follow what the woke hustlers say that are "the goods." The people who are doing what the regime says are treated like citizens and the people resisting are not. If you just come out and say that "the bads" are deplorables, people get it real fast.

Once you divide the population, what Mao would do is he would sell the people (who are on his side, aka "the goods") basically a bill of dreams. "We're going to have the great socialist society! It's going to work. There's going to be a reduction in the working day.

"Everybody's going to have bread and land and rice. It's going to be great! Whatever rumors you may hear or suspicions you may have that I intend to murder or starve to death 100 million of you is all fortune cookie nonsense. You can't believe notes inside of any pastry, especially a cookie where they always get the lottery numbers wrong. What kind of misinformation are we dealing with here? These fortune cookie people should be taken out and shot, and they will! But let's get back to you. Your day will shine like sun in sky; may there always be food in your pantry and may your jowls be fat with rice."

As they say in the fortune cookies, "Man who listens to great leader stays in own home and is not awoken in the middle of night (which scares wife and children) and thrown onto train to reeducation camp, still wearing pajamas and hotel bed slippers that were given out at last People's Republic party gala!"

Of course, they could never deliver on that perfect society — nobody can. But they promise a perfect society so that when it fails, they can blame the people who are "resisting" it. These are "the bads."

When it comes to COVID, they told the people, "Well, we had to close down the entire economy, and we'll be able to open the economy back up as soon as everybody gets their shots. But the reason we can't, and the reason you're losing your business, and the reason your family members are dying, is because these certain people won't get the shots!" You know, "the bads."

This creates a dynamic James and his consortium refer to as "hate crashing." What you do is you get the people who are going along with the program and convince them to make sacrifices for the movement. This makes them feel like they're doing what they're supposed to. They're sacrificing, they're giving up something. In China, that would mean giving up ownership of their land, their rights, working extra hard, being forced into labor, but it was all for the party. And in COVID, it was just stay home, take this shot, fifteen days to flatten the curve, we promise it won't be two years and you won't lose your businesses and your grandmother won't die alone. Still, even with all those sacrifices, the perfect society where every guy gets blown every morning while he drinks his espresso, and every girl gets their own makeup and hair crew, doesn't materialize. So, you get the people who are sacrificing to blame the people who *didn't* get with the program. Now, *the people* are mad because they did what they're supposed to, but the *enemies of the people* didn't do what *they* were supposed to, and the situation isn't improving so it's all *their* ("the bads") fault. Now there are no blowjobs, no espresso, and women don't even have their own makeup anymore. Or…fortune cookie number two says, "You will not gain from your toils but blame man who won't wear mask or get jab."

That's how you build out a politics of compliance. It's really that simple.

The goal is to brainwash as many people as possible to see through the lenses of the ideology. We could, for example, get past COVID immediately if people would just get their shots. We could, for example, have a society where policing isn't racist if we would just do a bunch of critical race theory riots, get rid of prisons, and defund the police. We could get rid of crime if we just got rid of, you know, prosecuting crime and gave people free stuff from the government.

In his formula, Mao called it unity, criticism, unity.[7] You start, he said, with a desire for unity. In other words, you make a situation polarized and awkward and contentious until people don't want that anymore. They want unity. So they're willing to sacrifice some of what they stood on before, some of their freedom, some of whatever, to have calm politics and so "we can come together as a country again."

Then you criticize the struggle (making scapegoats out of "the bads"). Criticize those elements that are preventing us from moving into unity — "We would have a country that's post-racial, but there are so many racists!" "We would have a country that supports full human rights, but there are always people who are transphobic who don't want to let trans people exist!" "We would have a country that could tackle the greatest challenges, except we have people that won't comply with public health responsibilities..." and so on and so forth. Global warming would be solved if it weren't for all those people who are selfish — not those in private jets flying around the world with Israeli models (you heard me, Leo!), or Bitcoin miners using more electricity than the nation of Italy,[8] or AI using more water than the inhabitants of a small city,[9] but the real polluters — the people still driving gas-burning cars, using gas stoves, growing their own food, using coal-powered plants to heat their house, just having a bad case of gas (from the animal they just ate that *also* gives off gas), and these assholes won't recycle their plastics on Tuesdays, even though it all goes to the same dump as the regular trash,[10] for God's sake! And let's not forget those terrible, irresponsible dickhead polluters known as volcanoes that spew ungodly amounts of $CO_2$ whenever they feel like it!

Once we criticize those elements that prevent unity from coming together, we can enter into a new, better unity (diversity, equity, inclusion, social justice, "Wear your mask for *me!*" etc.). This new unity is what Mao called democratic socialism.[11] Get people to give up their freedom so we can all march together in the same direction, and the people who don't want to are the reason that it doesn't work.

Now, if you're struck by all the similarities between Mao and our present life in this country, you're not alone. This is what they did to us, from identity politics to COVID to race. Remember, this is the same "racist" country that elected Obama two times in a row. Obama, who bailed out the banks, after their predatory loans sank our economy, and didn't stop the foreclosures of homes when he had the opportunity. They've done this to us in every single aspect of society, and the playbook is straight out of Mao.

The woke cultists are just using different identity categories than Mao used. We have them in terms of critical race theory as the "antiracist" versus, you could say, "white people." We have the imagined divide and identity politics with "queer activists" against normalcy, or you could say, "straight people." Token categories were mixed with activist categories and became *the people* while everyone else was made into an *enemy of the people.*

Before I ask the less obvious question — What can the average person do about this now? — let me first ask the more obvious question: How did we get here?

"The long march through the institutions" (institutions being academia, media, and the government) was a phrase coined by Rudi Dutschke to describe what Western Marxists saw Mao doing successfully and copied in the West. In 1966, Dutschke realized that what Mao was doing in his (successful) campaign to regain power in China was to stop trying to *fight* the system and start trying to *infiltrate* the system.[12]

Dutschke said that people (Marxists) need to go to school. They need to get educated and become teachers, computer programmers, engineers, professionals, accountants, or go into the government. If they keep their ideology and take it with them into the institution, they can force change in the institutions from within. Primarily, Dutschke said, that needed to happen in education at *all levels.* Now you see why there're some boys joining girls' sport leagues. It wasn't overnight, it was a long march, where the goal was to create the professors who would teach future teachers, future lawyers, future doctors, future journalists, and everybody that goes off to school is going to get exposed to at least some dose of this. Over the course of time, they'll get a bigger and bigger dose, and eventually they'll go off into the professions thinking, "This is the way the world works!"

That was their fifty-year plan, and it more or less was coming to fruition by 2010 and 2011.

The big bookmark years of this are 1970, 1990, and 2010 — kind of like in twenty-year increments. This plan began in 1970 when they started infiltrating the colleges and then the K–12 education in particular. By 1990, they believed that they had infiltrated and captured colleges of education. By 2010, they had an *entire generation of students that they'd educated, K through college*, that was coming out of schools and going into their jobs.

At the same time, the "enemies of the people" routine started with the Tea Party, which was the conservative side revolt. As the "enemies of the people," the Tea Party got framed as a bunch of racist, redneck, hillbilly, homophobic, blah blah blah blah blah conspiracy theorists. Every word we use today to denounce the "enemies of the people" was thrown at the Tea Party. This is the same thing we see happening with groups like Moms for Liberty, who have the crazy idea of taking pornographic books out of their children's grammar schools.

A big point nobody ever really brings up enough was that in 2013, Obama (according to the Associated Press) "signed legislation that changed the US Information and Educational Exchange Act of 1948, also known as the Smith-Mundt Act...[and] made it possible for some materials created by the US Agency for Global Media, the nation's foreign broadcasting agency, to be disseminated in the US."[13] Essentially what this legislation change meant was that it was easier (while still not "perfectly legal," as the Associated

Press refuted, but then again Project MKUltra was "illegal" too) for the intelligence community to use propaganda techniques on the American public. That's real significant because, all of a sudden, the entire media can go full blast and propagandize the American people through every possible channel, from social media to traditional media and corporate press. They can do the whole damn thing, just like they would do if they were trying to overthrow a foreign government they want to flip over and install a puppet dictator into.

That our own government could do that to American citizens, starting around the end of 2013, is when all the identity politics stuff went completely bonkers. For example, the Black Lives Matter movement blew up in America for the first time at the end of 2014, one year later, and has basically been a rolling narrative ever since. Thankfully, they're now being exposed as race hustlers and new owners of four lavish estates in the US while eyeing vacation homes in the Bahamas.[14] Coca-Cola quietly took them off their website in the fall of 2023.[15]

The woke movement first infiltrated the West through the universities, and then oceans of money started to flow into various causes to further propagandize Western society.

The money came from a few big sources. One was the nongovernmental organization (NGO) circuit — nonprofits like the Open Society Foundations, Rockefeller Foundation, the Chan Zuckerberg Initiative, and the Bill and Melinda Gates Foundation — who collectively are dumping hundreds of millions or sometimes billions of dollars into their initiatives. For example, the Human Rights Campaign received a $20 million grant from Open Society in the late 2000s[16] and started taking up the trans issue instead of just being a gay civil rights movement. Bill and Melinda Gates donated over $200 million to the Common Core educational initiative.[17] Essentially, you get these huge nonprofits that are run by these goofy un-laid billionaires that are throwing tons of money at these issues simultaneously with the advent of the environmental, societal, and governance (ESG) movement.[18] How did this ideology get so entrenched in the corporate hierarchy?

Well, ESG took corporate social responsibility and environmentalism and hijacked those ideas, transforming them into what we would consider woke agendas, and whether it's the environment, identity politics, or COVID, the ESG is all over it. Now, a huge amount of corporate money is getting directed toward craziness. For example, the Corporate Equality Index, published by the Human Rights Campaign and driven by ESG,[19] requires corporations to have a marketing budget for LGBTQ+ marketing, which culminates with transactivist Dylan Mulvaney on a Bud Light can, which made Bud Light sales plummet.

The Corporate Equality Index requires that corporations support Human Rights Campaign issues in order to get a high score as a company. They tell you which bills you have to support, they tell the airlines they have to fly gay activists around to pride events or their score will go down. If their score goes down on the Corporate Equality Index, then their ESG score drops. If their ESG score drops, they lose access to all the perks that have been constructed around high ESG scores by the gigantic asset firms.

My next question for Mr. Lindsay was this: What do we do? And what happens if we don't do anything?

James replied, "If we don't do anything, and if we don't succeed in stopping this woke takeover, the answer is actually really easy to predict. The answer is almost undoubtedly a variation of what's happening in China with their social credit system. It's not like old school Soviets where people were getting lined up against the wall and shot, those were twentieth-century solutions. Twenty-first-century solutions are social credit systems like we see in nations like China and Canada, where the governments are locking people out of their bank accounts, or preventing them from buying food, or preventing them from traveling until they 'behave.'"

Lindsay explained further, "What behaving looks like will be based off of ESG in the West. They're even talking about personal ESG scores, which is the social credit system. What that looks like will modify over time, according to what their needs are, because as we have noticed, they don't have a consistent ideology. One year they may need more race and less queer, and the next year they may need more queer and less race. They can flip it around as it suits them."

"Surely, not everyone is going to play ball with these loons. Like one of the good billionaires and future Mars colonizer, Elon Musk, right?" I asked.

"Well, look what they did to Elon." After Elon bought Twitter and said some things they didn't like, they said that he had a racist company and Tesla fell off the S&P ESG 500 Index.[20]

Boy, I don't think I like these ESG people anymore!

James continued, "They weren't able to march on us basically because we have our First and Second Amendments. Our Fourth Amendment, too [no unreasonable search and seizures], prevented our government from being able to do stuff like freeze people's bank accounts like [what China-loving-and-his-own-trucker-hating] Trudeau did in Canada. The Bill of Rights and our Constitution protected us *enough* to get us out from under COVID tyranny."

I interject — our Constitution is just a piece of paper. What really protected us was American citizens armed to the teeth with an estimated 466 million guns, including, dear reader, the author of this book![21]

"Is this social credit *Love, American Style* unpreventable at this point? If not, how can we good, God-fearing Americans help toss this Mao-redo woke nightmare back into the recycle bin of history?" I asked, proud that I was able to understand some of the things James was talking about.

"Totalitarian regimes fall very slowly, and then all at once, if you look at the history of them. The Soviet Union, for example, lumbered along for seventy years and then all of a sudden, by 1992, it was all over quickly. When a critical mass of people stop seeing legitimacy in the regime, the regime is over. When people start making fun of it [comedians!], flaunting the rules in a patriotic or comedic way, it all falls apart very fast. When enough people decide they are fed up with the corruption, regimes crumble." James' prediction is that we are, at most, eighteen months, maybe less than twelve months, away from the woke collapse ourselves. Still, Lindsay isn't sure exactly what will trigger it.

"The only thing they can do once we reach that point is to destroy as much as they possibly can before they're kicked out of power," Lindsay theorized. Kind of like how in the final days of World War II when Hitler wanted to blow up the Eiffel Tower and the rest of Paris, but thankfully the order was refused by Nazi general Dietrich von Choltitz, who realized there was nothing to gain from its destruction.[22]

"It's ultimately just a matter of learning enough about the history and techniques to be able to recognize it. When you see how a magician does their trick, it doesn't trick you anymore. You know where the card is hidden. You can tell if it's the magician that's robbing you when he's stealing your wallet because you know the *move*. When you can see the trick, it doesn't work on you anymore, and then you can tell your neighbor the trick, and then it won't work on your neighbor anymore either. By educating one another, we can develop a herd immunity to their tricks.

"The 'good ones' will ask for access and then demand accommodation. It's when they come in and say, 'You have to change the rules for me,' and *you* say, 'I don't want to change the rules,' and then they throw a fit and then you give in or you get sued. That creep of 'accommodation' is the problem. Finding ways to stand up to that personally, and then legally, so that you don't have to change the rules around somebody who's throwing a fit, is the path to stopping this."

As James explained:

Mao tells us that the revolution proceeds in stages. When they are pulling their magic tricks, they are attempting to destabilize us. Letting boys play on the girls' team destabilizes the situation. It creates people who are mad. It creates kids who are injured. It creates all this chaos and people fighting, and it makes lawsuits that sometimes they even win. It produces chaos, and that's precisely why they fund it — they need chaos to create system change.

"If you can destabilize a country from within, then that country stops making sense," James continued. "And if the country doesn't make sense, it doesn't have a politic. And if it doesn't have a politic, it doesn't have a nation anymore. In other words, you can de-constitute the nation by making it lose its mind and sense of identity."

We are one nation, under God, with one national anthem at

the Super Bowl, *not two*, and a vision of what we want our nation to continue to be for our children.

James concluded by saying, "While there is at least one nation that doesn't want to participate in some big, giant global scheme, because they don't want to give up their freedom to Brussels or to Geneva or wherever the headquarters should be, then the only possible way to take control at the global level is to destroy the capacity for a powerful nation like the United States to allow its citizens self-determination. If the World Health Organization [WHO] says that I have to wear a mask, as an American, it's my God-given and secure right to tell the World Health Organization to go fuck itself and jump in a lake!"

Thank you, James Lindsay.

As we will discuss further in the later chapters, it's unelected, unaccountable global groups like the World Health Organization that I believe are the greatest threat to our freedoms, and indeed to the freedom of all people.

I thought that James had finished but he was still on the line (which kind of weirded me out because we had already said goodbye to each other twice) and added this final, final thought to his final thought.

"While we all would prefer a better Bond villain than this, with some lasers or sharks or at least something interesting, instead what we get is a bunch of dorks in suits who have really kind of transparently dumb plans that, unfortunately, *could* work."

James and I agreed. To break through this closed system of propaganda, it comes down to the idea of engaging with your neighbor via podcasts, alternative media, books, and, well, stand-up comedy. These are the types of dialogues that are still free from the propaganda shackles and are the last honest channels we have to protect our freedom.

Whatever way the wind is blowing generally in society is how the disengaged people think, feel, and act. What we need, James estimated, is probably 10 percent of the population to be engaged. That's it! Just a measly 10 percent! You know how people say put in 100 percent effort? Well, we don't need that; we just need the bare minimum, people. We're talking a 90 percent discount here! You know, it's like a store that says 90 percent off, and then you come into that store, and they say in fine print *on some items* — well, this is on *all items*, as in your freedom to not live in a fifteen-minute city while they try to make you eat bugs! (How much did they pay Nicole Kidman for that infomercial where she ate bugs, and *who* paid, exactly? What is the going rate for an actress to sell her soul these days? I'm guessing high six figures. Whatever it is, it seems a step down from all that real estate porn.)

Ten percent, people! That's it! Just 30 million Americans who are willing to speak up.

CHAPTER TEN

# THE PATRON SAINT OF

# MEDICINE

During the George Floyd riots, I was in Chicago with my friend the great comedian Jamie Lissow, who joked, "I was just in Chicago, they had an incredible sale. Everything was free! All you had to do was break the glass."

This was during the scamdemic when most stores were closed, remember? People were paid to stay home. If you did find a restaurant that was open, only the owner and his wife were working there. "I'm sorry; we'll be right with you!" That was the single time busboys and dishwashers had the upper hand on restaurant owners. (In a Mexican accent) "Listen, jefe, I want to come back and help, but honestly, I'm getting paid more to stay at home and watch Netflix and occasionally some of David Spade's favorite dirty real estate lady!"

At that point in the pandemic in Chicago, I would wear a medical mask, one of the basic blue nurse masks, around my chin. You know, the ones that did nothing. That were later proved not to stop the virus.¹ I wore the mask on the bottom of my face, keeping my nose and mouth exposed to the (newly discovered) dangerous fresh air, because I'm pretty sure that most of my germs come out of my chin anyway. I needed to buy a shirt to work out in (also because like most people during that time, I was becoming quite the fatty), and to my delight, among all the boarded-up stores on Chicago's famous Michigan Avenue, there was one that defiantly remained open in the face of racially charged riots and an ongoing plague.

In the store was a Generation Z woman *actually* working and getting a check, and not a stimulus check, but a check from this possibly celebrity-owned activewear store. This store was similar to Lululemon, which recently (and regrettably) improved their leggings material thereby no longer exposing the puckered anus of the wearer during certain Ashtanga yoga poses. Warrior one position was no longer as illuminating ☹.

"Holy shit!" I thought. "We can go *inside* this establishment! This store is surprisingly open! They got somebody, probably a foreign exchange student, to throw caution to the Chicago wind and actually come in to work today!"

An aside — Lori Lightfoot, the reluctant Beetlejuice impersonator and former Chicago mayor, was often seen yelling at poor inner-city kids to go back indoors and stay away from the virus's most opportunistic breeding grounds (you know, the aforementioned fresh outdoor air and cardiovascular exercise).² Lightfoot has since been relegated to a position of shame that is behooving of someone with such a general mean and nasty demeanor, detrimental to businesses and individual liberties: Lori was awarded a teaching fellowship at the School of Public Health at Harvard

University.[3] An aside to the aside — how much would you have to despise your child to send them to Harvard in 2025?

So, I walked into this Michigan Avenue Lululemon knockoff and was immediately confronted. This masked twentysomething Gen Zer said to me, "Sir, I need you to put your mask on" and I was just about to explain how most of my germs come out of my chin or hoped that she'd recognize me from *Deuce Bigalow: Male Gigolo* or *The Hot Chick*, when she reiterated, "Sir, I need you to put your mask on" with renewed insistence. Still surprised that she hadn't recognized my uncovered face yet, she added these two words that struck me as quite telling of the era we were now living in: "Sir, I need you to put your mask on *for me*! *For me.*" Two words that I recognized from the totalitarian propaganda dictate and Democratic virtue signaling of 2020 where suddenly I was in charge of somebody else's health and safety, "We're all in this together!" Hmm, but I don't seem to remember this person helping me pack up and move my furniture from California to Arizona, but suddenly I find myself in this position of new (and unwanted) responsibility. She repeated them one last time: "*For me!* I need you to put your mask on *for me*!"

"Oh! For *you*?! OK…" I said. "Show me your tits. *For me!* We're *all* in this together! I'll put this mask over my face, just let me see those floppy things under your sweater."

Boy, security can get you out of a store very quickly if they want to. It's a quick move.

They grab your shoulder with one arm in a turning motion and at the same time shove you toward the exit, and the next thing you know you're back on Michigan Avenue once again looking at boarded-up stores. Boarded-up, meaning the "everything for free" sale is over! When it appeared that Lori Lightfoot was going to do nothing about the consistent riots and break-ins of Michigan Avenue, businesses like major property manager Sudler wrote letters threatening that they would all leave if nothing was done.[4] Unsurprisingly, the next day, the nonconsensual wealth redistribution plan ended when flashing police cars were placed on every block of Michigan Avenue. The smash-and-grab party was over! No more free Nike sneakers or Louis Vuitton bags! That's the way these Democratic cities operate; it's only when they are about to lose everything that they are forced to act in the best interests of people who live in their cities. Like California governor Gavin Newsom, finally cleaning up San Francisco for his Chinese leader pal Xi Jinping when Xi was coming to town to try the watered-down Chinese food where his fortune cookie read "Town only clean this weekend, good time to stop by." Maybe if Xi Jinping got a second residence there, the city would have a chance of staying clean!

To you social justice warriors that have made it to this part of the book, of course I never actually said "show me your tits" to that store employee. But when I tell that joke on stage, it gets a roar of laughter for what that exchange implied: We are each individuals, and another individual demanding that we comply to their dictates from what they perceive as a health threat is an impingement on our freedom.

Sorry, we're not "all in this together."

No. I'm not responsible for your health, your weight, your food choices, the drugs you're taking, how you treat your body, or if you've ever considered having a gym membership, or how difficult it is to get out of your gym membership, your carbs-to-protein ratio, how hydrated you are, your genetic predisposition to disease, and to quote Bob Dylan, "It ain't me you're looking for, babe, no no nooo." (All right, enough — okay, one more.) I'm not going to knock that Snickers bar out of your hand at Kroger because you're prediabetic.

While I want you to do well and be healthy, it ain't my responsibility! *At all.* Just as I'm not required to roll up your carpet when you get evicted, or take out your recycling bin on Tuesday nights, or make sure your boyfriend remembers your birthday, or make sure you're getting enough REM deep sleep, practicing your Duolingo, getting a streak freeze on your Duolingo, calling your mother after her fourth husband left her because she's a loser, or applying your toe fungal cream. Also, it's not my responsibility if you get one of the fifty different coronaviruses[5] that are all known as the common cold. FYI: One out of every five colds is caused by a coronavirus.[6]

I remember another time during the scamdemic when I was getting yelled at, well, maybe "yell" is too strong. I would say it was more of a bark. I got barked at by a woman who, being in Los Angeles, was obviously a science-loving, godless Democrat. For some still unknown reason the liberals were more susceptible to buying whole hog what the government was serving up. Tony Fauci, during his November 2022 deposition for allegedly colluding with social media empires (and infringing on every American's right to free speech), admitted (in the middle of his 174 "I don't recalls" [that's right, in the middle of his deposition he said, "I don't recall" *174 times*]) that the "six feet social distancing" idea was just something they made up, with no scientific backing behind it whatsoever.[7] Where's the liberal outrage when you really need it?

Where is the burning of cities? Come on, people! There's gotta be one or two more civil war statues left that we can tear down!

So here I am, in a parking lot in Calabasas, standing outside in a line to get into a grocery store wearing the mask I bought at

Maskfakefakefake.com. I'm trying to get into LA's most chichi grocery store, Erewhon, where you can get a protein shake for the ungodly sum of $30 — if you're lucky and if they don't run out of organic ghee butter, or MCT oil, or the blood of virgins. Standing in front of me also waiting to get her $30 protein shake was a woman who was wearing her obligatory Lululemon exact-ass-shape-revealing yoga pants.

She turned to me, left butt cheek visibly clenched, and barked, "Can you *back off*?!" Apparently, I had encroached on her unscientific six-foot bubble and needed to give her more room in the fresh (for Los Angeles) outdoor air, thus preventing her from instantly contracting the COVID plague. Imagine if she knew the danger she was really in with my mask being made of pantyhose material! I stepped back, thereby preventing her from getting put on a ventilator in twenty-four hours. Because remember, if they put you on a ventilator (which there weren't enough of... thankfully!), it would kill you (reported rates of mortality on ventilators ranged from 50 to 97 percent).[8]

But there was one thing we were told would save us all! The descendant of the greatest medical innovation of all time: medicine's holy grail, the unimpeachable, the savior of humanity, the patron saint of medicine — of course, I'm talking about the pus from cowpox lesions, or as it's known now, vaccines.

I asked my friend and vaccine historian Roman Bystrianyk, "What's the new book about?"

"It's the *Dissolving Illusions* tenth anniversary, and a companion book, which has, like, five hundred or six hundred pages of quotes from doctors and vaccine tragedies and all sorts of historical shit," he replied.

"That should be fun," I said. "Not exactly a comedy." To which he replied, "Actually, the whole thing's a comedy, a dark comedy…"

Ten years ago when I got attacked for my "heretical" vaccine views, I reached out to Roman after I read his book *Dissolving Illusions: Disease, Vaccines, and the Forgotten History*. We caught up again while I was writing this book so Roman could better explain than *I* could how we, humanity, got to where we are today as it pertains to the cowpox history.

I just want to say here, we're about to talk and debate things that you'd think in a free society shouldn't be sacrosanct or off limits for discussion and debate. I believe one of those things is vaccines. It's precisely because we were not allowed to discuss vaccines, and the suppression of that discussion, combined with the pharmaceutical companies' late-twentieth-century surge in power and omnipresence in media and politics that contributed to the recent global shutdown and quasi-religious medical idolatry that divides us today. So we must talk about this. If I'm going to write a book about suppression of free speech and don't talk about what led to the shutting down of the world, then I feel like I'm an asshole. I am an asshole, but for different reasons. You see, we're not allowed to discuss, dissent, or question the patron saint of medicine — vaccines — because, as Roman explains, they have become deeply entrenched into our medical belief system. Belief systems are the most hot-button things we can discuss with each other — whether it's religion, vaccines, or that you can still be a woman with a complete set of cock and balls.

Remember how in the 1970s the liberals would say, "Question everything!"? You'd see it on the bumper stickers of their Volkswagen vans (that were crawling with crabs from their untrimmed pubic hair that peeked out above their bell-bottom jeans) along with a peace sign and "Freedom over Fear." Cut to 2020, where the new liberal slogans are "Question nothing, absolutely nothing!" "Whatever you do, don't ask questions of your government, they know best, just do what they say already!" "Stop selfishly thinking for yourself!" "Masks save lives!" "It's just a shot, what are you afraid of?!" "Women have dicks, move on!"

When we question or challenge belief systems, we trigger hundreds of years of indoctrination and also step on the very large toes of the massive industries that make billions of dollars off those belief systems, like in this case, big pharma. (Uh-oh! No *Deuce Bigalow Three*!)

Vaccines became mythologized because they were a potential cure for smallpox, invented by the strange out-of-the-box-thinking Dr. Jenner. Even horror author Mary Shelley could never have imagined a real-life Dr. Frankenstein quite like Dr. Edward Jenner. Dr. Frankenstein didn't experiment on his *own* kids. However, *Jenner did*. "Hi Dad! I just got back from school, what's up?" In 1797, Jenner started making vaccines by experimenting on his eleven-month-old child using smallpox.[9] Back then, they would give the patient scratches of smallpox to test whether or not they were immune to smallpox.[10] So, Dr. Jenner did these scratches on his own lucky kid.

Presently, when you go to a doctor and get a vaccine, there's a needle, it sticks in your arm, there's a little alcohol, and it seems pretty clean. It's not that invasive, and it looks like there must be a lot of medical science behind it, and it must be perfectly safe and proven to scientifically work — I mean, how else would they get away with it?

Let's take the wayback machine to the late eighteenth century, to the beginning of this new "medical" procedure. At that time, the procedure required a sharp instrument called a lancet (similar to a scalpel), and they would scratch a bunch of hash marks into your arm. ("Ouch, Dad! I'm gonna tell Mom you're experimenting on me! I'm not even a year old yet!") Then they would take pus from a cow or horse or somebody else's arm and squish it into those cuts.[11] Without any alcohol, they would cut you up and give you the disease by smearing it into your wounds. (Vomit emoji 🤮!) I'm sure there wasn't a big long line for *that*. "What are those people waiting in line for?" "Oh, the town healer will cut your arm up and give you horse herpes." "Well, I don't know about you, but I know what *I'm* going to be doing the rest of the day. Standing in that long line waiting to get *my* horse herpes! God, I hope they mandate this soon, so everybody has this opportunity! Hey, no cuts! Except the cut on my arm giving me horse herpes!"

Somehow, if you dare question this procedure, you are viewed as an ingrate. Well, of course, you pretty much got sick within a week. Everyone got sick. That was like standard procedure. Of course many people got really, really sick and died. You were supposed to get sick, and that was how you had to go through the cowpox illness before you were "immune," supposedly.

It's just a silly idea, but they had a lot of silly ideas back then. They used mercury to help people,[12] you know, mercury, the second most poisonous thing on the planet next to plutonium. They used to hand that out like it was candy! Another big thing at the time was "bleeding," where they would intentionally make somebody bleed to "cure" their illness.[13] In fact, they bled George Washington to death.[14] I'm sure if Washington had refused the bleeding, he would've been labeled an antibleeder. His obituary would've read "George Washington, first president of the United States, general, Founding Father, and antibleeding activist." Thankfully, he didn't question the bleed-your-way-back-to-health belief system. Instead, he was bled to death and was quickly buried.

Bleeding and mercury both killed lots of people, and the idea of the smallpox cure was just another dumb idea, potentially the dumbest. But the unsurprising reason it stuck around was because the medical profession, or what was referred to as the medical profession, grabbed onto it. The myth of this post-medieval barbarism providing immunity became so powerful that the medical profession began mass vaccinations, sweeping the world over.

Now, we're talking several hundred years ago, people. Forget about your pre-scratch cow pus alcohol swab. We're talking filth here. Real filth. The doctor's office was a very dangerous place to hang out. To quote the NIH, "Doctors did not routinely wash their hands until the mid-1800s, and they would proceed straight from dissecting a corpse to delivering a baby, providing the basis for the spread of puerperal fever."[15] Puerperal fever was killing one out of every three babies in 1841, not even counting the mothers.[16]

"What is it, a boy or a girl?"

"Neither, anymore..."

"What do you mean?!"

"There was nothing we could do..."

"You could've washed your hands, you fucking *animal*!"

"Also I have other bad news for you: we just bled your wife to death..."

"WHAT?!"

Not only was vaccination unsanitary, but there was also the challenge of delivery. Before they had syringes and vials (the hypodermic needle was invented in 1853), all they had was either the four-legged cow where the pus was cultivated, or the arm of another "vaccinated" person had to come to you (lucky you!).

Essentially, they turned people into walking vaccine needles. And, when the industry took off and spread around the world, they needed to get those needles (ahem, people) around the world, too. I know what you're thinking: "But Rob, where are they going to get these people to act as vaccine syringes?" Well, luckily, they thought about that, and eight seconds later they had the answer, and luckily they had a lot of them — orphan children! Yep, they rounded up orphan children and children from working-class minorities from the slums in England, put them on ships (probably not in business class — more like economy minus, or wherever they put the human guinea pigs), and sent them to foreign lands. The children were the preferred tools of this new trade because they were thought to be less likely infected with syphilis or tuberculosis and other diseases that the adults had at the time. (Perhaps the beginning of child trafficking.)

The medical profession knew there was money to be made here. But they still had one problem, and it was rather a biggie. When a potential "vaccine recipient" was asked if they wanted to rub cuts with a recently imported British slum child, the person could say, "No thank you. I'd rather not." Or, "The last time I saw you, you bled my father to death, and he was the president of the fucking country!" said George Washington Jr.

So, the medical profession needed to force people to get the vaccine — whether they wanted it or not — which they managed to do in the early 1800s. In Britain, they made vaccines legally mandated in 1853[17] and 1867.[18] So by 1870, fan of cow pus slum children or not, everybody was vaccinated.

If you thought that the vaccine mandates to keep your job during COVID were crazy, back then everybody was vaccinated, like *everybody*.

If you didn't get vaccinated, you would be fined.[19] Of course, the poor people couldn't afford the fine, so they were sent to prison. Prison then wasn't like the fun semi-consensual prisons of today either. Prisoners were subjected to hard labor and horrible circumstances, sometimes going without food. Truthfully, it was either get vaccinated or die.

Curiously, a massive smallpox pandemic enveloped the world in 1872, despite the fact that almost everybody was vaccinated.[20] There was, obviously, an uproar and finally the government realized they had to act promptly. And sure enough, *twenty-six years later*, they did. In 1898 they allowed for conscientious objector status.[21] Poor bastards could now say no! Because of this new ability to object to the jabs, vaccination rates dropped like a rock, from 100 percent down to 70 or 60 percent in some places.

Yet while the vaccination rates dropped, so, too, did the disease's prevalence. Which is counterintuitive to the idea of vaccines. If the vaccination rate dropped, shouldn't the disease rise? Isn't that the point? The medical industry, while not all that smart, simply couldn't figure out inoculation. Keep in mind, this is fifty years before the medical profession figured out the cure for mild depression — giving the patient a lobotomy by scrambling their frontal lobe with a needle through the eye. Who was the first person that said yes to *this*?

"We can fix your depression!" "You know what, I'm suddenly not depressed about anything in my life anymore! Thank you, but I'll take a mid-twentieth-century pass on this new psychiatric treatment."

However, we are still very much gripped by the cowpox procedure.

Question, dear reader: If we have had a decline of 90 to 100 percent in mortality of the diseases we wanted to vaccinate for, why do we have to mandate vaccines? No one's dying from measles or smallpox or scarlet fever (which there isn't even a vaccine for).

Starting in 1912, measles became regularly reported in the United States and at the time was killing six thousand people a year.[22] The measles vaccine was introduced to the US in 1963, but at that time, the mortality rate had dropped by 99.8 percent.[23] While the vaccine came out after the disease had dramatically stopped killing people, the vaccine still gets all the credit. It's kind of like how Adam Sandler gets the credit for all the laughs in *50 First Dates* when he's off doing romantic scenes with Drew Barrymore, while after two hours of hair and makeup, I'm dressed up as a Hawaiian stoner going, "This one's my good eye!"

In 2000 the World Health Organization announced that measles had been eradicated from the US — and gave the recognition to vaccines. Yet in 2018 to 2019, a measles outbreak in New York resurfaced with 1,249 cases. Of those 1,249 confirmed cases, not a single person died from the measles.[24]

Using the tried-and-true scapegoating technique, the medical industry and their paid sycophants in the media, of course, blamed the measles outbreak on the unvaccinated while conveniently ignoring the fact that the outbreak didn't kill anybody, or that measles had been, in fact, *eradicated* nineteen years earlier. They used a tactic of demonization to shame those that weren't vaccinated. Their tactics were punitive and meant to be embarrassing — they prohibited unvaccinated students from coming to school, unvaccinated children were banned from public places for thirty days, and parents that *didn't* vaccinate their kids could get six months in jail and a $1,000 fine.[25] It was a precursor for the big party that big pharma had in store for all of us in 2020.

What really mattered to lower the death rate of these diseases was the health of the people and child labor laws. Fresh fruit and vegetables, some exercise, a clean place to live, economic development, and indoor plumbing — that's what made the difference. It had nothing to do with the medical system or the patron saint of medicine whatsoever.

Society cleaned up tenement slums. Fourteen families weren't forced to share one toilet.

People were no longer living in damp cellars. People had access to nutrition. Refrigeration kept food from rotting while in the 1800s people were eating mostly inedible garbage and spoiled foods.[26] (You know, basically like college dorm life.) Back then, there was no plumbing or sanitation, so all your human, animal, and industrial waste went right into your water supply. "Drink up, people! The water's fine! Don't worry about your neighbor dropping dead. Stop asking irrelevant questions like 'What's that thing floating in my drinking water?' Or, 'But I just saw my neighbor's horse take a shit downstream.' Stop doing your own research! Just grab a cup!" "It's not research, I can smell it!" "Stop spreading your disinformation, you anti–water drinker!!" Thanks to sanitation (toilets), clean drinking water, and better nutrition, life by the 1940s and 1950s was a whole new world.

We shouldn't induce disease to prevent disease. To prevent disease, we need to make sure the person is healthy, and that they have sunshine, fresh air, some exercise, decent food, and here's a crazy idea... don't drink out of your own toilet.

By 1950, no one was dying from scarlet fever, which was a bigger killer than smallpox. Where's the scarlet fever vaccine? There never was one. Tuberculosis killed more people than any disease in the nineteenth and twentieth centuries, but who gets the tuberculosis vaccine? Practically nobody. Why isn't there a tuberculosis pandemic? one might ask.

But like I said, we are not allowed to speak freely or challenge the belief system of vaccinology.

Like Roman, I think Western medicine is great if you fall down a flight of stairs, get in a car accident, get stabbed, shot, have a heart attack, get hit by a bus, or have a heart attack while you're getting stabbed and hit by a bus, but for anything else, they really don't know how to cure anything. Our nation suffers from chronic illness and we should live in a healthier way where we don't need medicine in the first place. Instead, our medical systems should be built around educating people and guiding people to live *without* them, instead of keeping us reliant on them and their billion-dollar-earning cholesterol and heartburn pills.

The medical system makes up 17.3 percent of our GDP, with a spending of $4.5 trillion a year.

It should go down to 1 percent of our GDP, which would be $254 billion — or $771 per person per year.[27] It's not like they're dramatically improving our life expectancy anyways — our life expectancy in the US has only gone up four years in the last *four decades*.[28]

There's also a demonstrable emotional component to all this. Stress and fear make you sick. Scaring people continuously is not a good idea. Instead of empowering people, which of course our governments and media don't like to do, and saying things during the pandemic like "Go out, have some good food, a cup of coffee, enjoy your day, get some sunshine, and exercise!" they instead tell you to stay home and be scared.

The difference between smallpox and COVID, both of which created a frenzy, and scarlet fever or tuberculosis (which despite being much bigger killers did not incite frenzied times for society) is that during smallpox and COVID they *believed* they had something they *could* do — vaccines. The reason we have vaccination is simply because it makes us feel in control.

As Alan Watts says, "You know how, when you're on a plane and there's turbulence, so you grab the armrest as if that's actually doing anything?" In other words, you think you are controlling something when you're not doing anything at all. The fact remains that we are on a watery rock that is careening around a giant fireball at a thousand miles an hour. We control virtually nothing. This lack of control induces fear, and fear creates a vacuum that can be filled with irrationality. Feeling that somehow we could control a disease is what got the human psychology behind this medical intervention. If you can make people fearful enough, you can get them sucked into the Dyson of irrationality. (All kidding aside, that's a great fucking vacuum. That's a vacuum that can change your life or, hopefully, the life of the person who cleans your house!)

It's pretty genius if you think about it. For centuries they said, "Don't fear, be grateful, we have vaccines."

For centuries there's been this blind belief in healers, witch doctors, and wagon-driving, all-disease-curing snake-oil peddlers. Especially this new twenty-first-century version. You know, the ones that have diplomas, a nice house, wear white coats, so they must know *something*. They went to medical school where the president was a plagiarist! This centuries-old belief is built on top of this idea that there's a certain group of people that know something about health — and you don't know jack shit! And don't you dare try to read about it either!

The people that "know" come out with these ideas and you basically go along with them because you're an ignorant person in need of their saving. Next thing you know, dear reader, three hundred cow pus years later, we now have a schedule of all the shots our kids "need" to take. Currently seventy-two different shots of sixteen different vaccines before the age of six. (Why are so many kids sick again?)

In a 2023 paper about flu vaccines, Fauci and two other health officials admitted that "after more than 60 years of experience with influenza vaccines, very little improvement in vaccine prevention of infection has been noted."[29] After the paper was discovered and shared online, one of the authors insisted the paper wasn't saying "these vaccines don't work, just that they don't work as well as we want them and need them to work."[30] It's funny how they'll admit things in journals that they'll never tell the public.

Well, holy shit, here you are admitting it in your own journals that it doesn't work, but they don't tell that to Grandma — "Roll up your sleeve, bitch, and take this flu shot!"

Here's something that very smart doctors recognized over the centuries: medicine is nothing but empiricism. They would call it experimentation. They would try things over and over and over again, and it's always an experiment because they don't really know, despite the top hats and the white coats, how the human body works. No one knows. It's always an experiment.

They'll take whatever idea they have, like mercury or cholesterol-lowering medication, and they'll just put it on to the public and then see what happens. If it works, fine. If not, they move on to something else because they know the public doesn't pay attention for long anyway.

And here's something you won't read in David Spade's book...

There is no such thing as a side effect. When you put something in your body, it has effects. The effects they like, they explain, are the outcome of the medication. The effects they don't like, they call them side effects. It's simply all an experiment. When you go to the doctor, you try this medication. You go back, "Oh, you know, it's really giving me nausea." "Oh, okay, we'll switch to a different brand, then!"

Where's the science? There is no science. You just try different things until you get something that works or seems to work. No one truly understands how the human body functions because it is vastly more superior and intelligent and complex than any collection of doctors.

You can ask 100 different doctors what the optimal human diet is, and you'll get 110 different answers.

At the end of the interview I asked Roman if he had one thing to say to the reader what it would be, and here's what he said, which is witch doctor approved:

"Ninety-nine point nine percent of your health is in your hands. You just need to go into the sunshine. Don't be afraid of the sun that gave life to everything on the planet, including us...Exercise. Get plenty of fresh water. Hydrate, eat good food, organic foods (and everybody has a different idea what that is), but stay away from processed foods and de-stress. Don't worry. Live a life. Have a nice day. And then suddenly, you know, you're doing good. You got everything done. You don't have to worry about all sorts of horrible things happening to you, and then eventually you're going to die. Have a good life until you die because everyone dies eventually. Just don't worry about everything."

I'd like to thank Roman for his help writing this chapter, and I'll be sure to send all the hate mail and career-ruining stuff from the pharmaceutical industry directly to him. Speaking of hate mail, in chapter 12 we will discuss how an industry like big pharma will stop at nothing and violate all the freedoms you have in order to keep pushing their cow pus syringes into everybody's arms.

## CHAPTER ELEVEN

# GLOBAL BARBECUING

My these-fucking-liars-are-fucking-lying-again detector was slow to pick up on the global elite's big-budget Hollywood sequel to COVID, global warming, which wasn't alarming the plebes sufficiently enough to get us all to give up living in our modestly fossil fuel–heated homes and move us back into batshit-encrusted caves, where we could freeze in winter and simmer to the point of evaporation in summer. So they doubled down, upgraded and rebranded "global warming" to much more alarmist-sounding "global boiling."[1] I am not fucking kidding you. They are actually calling it that. I must admit, global warming sounded way too comfortable, snuggly, and cozy. Like, "Hey, now that the planet is safe from a new ice age, let's take advantage of this global warming and make some popcorn, sit on the couch, and watch Dave Chappelle's new comedy special on Netflix!"

But, as we've painfully learned, there's no money to be fleeced from leaving us alone. Luckily, we have super-duper-party-pooper smart people who have figured out that *we* are definitely the reason why there are bad hurricanes in the Bahamas! Now that I have your attention, please turn off your gas-burning stove, plug your car into the electrical socket (which I fucking guarantee you is powered by fossil fuels or coal!), and listen to this other scientific drivel.

The fearmongers always need a scapegoat. It's either "The Russians are interfering in our election," or "If Trump gets elected again, he's going to round up all his political enemies and put them in jail like *we're* doing!" If I could speak for the global COVID plunderers, their trillions of dollars of transferred wealth (from us to them) was a middling success for two reasons. One, it ended. And two, their globalist reset button was not pushed by all the planet's inhabitants. In other words, there were enough people that politely said, *No more*!

As well planned as they were, there were enough doubts raised from all the outright lies and bullshittery, that eventually even the most dull of mind turned off their fear switch.

But what if, between pandemics, there could be an everlasting emergency that could (they hope) never be turned off and, no matter the weather, warmer or cooler, no storms or way too many storms, could be blamed on this new all-consuming existential threat to humanity?

CUE: Outraged alarmist Swedish teenage girl, *"How dare you!"*

You've heard it before. "The science is settled." But once someone says, "The science is settled," be very careful. Because they now have a closed system of thought, a belief system. A dogma that cannot be questioned. Science is the new religion. If you dare question any aspect of what is now suddenly called "settled science," you are labeled an antiscience flat-earther and a "denier."

In other words, asking any questions or challenging the prevailing narrative is off limits. But science is permanently unsettled. We are really not too sure about anything. Doubt is the most important part of expanding your knowledge. The most important principle in attaining knowledge is being unsure.

We absolutely must leave room for doubt or there is no progress and no learning.... People search for certainty. But there is no certainty.

— physicist Richard Feynman[2]

In this chapter, I am going to highlight one free speech hero who isn't afraid to go against the grain, ask questions, and raise alternative theories about "settled science," despite a lot of pressure to shut up.

Now, I'm not saying there isn't climate change. To the contrary, I believe climate change is very real and indeed happening right before our eyes! Why, right here in Arizona, this very morning, the temperature changed from 57 degrees Fahrenheit to the present (and lovely) 73 degrees Fahrenheit (which is why I moved here).

The scapegoat, of course, is *us*! Well, specifically they point to one single gas, $CO_2$, that, because of our pesky habit of continual survival, we apparently are making too much of. Never mind the amount of $CO_2$ that is being rereleased into our atmosphere by that offensive polluting powerhouse known as our planet's oceans.[3] I have yet to witness even a single protest at my nearest beach, the Pacific Ocean. Nope! Not even one climate-warming warrior has bothered to toss even a single can of soup into the world's largest body of water. Remarkable.

Not to mention that other Earth-warming climate twat,

volcanoes! I am telling all my climate alarmist friends to get on the first (gasoline-powered) plane to Reykjavik, Iceland, and hightail it up the Fagradalsfjall volcano, can of soups at the ready! Toss in as many as you can, and then get the fuck out of there because it's spewing huge amounts of planet-warming sulfur dioxide ($SO_2$, so we're okay with that, phew!) and unfortunately also that naughty $CO_2$ into the atmosphere!

Global-boiling proponents blame the life-giving gas $CO_2$ for Earth's temperature rise, ignoring the fact that $CO_2$ allows all plant life to flourish, like the lungs of the planet, the rainforests, to breathe and create oxygen, which allows these same $CO_2$-deniers to (unfortunately) keep breathing. They don't seem to realize that the thing most affecting Earth's temperature for the last several billion years is probably that giant fireball in the center of our solar system that's 109 times the size of Earth — our sun!

But don't listen to this junior college dropout. Have a listen to a much smarter dude, Ned Nikolov, a PhD physical scientist.

As we learned about the human belief system as it relates to vaccines, when we are taught and believe that we have the power to stop suffering, we will vehemently defend it. Those who believe vaccines are something that *can* stop disease get set off when you challenge that belief system. The same goes for those reusable grocery bag–using, Prius-driving, recycling environmentalists. Save the planet!

The problem is, $CO_2$ is just the environmentalist's version of the vaccine.

For the last 700,000 years, the global temperature through geological time, as referenced from a declassified August 1974 CIA document titled "A Study of Climatological Research as It Pertains to Intelligence Problems," has fluctuated between a temperate, warm climate where life exists, before dipping into a cold period that caused much of the land to turn into glaciers. For the last ten thousand years, the CIA says, we have been living at one of the warm temperature peaks. The CIA said confidently in 1974 that "the northern regions, such as Canada, the European part of the Soviet Union, and major areas in northern China, will again be covered with 100 to 200 feet of ice and snow. That this will occur within the next 2,500 years they [scientists] are quite positive; that it may occur sooner is open to speculation."[4] What this means: climate change has been a constant factor, way before we had the combustion engine, landfills, and cow farts.

Just like with vaccines, humans are determined to convince themselves there is something we *can* do, and just like how vaccines were developed as a way to control disease, global warming and the climate-change movement was developed as a "way to control" Earth's natural warming and cooling.

$CO_2$ just became the scapegoat.

Until 2010, Ned, an accomplished scientist and theorist with a PhD in ecological modeling and a master's in forestry, was a firm believer in human-caused global warming. Over the course of his career, he has worked at the USDA Forest Service to improve fire-weather forecasting, and developed methods to predict fire danger and wildland fire activity. Ned used to argue with some colleagues that didn't believe the greenhouse theory or the global-warming agenda. He would tell them that they have to be crazy to not believe it, because thousands of scientists have signed up for this — how is it possible that they are all wrong?

Then came Climategate. The head of the University of East Anglia's Climate Research Unit, Phil Jones, had his email hacked.

In the emails between him and other top scientists, including Michael Mann, they openly discussed using a "trick" to "hide the decline" of temperature data.[5]

Ned started realizing that something was amiss.

In the 1970s, and part of the reason for piquing the CIA's interest in the climate, there was a cooling period. The CIA feared that this could impact crop production, which would assuredly impact national security. The same CIA document outlined these other climate impacts:

> Early in the 1970s a series of adverse climatic anomalies occurred:
> The world's snow and ice cover had increased by at least 10 to 15 percent.
> In the eastern Canadian area of the Arctic Greenland, below normal temperatures were recorded for 19 consecutive months. Nothing like this had happened in the last 100 years.
> The Moscow region suffered its worst drought in three to five hundred years.
> Drought occurred in Central America, the sub-Sahara, South Asia, China, and Australia.
> Massive floods took place in the midwestern United States.
> Within a single year, adversity had visited almost every nation on the globe.[6]

So how could it explain that while the $CO_2$, which was dubbed the culprit, was still going up, that it was possible that the temperature would drop? This, of course, was troublesome for the climate-change activist community ("the people," or "the goods" as James Lindsay would say), and they needed to quickly address it. Committing a cardinal sin of science, instead of revising the theory, they instead...revised the data.

Ned sought to better understand how we got to the current climate-change dogma, despite being a believer (and defender) of it just a few short months earlier.

That was when Ned started to question the greenhouse gas theory entirely.

Thermodynamics, the study of heat transfer and gas behavior, is something we all know to be true. The greenhouse theory claiming that $CO_2$ and other greenhouse gases are responsible for global warming because they trap heat in our atmosphere is a nineteenth-century concept proposed as a conjecture by earlier scientists.

French physicist Joseph Fourier theorized in 1827 that the atmosphere works like a blanket. He correctly concluded that the presence of atmosphere makes us warm. Given how far away Earth is from the sun, our planet should be much colder without this gaseous blanket.[7]

Then in the middle of the nineteenth century, John Tyndall in England did the first experiments, testing how different gases absorbed visible and infrared radiation from artificial light sources. He found that carbon dioxide and water vapor absorb infrared radiation a lot more than other atmospheric gases such as nitrogen and oxygen.[8] However, he incorrectly interpreted this heightened infrared absorption as an ability of these gases to "trap" heat in the atmosphere. No gas in our turbulent atmosphere can trap heat, because any thermal energy absorbed by air parcels is quickly dissipated through convection. Even to this day, climate scientists erroneously assume that just because a gas *absorbs* infrared radiation, it can prevent heat from escaping to space. Which is fancy science-y talk for "fuck off, Al Gore."

Our atmosphere works off *convection*. The sun heats the ground, and conduction and convection warm the air. The warm air rises and is replaced by cooler air coming down. A missing part of the greenhouse theory is that a gas alone couldn't trap heat to make the air warmer unless the gas itself is physically trapped in a *container*.[9] Heat trapping is impossible in an open atmosphere without a lid on top. The simplest example is in the middle of the winter, if you took off the roof of your house, how much heat would you lose? This idea of trapping heat in the atmosphere through greenhouse gases is the most fundamental premise of the current climate theory, but it makes no physical sense. When you open your convection oven door, does the atmosphere of your kitchen keep the heat *inside*?

Instead, there are other explanations for the variation of temperature in our atmosphere, like albedo. (At this point my brain hurts! But methinks this albedo shit has something to do with clouds or some cloud-cover shit!) Albedo is the scientific term for the fraction of light that a surface reflects; it explains how much of the sun's heat gets absorbed by Earth. If the albedo is 1, it means all light is reflected. On our planet, we can track how much light is reflected back into space. Over Europe, about 29 percent of the incoming sun's radiation is reflected to space (though it is different all over the planet, as some parts of the world are darker and absorb more light). Clouds also impact how much sun our planet gets.[10]

If greenhouse gases do serve as an invisible "roof" to trap heat, then what causes the atmospheric thermal effect? Ned set out to find the answer and published a paper in 2014, where his team compared Earth's temperature to the temperature of our moon. While the moon is at the same distance from the sun as Earth, it has no atmosphere. Ned and his team demonstrated using math that, without an atmosphere, Earth would have the same global temperature as our moon. They also discovered that the way climate scientists calculated the thermal effect of Earth's atmosphere was mathematically wrong.

Ned derived a universal mathematical model that accurately describes the long-term global surface temperatures of diverse planets and moons in our solar system (including Earth) using only two predictors: incoming solar radiation received above the atmosphere and total atmospheric pressure at the surface. The model describes Earth as a part of a cosmic continuum that relates our climate to the climates of other planetary bodies with rocky surfaces such as Venus, the moon, Mars, Titan, etc. A key implication (consequence) of this discovery is that the global climate is *independent* of atmospheric composition. This means that human carbon emissions cannot in principle affect Earth's global temperature, because such emissions have no measurable effect on total air pressure. Therefore, attempts to control the climate through reduction of carbon emissions are physically futile and practically pointless.

Ned then published a paper in 2017 that describes this thermal effect on the atmosphere, a paper that raises legitimate questions about the greenhouse theory.[11]

The response from the scientific community was...silence.

SURPRISE!!!

Ned was largely ignored, like other free speech heroes we've covered in this book, and we see once again an individual going up against an entire machine. This time it's the climate industry.

So why didn't the climate-change greenhouse theory model face more scrutiny when other scientists, like Ned, published their findings that there were other explanations for how heat gets trapped in our atmosphere? Between other things trapping our sunlight in our atmosphere (like clouds) as well as atmospheric pressure, it seemed that there were other things besides greenhouse gases keeping the planet warm. Besides, the CIA documented that Earth's ebb and flow of temperature is a natural occurrence from 700,000 years ago!

The answer is because we can do something about $CO_2$ emissions, and we must believe we can do something about the planet's temperature because we need to feel in control. So, anything we can't control that could be causing the temperature rise is discounted.

Plus, when there's fear, there's money to be made...

Now, like with the ESG rankings, there is a whole business built around the fight against $CO_2$. Instead of a social credit, we have the carbon footprint, where we are judged to be good or bad by how much we follow the rules of reducing carbon. Businesses, and even individuals, are regulated, and there's a massive push to get to alternative, less-$CO_2$-producing energy. Greenwashing is everywhere, and just like with COVID, when it comes to $CO_2$, "we're all in this together!"

Those that ask questions, or propose *alternate* theories, are once again the enemy of the people. Those that go along with the narrative are "the goods," and they get to enjoy the perks of going along with the climate-change story — like using the HOV lane even when it's just you in the car because your car is electric, or getting your ten-cent deposit back when you return a beer can in Michigan — and the only price they have to pay is living with the existential fear that they are somehow contributing to humanity's ultimate demise because they used the washer and dryer at three in the afternoon.

There! Take that, global-boiling assholes!

## CHAPTER TWELVE

# RUNNING OUT OF

# ACTUAL TERRORISTS

The ever-growing spy agencies and intelligence community are big business. The United States government has several agencies to deal with terrorism, both foreign and domestic. Like the CIA and the FBI, which would seem adequate for this endeavor. But we also have the National Security Agency, and after 9/11, America was gifted with another, the Department of Homeland Security, which sounds like something that came out of Germany in the 1930s. By the way, there's no longer any school course in Germany on "leadership," because "leader" in German is *Führer*, and that word is no longer welcome in polite German society.

There are also many private security groups in the United States, like former vice president Dick Cheney's former group, Brown & Root Services (where Cheney was the CEO of the parent company Halliburton and the single largest shareholder in a company with a vested interest in war).[1] The private security industry's largest region is North America, and globally the industry is projected to be worth *$446 billion* in 2030.[2]

In a book on free speech, I have to mention the former Dell employee that was contracted for a private security gig with the United States for an NSA base, the infamous Edward Snowden, who now has a Moscow address after he revealed global surveillance programs. Director of national intelligence James Clapper falsely testified under oath during a congressional hearing where he was asked if the NSA was collecting millions of Americans' data and he answered, "Not wittingly."[3] Now we know that millions of Americans had been spied upon *wittingly*.

The same idiotic logic that was used in COVID was used about spying. "Well, if you have nothing to hide, what are you worried about?" That's not the point, dickhead. It's wrong and illegal for the US government to spy on its citizens without a warrant. The Constitution protects citizens from unreasonable searches and seizures by the government through the Fourth Amendment. Whether I'm going online and planning to put a bomb in my shoe like Richard Reid,[4] the half Islamic terrorist, half retarded English bomber, is not justification for illegally spying on every citizen. The potential for a crime is not, and has never been, justification for a warrantless search. By the way, Reid put a bomb in his shoe with wires sticking out, you know, like a half retard Islamic terrorist would do. Now, because of this one loony individual's actions, *you* have to take your shoes off at every airport for the rest of your life. It's worth noting that every infringement on liberties that they have taken from you, including taking your shoes off, you don't get back. Once they get people used to taking their shoes off, it becomes entrenched and another "accepted" inconvenience.

The "accepted" inconvenience... That's the opening right there. Get people used to small, seemingly inconsequential inconveniences and increase them over time, find new justifications for additional seemingly inconsequential inconveniences, and you're conditioning people to eventually allow themselves to be X-rayed so some TSA officer can masturbate to their image. Remember how, in 2010, you had the option to stand in a full-body X-ray machine, that apparently made a very sexy image of you, or go for the back-of-the-hand crotch-groping "enhanced full-body pat down" ("enhanced" meaning touchy-feely)?[5] But that sounded a tad invasive, so, needing to make your flight in fifteen minutes, you opted for the X-ray machine, only to find out some rogue TSA officers were drooling over the photos of your surgically enhanced titties?[6] Do you notice how when the government fucks up like that, and after they get caught, they don't *stop* taking pictures and just go back to the old tried-and-true metal detectors? Yep! These machines cost a lot of money and, more importantly, are making someone a lot of money. So let's keep X-raying people, and now just make the pictures a little fuzzier, causing the TSA masturbator to use more of his or her imagination. That's actually what fucking happened, people! At the same time they created a new revenue stream, the TSA PreCheck, so if you pay the TSA money, they won't take pictures of your balls, which I think is worth the hundred bucks. Thank you, United States government!

When the government and other captured agencies — like academia, pharmacology, and the media mob — run out of actual terrorists, they'll just create their own for their job protection. They'll change the definition of what they construe to be a terrorist. They need an excuse to keep their cash flow coming to justify their existence and keep the fear machine going. No perceived threat, no matter how small, can go unpunished, even if, or especially if, all the information is fact-checked and true and indisputable. They don't need to dispute facts, they just need to demonize the one telling them. In this case, me.

In 2012 (eight years before COVID) I helped narrate an informational animated piece to inform parents about the reality of what you have to go through if you do the "right thing," and listen to your doctor, and your child gets injured permanently by an approved drug. And people do get hurt — over $5 billion (that's billion with a *b*) has been paid out to families of vaccine-injured children and adults. Through the Vaccine Injury Compensation Program, $4.6 *billion* in compensation and $450 *million* in attorneys' fees were paid out to victims and their families,[7] like Hannah Poling, a child whose autism, the courts found, was indeed caused by vaccines and was awarded *just* $1.5 million.[8]

I chose to, and still choose to, believe parents who know their children more than anyone else and knew their children were fine and then weren't fine after being given a product medical professionals assured them was perfectly safe. The pharmaceutical industry, to put it lightly, didn't care much for this additional information I was providing potential new customers of their products.

In 2014, against my better judgment, I appeared in a State Farm commercial reprising the *Saturday Night Live* character the Richmeister (the Making Copies guy). I had a lousy attorney at the time, and it was a mistake not firing him earlier. He worked on commission and, along with my greedy agent who also worked on commission, didn't make money unless I was working. They talked me into doing this commercial for State Farm with football quarterback great Aaron Rodgers (who would later famously become vaccine hesitant as well). The CEO of State Farm at the time, Edward B. Rust Jr., happened to be a fan of *Saturday Night Live* and the Richmeister character I created. Anywayyyy, I did the commercial. In all seriousness, I am the only person responsible for my own decisions, and while I would prefer to blame my attorney and my agent, I am a big boy and I am responsible for my actions. Nobody tied me down and forced me to make that commercial. It was a far more insidious and coercive kind of pressure. A pressure that Hollywood is notorious for... They paid me a shit load of money. That's right. Those evil bastards gave me $400,000 for three hours of work. What a bunch of dicks! Truthfully, I needed the money to help finish paying for my own TV show that I was producing.

By the way, Aaron Rodgers got into a kerfuffle because he chose to "unscientifically" (but logically and completely rationally) use his own human, natural, immunological response, which took human beings hundreds of thousands of years to develop, instead of a drug that was developed at quote "Warp Speed." You may notice you haven't seen any new Aaron Rodgers State Farm commercials, but what you also haven't seen is Aaron Rodgers in a Jets uniform collapsing face-first on the turf, requiring a defibrillator to get his heart started again... yet. The Jets offensive line is terrible!

A decade ago, cancel culture was first getting its feet wet in ruining people's lives, careers, and relationships by finding old tweets, yearbook photos, or the occasional hot mic recording: "And when you're a star, they let you do it. You can do anything... grab 'em by the pussy."[9] Trump did use the word "*let*," by the way, just for clarification. CNN never did a program focusing on that, because if Trump used the word "let," as in "*let* you grab them by the pussy," while still not very nice, that would confer some measure of consent.

But I digress. Back when cancel culture was just getting good at helping people get over the hump of whether to kill themselves or not, companies, especially, were vulnerable. A handful of people can appear like it's many people online, and the online uproar seems more magnified than in reality. When the commercial featuring me and Aaron Rodgers aired, a few pro-pharma trolls and their followers started their own social media campaign on Twitter to tell State Farm to fire me. State Farm quickly removed the ad, even though the information I had given out was correct and easily verifiable about the painfully arduous system of how vaccine injury compensation gets metered. State Farm, being an insurance company (that sells life insurance), was vulnerable to the perceived online attack. I wasn't fired (I was paid in full and so was my greedy lawyer and agent) — they just removed the ad — but that was not the public perception. The cunts celebrated and then the pile on and vilification from the mainstream media was truly head spinning. I was vilified as if I was someone who was putting children in jeopardy, or even trying to kill children, *like I was a terrorist*. The ramifications and threats on my career were obvious and real. They don't want to only silence you, they want to make you an example.

After my State Farm debacle I got a phone call from a very good friend who was the CEO of a Fortune 500 company. He called me after I just got off stage from a sold-out show in Boston. I remember this now, as I write it, clear as day, like it was just happening right now — it's seared into my memory. He said:

"Listen, you're just a nuisance now. But you're really famous. If you hurt them, if you cost them money, you will never work again.

They will sue you, but not only you, they will sue other companies just to prevent you from working. Is that the battle you really want to fight?"

"But what I'm saying is true!" I said. "Somebody has to fight this."

And he said, "Well, Rob, you have a young daughter. Is it fair that she has to fight this battle, too?"

My stomach hit the floor, which is what they want.

They want you to fear them. They want to make sure other people know what will happen to them if they dare ask the same inconvenient questions.

Big pharma, the pharma-paid medical boards, and our pharma-captured health agencies didn't feel obliged to counter any of the points I made. This was public relations carpet bombing. There would be nobody coming to my aid.

That's how powerful the real, legal drug cartel is. Forget about the Mexican drug cartels. That's small time. Big pharma is *the* drug cartel. The Mexican drug cartels just make a few measly billion dollars. The pharmaceutical cartels globally *legally* rake in hundreds of billions of publicly paid dollars annually. *Annually*. Sometimes when you're attacked, you either succumb to it and crumble or if you survive, you become emboldened. That was their mistake. They fucked with the wrong Filipino. A guy who didn't crumble...yet. If they paid me enough, I'm available for crumbling, because not only am I a free speech advocate, I'm also a whore.

CUT TO: five years after the State Farm experience. The pandemic rehearsals took place in October 2019 at something called Event 201, a conveniently described pandemic "training tabletop exercise based on a fictional scenario" at Johns Hopkins

University[10] — in costume, by the way, replete with official name tags of governmental health officials, who would be the same officials that would use these "fictional" procedures to shut down the world a mere 136 days later. For the previous eight years leading up to the rehearsal, big pharma had been on a full-court press offensive to silence, punish, and eliminate any and all would-be objectors, using the derogatory term "antivaxxer." So much so that the World Health Organization labeled "vaccine hesitancy" one of the major global threats in 2019.[11] That's right, people questioning a vaccine is right up there with nuclear war, famine, and genocide! By being labeled an antivaxxer, you were automatically looped in with the other science-denying (and frankly ungrateful) flat-earth loonies. They blamed the antivaxxers for causing a measles breakout in 2014 in Disneyland, yet they found out later that over half (55 percent) of the cases were vaccinated, partially vaccinated, or their vaccination status was unknown, but that crucial piece of information was deemed unimportant to the narrative of wanting to frighten people and at the same time scapegoat unvaccinated people, so it didn't get much press coverage.[12] The term "antivaxxer" is problematic in and of itself. It's too all encompassing. It's like if you question the fact that the Boeing 737 Max airline may have problems, nobody labels you antiplane. The same thing with a woman. If a woman doesn't want to have sex with you, that doesn't make her antidick. She's just anti–*your* dick.

When there is no firewall between the pharma industry and the agencies that are supposed to regulate pharma, like the FDA, CDC, etc., there is a loss of impartiality. Without firewalls, those with something to gain from the industry can influence those bodies that should be regulating them. Without a fair and impartial referee, those in the industry will do whatever will line their pockets the best — like the media sensationalizing the news they must deliver to the public, or like a baseball manager betting against his own team in baseball. This is the slippery slope to tyranny that creates these different cartels and reinforces a new oligarchy.

Unfortunately, an edutainment book like mine, or a writer like I am with such a low attention span, cannot cover the full range of everything that is captured in our society, but I will mention that we're having to deal with captured media, technology, pharmacology, healthcare, and academia. These captured agencies are where the suppression of free speech thrives.

Is it just the junior college dropout or does it seem overtly corrupt that someone like Julie Gerberding — who was the director of the Centers for Disease Control and Prevention — can leave the agency and then five minutes later (eleven months to be exact) become president of the vaccine division for one of the major providers of (publicly funded and mandated) vaccines, the well-funded Merck?[13] Through Gerberding's connections at the captured agency she just left, the CDC, she can influence legislation and oversight to make it friendlier (and more profitable) to her new employer.

Around this time, the founder of the National Vaccine Information Center (NVIC), and real hero in my life, Barbara Loe Fisher, reached out to me.

She assured me that what I was going through was not new. The demonization of and discrimination against those who declined to get a government-recommended vaccine, or those who spoke publicly about how they or a loved one were injured or died after vaccination, has been going on since the nineteenth century. John Pitcairn Jr. and Alfred Russel Wallace were two pioneers that were against mandatory smallpox vaccination laws.

Their legitimate scientific and ethical arguments that they were making regarding forced smallpox vaccination are absolutely valid today.[14] (For more on this chapter and to see my whole conversation with my dear friend Barbara Loe Fisher, please go to my website, RobSchneider.com, if it hasn't been crashed by the government or the pharma cartel.)

Now, vaccines have become so important and engrained in our society, government, and individual belief systems because they are painted in the name of disease control and now, God forbid, national security (how did this happen?) and, of course, for the greater good. By default, if you have questions about vaccines, you are anti–disease control, anti–national security, and anti–greater good.

This is, unsurprisingly, exactly how we would define a terrorist.

What happened? How did we get here? In a short time we seemingly traded natural childhood diseases that strengthen and inform the human immune system for generations of sick kids.

An NIH statistic shows that 54 percent of our children suffer from chronic illnesses that were unheard of just a few short decades ago.[15] There has never been, to this day, a study of a thousand kids that have taken the vaccine schedule and a thousand kids that have not, to see who has better health outcomes.

The only way that this is possible is because pharma has the rule makers in their back pocket. In 2021, at the small sum of $1.1 billion, big pharma accounted for 75 percent of the FDA's operating budget.[16] You know, your Food and Drug Administration, which is responsible for regulating every one of pharma's new drugs, is financially beholden to the pharma cartel.

The pharma cartel continues to expand. They embedded

themselves in government lobbyists, they became the largest donor for both federal and state elected officials, and their tentacles fondle every level of government balls (they were the largest industry lobby in the US by more than $140 million in 2023).[17] They pay for medical boards, committees, and candidates in every state.[18] They advise (and actually write!) legislation through the medical boards that they finance. Bills that are printed and voted on are near verbatim what the pharmaceutical industry dictates.

The power that big pharma wields is easy to understand once you know this fact: pharmaceutical advertising for their drug products made up an astounding 75 percent of all the internet, television, and radio ad spending combined during 2020.[19] When you see "ABC News brought to you by Pfizer," it is because ABC News is bought, paid for, and brought to you by the pharmaceutical giant, Pfizer, who, not coincidentally, paid the biggest criminal fine of any kind ever in history in 2009 — $2.3 billion.[20] But for Pfizer, that's just the cost of doing business. By the way, we're one of only two countries in the world that allows this direct-to-consumer pharmaceutical marketing (New Zealand is the other).[21]

Question, dear reader: If something goes wrong with a government-mandated vaccine — I mean, my kids need it to go to school after all — and my kid gets injured and needs to wear a helmet for the rest of his life to stop himself from hitting his head against the wall, I can sue the manufacturer, right?

WRONG!

That's right, you can't sue them! Why? Because they have complete product liability immunity.

What? But vaccines are drugs! And in the history of drugs, there is not, and has never been, a drug that is 100 percent safe,

100 percent of the time, for 100 percent of the people. So why are we both giving product liability immunity *and* mandating that everybody take these drugs? Barbara's message is a very simple one: If there is risk to any medical intervention, we must have choice, or we don't have freedom. The discussion on drugs needs to be pragmatic and about weighing benefits against risks for the individual. This is how every drug needs to be considered legally, ethically, and morally. What exists now is medical tyranny. We find ourselves in the same situation today as we were two hundred years ago.

As the public became more aware of the dangers of vaccines, thanks to the PBS program *DPT: Vaccine Roulette* (1982)[22] and Barbara's book *A Shot in the Dark: Why the P in the DPT Vaccination May Be Hazardous to Your Child's Health* (1985), the number of vaccine lawsuits increased twenty-two times in the 1980s.[23] Because the pharmaceutical industry was getting the shit sued out of them, they went to Congress and pleaded with them and threatened that if they didn't get liability immunity for their products, they were going to stop manufacturing vaccines.

The result was the 1986 National Childhood Vaccine Injury Act.

In a nutshell, the act was originally designed to be an expedited, less traumatic, less expensive, more just, no-fault, *administrative* vaccine injury compensation system alternative to filing a civil lawsuit against vaccine manufacturers or negligent doctors/vaccine administrators. It was never designed to be an "exclusive remedy" but an *alternative* to a lawsuit. If a vaccine victim was turned down or offered too little compensation, that person could still file a lawsuit, but it was made more difficult.[24]

Of course, the government didn't even want the bill passed in the first place during the Reagan administration because each and every award to a child that has been injured or died from a vaccine is an admission that vaccines *can* hurt or kill. They did not want all these children compensated because they felt it was a confirmation of the toxicity of vaccines. As imperfect as it was, when this bill was passed into law, it was at long last an admittance by the government, medical establishment, and vaccine manufacturers that not only do vaccines carry risk, they can and do injure and kill people. In the act, Congress affirmed and stated for the first time that vaccines were unavoidably unsafe.[25]

Throughout the hearings and the negotiations, the only people representing the interests of every future child in America were not a group of lawyers, highly paid medical professionals, the vaccine manufacturers, or well-funded lobbyists, but a handful of parents of injured children. At the forefront was my friend Barbara, and the parent group the National Vaccine Information Center. Despite the parents fighting alone against the hugely powerful combined forces of the United States government and the pharma cartel, they won some safety provisions of informing, recording, reporting, and research on vaccine development. This was quite an achievement.[26]

However, in just a few short years from that, the pharma cartel was able to lobby their way to the Supreme Court and gut nearly all the safety provisions and close any manufacturer vulnerabilities. Just like that, blanket immunity was here, and there was full liability protection for vaccine manufacturers.[27]

Cruelly, when the Supreme Court gave vaccine manufacturers full liability protection, that same week they held car manufacturers liable in a court of law for defective seat belts.[28]

Even big auto couldn't get what big pharma got.

Unfortunately, instead of the intention of making safer

vaccines for our nation's children, or educating the people about the dangers of vaccines, or making it easier for parents of vaccine-injured children to get compensated, this act opened the floodgates for more and more liability-free vaccines. Now, all they had to do was work with state legislatures and state health authorities to make sure their drugs were mandated and all children would have to take them if they wanted to attend school — and that's exactly what happened.

We saw that played out with the scamdemic.

Pharmaceutical companies would only provide their heavily hyped "miracle" COVID-19 shot in countries that gave them blanket immunity. In other words, unless a government gave them free liability from lawsuits for this new jab, your people don't get the "miracle."

Politicians, media personalities, and health officials assured the public that the "miracle" drug would get us "back to normalcy" by promising, *"It stops with you!"* Whether it was MSNBC's Rachel Maddow's direct-to-camera assurance, or the president of the United States, or the famous Tony-174-times-I-don't-recall-Fauci, or CDC director Rochelle Walensky — they misled us on what the drug was even promised or designed to do. And through a miraculous state of emergency, they were given extraordinary power to bring the "vaccine" to market faster than ever with Operation Warp Speed.

What that meant for you was that if you're one of the unlucky people that got myocarditis and collapsed on a soccer pitch or an NFL football field (how scared was *that* motherfucker?! He didn't want to say shit, and his heart almost exploded!), you can't sue because they've been given blanket immunity. Maybe my friend from the Fortune 500 company called his ass, too!

Even though children were not susceptible to COVID-19 and only at risk if they had a precondition — you know, precondition, like, you're a little kid getting cancer treatments — no matter, the pharmaceutical companies desperately needed to get it on the childhood vaccine schedule. The childhood vaccine schedule was their get-out-of-jail pass if (and when) people started dropping like flies (which ended up being "tested" at warp speed anyways on half the human population on the planet). The reason you're able to read this book is because I wasn't one of them. #DiedSuddenly.

Let me get sidetracked (again) for un momento.

No one has ever written a book like this. How did this happen? People may get fired, but by *then* (hopefully) I'll be on my little island, growing vegetables under an assumed name (David Spade) with my huge arsenal of weaponry.

*But wait, Rob, you were talking about terrorists. How do they make the jump from making us take vaccines to those who "say no" are terrorists?*

There's money to be made off unhealthy people. The sick and the weak "need" medicine and are thus a money generator for the health industry. Their plan is "from-cradle-to-grave drugs." Nice! Fortunately for them, America is full of the sick and the weak.

America has the greatest share of obese people (fatties) of any industrialized nation. But, let's be honest, if you're really fat, *be fat in America*. Because no matter how fat you are, you only have to wait four minutes, five tops, before *you* see somebody that's WAY fatter than *you* are. "God, I feel terrible, but look at *that piece of shit*! I didn't even know skin could stretch *that* much! That guy is like one of those Chinese balloons!"

But you don't hear that on the evening news!

Instead, what you hear on the evening news is if you declined to get every government recommended vaccine, you were "self-ish" or, according to the Department of Homeland Security, the CIA, or the FBI, you were a domestic threat actor.[29] Now, the FBI and the Justice Department, running out of actual terrorists, will investigate anyone as a terrorist, like mobilizing agents at the request of the National School Boards Association, who compared protesting parents to "domestic terrorists."[30]

When we have run out of actual terrorists, we need to create more, to continue to stoke fear and control people. The word "terrorist" is almost as watered down as the word "Nazi." As a matter of fact, they actually sound pretty good together: "Check out that Nazi terrorist asking the school board to take pornography books out of his kid's grammar school! Doesn't he want his third grader to know how people blow each other?!"

My right as a parent to do what I feel is in the best interest of my child cannot be superseded by the government. Certainly, standing up for those rights doesn't make me a terrorist, either. These are my natural rights.

Human rights are blessed by governments. Natural rights are a grace given to you by God. When you become informed and think rationally about a risk that you or your minor child may take and then follow your conscience, you *own* that decision. And when you own your own decision, you can *defend* it. And once you can defend it, you'll be ready to do whatever it takes to fight for your freedom to survive, no matter who tries to prevent you from doing that. There's no liberty more fundamentally a natural right than the freedom to think independently and follow our conscience when choosing what we're willing to risk our life or our child's life for.

The journey we take on this earth is defined by the choices we make, and if we are not free to make choices, the journey is not our own.

To the extent that I was able to keep my journey my own, I regret nothing. Maybe it means I don't get to make *Deuce Bigalow 3: Mexican Gigolo*, but I think I can sleep tonight...While I write this book about free speech, I am also writing it to help you, dear reader, recognize when tyranny is afoot.

When you stand up for your natural rights, they may call you a terrorist.

When you stand up to protect your child, they may call you a terrorist.

But when the government tries to force you to do anything against your conscience, it is not you, but the government, that is the actual terrorist.

## CHAPTER THIRTEEN

# I DON'T WANT TO BE
# LENNY BRUCE

The only people liberals like to attack more than conservatives are liberals that step out of line and challenge some of the woke constructs (and any of their new woke terminology) that we're being force fed through our cultural feeding tube. Like foie gras, where ducks or geese are intentionally overfed through a long metal tube so we can eat their fatty (and delicious) liver, we have the woke movement and all their ideological claptrap stuffed down our gullets until our intellectual livers are close to exploding as well. Louis CK, Dave Chappelle, Elon Musk, and Joe Rogan are the traditional liberals that are accused of being right-wingers today. Liberals want to keep everybody in line, and you're always allowed to speak freely as long as you don't question the dictates of the illiberal politburo. Like we said before with Hitler and Stalin, you have all the free speech you want, as long as you agree with them.

If you're a conservative, and you have something crazy to say like, I don't know, "Men can't have babies," or something, don't say that on Facebook! If you have something *that* crazy to say, like "Men can't have babies," say it in *person*, so there's at least some plausible deniability. If you say *tonight* on your Facebook account, "Men can't have babies," tomorrow *you won't have a Facebook account*. And here's the weird thing, dear reader: men can't have babies. I don't care what they say.

*"I feel somethin'!"*

*"It's a turd! Trust me, take some Metamucil and call me in the morning, you won't have this problem anymore, I guarantee it."*

If you parrot the left's talking points, you are in the protected class and if (and when) you're proven wrong, you *won't* get tarnished. If Democrats and liberals get something completely wrong, like COVID, they pay no consequences whatsoever.

If you're like my *Saturday Night Live* and *Grown Ups* costar Chris Rock, who genuinely thought that he and Governor Andrew Cuomo were doing the right thing, you can sit next to the former governor and serial groper and say in front of news cameras, "I agree with whatever he says," and later not get called out for agreeing with New York's former commander and chief groper.

However, if I, Rob Schneider, would have sat next to Florida's governor Ron DeSantis during COVID and said the same exact thing that Rock said about *his* governor — "I agree with whatever Ron DeSantis says!" — I'd be labeled a racist, science-denying, right-wing, ultra-mega-MAGA-Muga grandma killer!

If Cuomo was in a different political party that didn't have a *D* next to it, he would have been brought up on criminal charges. I know, like Cuomo explained, for Italians, "groping" is part of their, quote, "culture."[1] I know the wandering hand of Italian men has a "mind of its own." For most of the 2010s, guys like Cuomo got away with it! Up until pretty recently, your *free hand* was given a *free hand*. Like my friend, the great Jay Leno said, "I don't know why it's so hard to believe women. You go to Saudi Arabia and you need two women to testify against a man. Here, you need 25!"[2]

May I remind you, dear reader, that Governor Cuomo is the same governor that sent thousands of elderly people with COVID back into nursing homes to die and give the other old people in the homes COVID so they could die as well.

If you're on the "wrong side" of the nonliberal media and you're actually correct, well, you're still on the wrong side. There is tolerance and forgiveness for mistakes *only* if you're on the *liberal* side of the nondebate. Remember, when free speech is attacked and everything is "settled," like science, race, gender, or sexuality, we don't get debate. Instead, what we get is a bunch of "you're wrong, now let's kill your career, you (insert new specific term for specialized bigot here)."

Here's the deal: no one is safe. Even if you're a mask-wearing true-blue always-voting-Democrat *liberal*, you're still in jeopardy if you don't go along with all the newly minted leftist ideological gobbledygook. If you object to *any* of it, you will get tarnished just as if you were a MAGA-hat-wearing minority strategically placed behind Trump at one of his overflowing rallies.

Until the conservatives somehow break this hegemony of the liberal monopoly of technology companies, academia, and the media, conservative voices will continue to be marginalized. They even want to get rid of Fox News, which would leave conservatives with basically just the guy who sells pillows. "And you're looking gooood!"

This is how Jimmy Kimmel and other liberal hosts still have their late-night shows. On all the reigning late-night shows there is no individual point of view. It's all interchangeable. You can put the words of Jimmy Kimmel's monologue into the always laughing mouth of Jimmy Fallon, and you can take Fallon's words and put them into Stephen Colbert's mouth. Whatever's left over can be rechewed and spat out by Seth Meyers for the few people that are still awake and haven't already intellectually thrown up.

It was never more obvious than during COVID how these late-night hosts churn out state propaganda and governmental talking points. Worse yet, the audience cheered on this propaganda, and they didn't even know that what they were lapping up was just Fauci's talking points in the guise of comedy. As I famously said on Twitter, "Much late-night comedy is less about being funny and more about indoctrination by comedic imposition...People aren't really laughing at it as much as cheering on the rhetoric. It no longer resembles a comedy show, it's more like some kind of liberal Klan meeting."[3]

The audience wasn't prompted to think, be nudged, or come to any conclusions on their own. They were just reconfirming their bias. The hosts were just throwing liberal meat to the liberal lions. They weren't really telling jokes as much as they were just cementing what the government was demanding of their people. Any former Soviet Union government officials still breathing must be envious at how well behaved these propaganda late-night talk-show performing seals were.

In their defense, the hero to all late-night talk-show aspirants — the *Tonight Show* host extraordinaire Johnny Carson — never came out against the Vietnam War. But you didn't really ever know what side of the political aisle he was on.

(By the way, Carson had on average 17 million people watching him at night, including 45 million on December 17, 1969, for the Tiny Tim wedding.[4] That's how fucking big Johnny Carson was! Whereas now, the number-one show, *Gutfeld!*, which happens to be a conservative talk show hosted by my good friend, the very funny Greg Gutfeld, gets 2.5 million.[5]) The same goes for David Letterman and Jay Leno. You knew they leaned left, like most people in entertainment do, but at the same time, whoever was in power was fair game and the usual target of their monologues.

Something changed.

Donald Trump became president of the United States.

Donald Trump changed some liberals and their ability to reason and apparently write jokes.

After Trump, there was no longer any differential teasing ratio between Republicans and Democrats. Any jokes about the liberal intelligentsia, or jokes about Democrats, especially Joe Biden's mostly Ben & Jerry's for brains, became a no-go area. I don't like the term "Trump Derangement Syndrome," but Trump did seem to genuinely damage some people's brains. Sometimes, a mean tweet or something Trump would say or do would cause a liberal, much like an NFL football player with an injury, to leave the playing field and go into the *blue tent* and get their head checked. The unfortunate liberal would suffer these *dingers* that would stop their mind from thinking coherently and they would need a time-out of sorts before they could be allowed back in the game.

Glenn Greenwald (along with Tucker Carlson, Matt Taibbi, and Michael Shellenberger) is the last great American journalist (so of course he now lives in Brazil). He summed it up perfectly when he said, "The cultural left (meaning the part of the left focused on cultural issues rather than imperialism or corporatism)…has become increasingly censorious, moralising, controlling, repressive, petulant, joyless, self-victimising, trivial, and status-quo-perpetuating."[6]

In the '60s, '70s, and even the '80s, journalism was a vocation for people who grew up in the middle class and were trying to make the world a better place. What you have now, as opposed to middle-class kids trying to make the world a better place, are upper-class wealthy kids going into journalism with a politicized agenda, like they were climbing into the *grudge* Octagon. They're advocating for this very partisan Democrat system of control and authoritarianism in the guise of progress. Their agenda is dressed up as tolerance and they call it fancy words like diversity, equity, and inclusion, but really it is the opposite of that — exclusion, dis-unity, and cancellation.

One of the perks of being famous (me!) is your access to important people, like former *60 Minutes* producer Lowell Bergman. Bergman coordinated an interview with tobacco whistleblower Jeffrey Wigand where Wigand explained that the tobacco industry and executives were knowingly tampering with their tobacco to increase the effects of nicotine. However, CBS executives didn't release the story when they had it, they only aired the *60 Minutes* episode *after* Wigand's findings were already made public by others. Bergman said in an interview with PBS, "The original *60 Minutes* story was stopped in mid-stride. It wasn't done. We were still reporting it…In this case, it was really pre-censorship. This was self-censorship." The story ended up winning a Pulitzer Prize, but not for *60 Minutes* or CBS — the *Wall Street Journal* won it when they ran it on the front page while *60 Minutes* sat on the story. The *60 Minutes* episode finally aired months later, with no Pulitzer in sight.[7] This even became the plot of a Hollywood movie, *The Insider*, which chronicled the internal censorship that CBS employed, with Russell Crowe as Wigand and Al Pacino as Bergman.[8]

When I met the legendary Bergman, he asked me a question that I didn't have the answer to. He asked, "Why do you think news vans are allowed to park in the white zones without getting a parking ticket?" I couldn't think of a reason. Bergman explained, "It's because the news, the media, are in the public interest." In other words, the news is supposed to look out for the little guy... you and me, the public.

When I first started in television, I worked with people who were there working for the networks in the 1960s. In the '60s, you had three networks — ABC, NBC, and CBS. That was it! No cable TV, no HBO, no David Spade–pleasing Spectravision. This was decades before streaming services. It worked like this: the network would need to get a license from the FCC to broadcast because the airwaves were *publicly owned*. For that license, a network would have to give something *back* to the public. At that time in the 1960s, a significant portion of all broadcasting time had to be news.[9] Hard news. Actual news. News that was informative, news that served the public. ABC, NBC, and CBS were congressionally required to provide a good portion of their programming to benefit the public interest.

That was before the so-called disease-of-the-week "news" shows like ABC's *20/20* and NBC's *Dateline*. This became the worst kind of "news," news as entertainment, where the story would be in some town like Gilbert, Arizona, and the majority of its inhabitants contracted chlamydia from the neighborhood diner. The ratings success of shows like *20/20* and *Dateline* led to other entertainment news that was "technically" news but was much more entertainment, more resembling shows like *Forensic Files*, etc. This began the "need" for these major networks to sensationalize their news and make it as entertaining as possible.

Now, with the sensationalized entertainment news becoming common practice, we've seen the quality of everything—from breaking news reporting to the weather to late-night comedy— deteriorate and become the left's mouthpiece. It's a far cry from why news vans are allowed to park in the white zone. Remember watching news where the person just read the news objectively and didn't tell you how to think by shaking his head disapprovingly?

Speaking of shaking your head disapprovingly, how about the social media assassination of Eric Clapton? Eric Clapton, recovering alcoholic and rock and roll legend. Clapton did everything right: he listened to the medical professionals and elected officials and took the required jab, which immediately caused a reaction so severe he couldn't play the instrument that brought him so much fame and adoration. But he fucked up! Not because he *took* this experimental vaccine that caused his immune system to go berserk and attack his own limbs, but because he *recklessly* and *shamelessly went public* about his injuries. That's not allowed! "Shut up and take it like a man, Eric!"

Soon, the media was digging up four-decade-old audiotapes of him drunkenly saying publicly what a good proportion of English people were thinking privately about the wave of new immigrants forced upon their population in the late 1970s. Getting the jab wasn't the only thing that was mandated, it was also apparently mandated that you should *shut the fuck up* if anything went wrong. Your own personal tragedies have no importance and could get in the way and make other people leery of the new mandated procedure. "C'mon, Eric, we're all in this together!"

"Yeah, but my fingers don't work anymore..." "Shut up, Eric. You said something racially insensitive over forty years ago and we have *proof*!"[10]

For those of us who greatly admired Noam Chomsky, American intellectual, human rights advocate, and coauthor of *Manufacturing Consent*, Noam didn't offer much human rights or consent during COVID when he said that the *unvaccinated needed to isolate themselves from society* and quipped, "How can we get food to them? Well, that's actually their problem."[11] Thanks, Noam!

Sometimes you learn that being smart is no inoculation against people discovering that you're a complete sociopath. Ladies and gentlemen of the jury, may I present podcaster, author, and intellectual — the morally vacuous Sam Harris. Seeking validation for greater societal shutdowns and vaccine mandates, Harris seemed genuinely disappointed when he famously said, "If kids were dying by the hundreds of thousands from COVID... there would've been no patience for vaccine skepticism."[12] Aww, sorry Sam, you didn't get your hundreds of thousands of dead kids to justify your preference for authoritarian Nuremberg-code-violating forced human experimentation!

Luckily, Hollywood took the high ground and didn't shame people who wanted to make their own individual health choices.

Nahh, just kidding. Here's a list of some assholes:

Being unvaccinated is like pointing a gun at someone.
— said nonphysician thespian Sean Penn[13]

I think every company should do [mandatory vaccines]. Listen, I don't care. To me, it's really simple.
— said the TV *ER* doctor (not real-life doctor) George Clooney[14]

Those who refuse to be vaccinated, with no medical reason not to, should be refused NHS care if they then catch
covid. I'm hearing of antivaxxers using up ICU beds in
London at vast expense to the taxpayer. Let them pay for
their own stupidity and selfishness.

— said the fearless Meghan Markle attacker Piers Morgan[15]

When are we gonna stop putting up with the idiots in this
country and just say it's mandatory to get vaccinated? Fuck
'em. Fuck their freedom.

— said freedom minimalist and radio host Howard Stern[16]

Screw your freedom.

— said weightlifter and body autonomy Terminator
Arnold Schwarzenegger[17]

John Oliver, who has often been misgendered as a comedian,
and whose American success my British comedy friends are genuinely mystified by (America has always been a sucker for a British
accent. "They sound so smaaaaart!"), openly mocked those like
me, Robert Kennedy Jr., and the parents of injured kids, who wondered if there could possibly be a connection between children's
lifelong neurological problems and all those mandated childhood
drugs.[18]

Late-night talk-show host and apparent pharmaceutical sales
rep Stephen Colbert had an entire choreographed dance routine
with the dancers dressed up as syringes.[19]

And how can we forget when Kimmel infamously said, on the
topic of tough choices in the ICU:

That choice doesn't seem so tough to me. Vaccinated person having a heart attack? Yes, come right in. We'll take care of you. Unvaccinated guy who gobbled horse goo? Rest in peace, wheezy.

— Jimmy Kimmel[20]

I can't speak for George Carlin, but I'd like to think this is the opposite of what he would have done. I'm pretty sure Carlin wouldn't have reinforced the idea of keeping people in their homes, closing down schools, and not treating unvaccinated men, women, and children in the hospital.

After advocating for no emergency care for the unvaccinated, Jimmy Kimmel still gets to keep his talk show and host the Oscars (with its ever-diminishing viewership), but Aaron Rodgers or I don't get to make any more State Farm commercials. With the Oscars, the best performance in your field will *now* only be considered if you have the required diversity-hire ratio in your film. Here's something you never hear: "Let's go see that new movie! I've heard it's really diversified and forty percent of the cast and crew is LatinX and queer!" "Forty percent queer?! Let's GO!" Meanwhile, Eric Clapton gets to keep his vaccine injury, which damaged the hands of one of the greatest guitar players of all time. If you like the Beatles, and appreciated the guitar solo in George Harrison's "While My Guitar Gently Weeps," you were appreciating the genius artistry of the pre–vaccine injured and media-shamed Eric Clapton.

I don't set out in my comedy routine to be mean to anyone. However, the government and people in power, when I believe their power is abusive, need to be addressed comedically like the court jester of old would do to the king. He would say out loud what people were thinking, with the caveat being, in this format, he would be protected. Most times, he wouldn't lose his head. People without the jester's headdress wouldn't be so lucky.

Therein lies the rub. As George Bernard Shaw said, "If you want to tell people the truth, you'd better make them laugh or they'll kill you."[21]

Just like what happened to Mort Sahl and Lenny Bruce, I'm not invited to the late-night shows because they don't want an opposing point of view. They want diversity but not diversity of thought or opinion. They want the illusion of diversity — they want people who *look* different but don't think different. They want diversity for your eyeballs. They'll never invite African American historian and intellectual Thomas Sowell to sit next to their talk-show desk. If you are a person of color who happens to think with a diverging viewpoint, you are not only vehemently disagreed with, but you are also accused of being a race traitor. See Clarence Thomas and Candace Owens, to name a few.

They want the *illusion* of tolerance. They are only pretending to speak truth to power, knowing full well *they* are the powerful ones. Fear is their tool, and those who are not cowed are canceled. Imagine losing your job in 2020 as a thirty-year sports commentator in Sacramento, California, because you said something outrageous like "all lives matter" instead of "black lives matter."[22] Fired!

None of these realities are at all covered by today's establishment comedians, because they are indoctrinated the same way *New York Times* writers are. As Noam Chomsky once said, "The indoctrination is so deep that educated people think they're being objective."[23]

"Nobody tells me what to write," a *Times* journalist may say. Well, that's because nobody has to — you wouldn't even be in that position if you weren't already indoctrinated and brainwashed into their way of thinking. Whether you know it or not, you write what they want you to write.

When you *do* realize they're telling you what to write, like the Peabody Award–winning journalist Uri Berliner of NPR did, and your journalistic conscience can't take it anymore, you publicly acknowledge it, like he did when he wrote "[NPR] lost its way when it started telling listeners how to think."[24] Of course, NPR took this to heart. Admitting they had erred and lost their objective rudder, they promised to do their best to rebuild the public trust and once again be a respected journalistic outlet.

Nahhh, I'm just kidding. Uri was suspended by the new woke mask-wearing CEO Katherine Maher after exposing the network's liberal bias. The fact that he is, by his own account, "Sarah Lawrence educated," and "was raised by a lesbian peace activist mother," or spent twenty-five *years* at the network, was not enough to protect him.[25]

This experience is similar to what happened to the comedians in the early part of the twenty-first century: they think they are telling their own jokes, but they are just regurgitating for the establishment. Not just late-night hosts, this covers a lot of the comedians. But thankfully not all.

I hold no grudge against any of these comedians who went along with the system, and I completely understand how they can be swept up into it. I genuinely hope that they don't feel from me the shame that they tried to give others, because they are my brothers, and like any brother, I'd like to cajole them back to a state of reason and give them a hug because I understand what they went through. I hope and wish nothing but the best for them. (Except for John Oliver.)

I don't want to be Lenny Bruce, who, we remember, was found naked in his bathroom dead of that suspicious morphine overdose. Just for the record, if I'm going to OD on morphine, I'm going to do it with all my clothes on. Actually, I'm going to wear a wetsuit, so it's really difficult for the police to take it off and let the press photograph me naked before the coroner gets there. I mean it's still possible but very difficult, especially when you get down around my large ass region, and if I'm dry.

I only want to be a comedian. I didn't enter show business to be a free speech advocate. I entered it to get laid, or at least, improve my chances. I mean, look at me, for cryin' out loud! I knew I needed something.

You know how if you have a brother, a sister, or somebody you love and care about who is an alcoholic, or maybe addicted to gambling, sex, or porn? (I'm not saying David Spade, but I could see how you'd think that.) If you really care about that person (like I do David), at some point you have to confront them (like I'm eventually going to confront David) about this new destructive behavior that is causing so much havoc in their lives and the lives of the people around them before it gets to a place beyond repair. It's a loving thing to do. To not do so would be unloving.

That's the way I feel about the woke's current attack on Western civilization, specifically the country that I live in, the United States of America. This attack on America is an illness that is self-inflicted. The attack on America is coming from Americans themselves. They have no problem in condemning and accusing America for being steeped in racism and white supremacy, when in fact it is the freest nation on Earth. At the same time, they would never criticize China, which currently holds over a million Uyghurs in concentration camps. This relatively new self-destructive behavior, which we have all witnessed, is having detrimental effects on our society and to not speak up would be unloving. The trick is, can you speak up and still be allowed to work without ending up with a needle in the wrong arm (Lenny Bruce), or ending up in your eighties in front of forty people at a coffee shop (Mort Sahl)? Because, dear reader, my favored addiction is to continue keeping my family eating and sleeping indoors, in my swanky Arizona abode, complete with gas cooking stove and my (practically) always heated pool.

## CHAPTER FOURTEEN

# BUT THERE IS MORE

# THAN HOPE

In my final chapter, I offer more than just hope.

I've got good news. Thanks to people like you who purchased this book, apparently there are people who *do* want to hear opposing views, and I think people are starving for it. There is not one club or theater where I performed in America in 2023–2024 that wasn't completely sold out. There is an audience, and your voice, and your right to speak freely, matters tremendously.

I'm able to say what I want even though pharma-sponsored television networks and nervous streaming services feel that I may be too mouthy to have on their platforms, because I am still able to sell tickets and tell my filthy jokes to corruptible malcontents, like me, in darkened drinking establishments. And also because I can say whatever I want on Twitter, because one of those malcontents happens to be the owner of the company and the richest man on the planet, Elon Musk! Thanks for reading, Elon!

In fact, now Elon Musk has emerged as the last of the tech bros that will still fight for free speech. The Brazilian Supreme Court justice Alexandre De Moraes announced there will be a criminal investigation into Musk, because in their eyes, X is allegedly spreading disinformation and obstructing justice within the country.[1] Since when, outside of 1930s Germany, does a Supreme Court justice launch an investigation? Musk, in his miraculous defiance, said, "We are lifting all restrictions. This judge has applied massive fines, threatened to arrest our employees, and cut off access to X in Brazil. As a result, we will probably lose all revenue in Brazil and have to shut down our office there. But principles matter more than profit."[2]

What other billionaire would say *this*? I can't imagine Mark Zuckerberg interrupting one of his karate lessons, the images of his childhood beatings still fresh in his mind, to lose revenue from the biggest economy in South America to stand up for free speech. (One may wonder what censorship compromises Facebook may have made in Brazil.) Musk is one man that is literally saving free speech, and Musk said he will do a "full data dump," which *Forbes* magazine inferred meant "[X] will do 'a full data dump' of information on the Brazilian judge — who Brazil's political right frequently criticize as overstepping his authority to censor free speech."[3] I would happily help pay for Musk's own 24/7 security guard, so he doesn't pay the ultimate price for standing up for our freedoms. (Obviously I can't afford a Monday-through-Friday guy, but for special Jewish holidays I'll be more than happy to loan him my muscular gardener.)

Standing up does come at a price. It will cost you to stand up for your freedom and speak your mind. Be judicious but stand up when your bullshit detector goes off and you know something to be false. Call it out for what it is! The price to *not* stand up for your freedom is much higher. Like I said, it has cost me money and work, but in the grand scheme of things, who cares? Sure, I get the usual derogatory labels, but it's like I always say, sticks and stones may break my bones, but living in a Democrat-run city can kill you.

While I love making Hollywood movies (it pays well and the rewards are incredible!), you know what's even more rewarding? Doing everything I can to make sure my daughters grow up in a free society, like being able to speak their mind on their college campus and not being shamed if it deviates from what most of their classmates think, or not having to play sports against biologically stronger boys. I do this by practicing my right to dissent. Dissent *is* democracy. *Not* allowing dissent is tyranny.

We are dangerously close to preventing dissent in our own nation. The Supreme Court will be hearing this year a massively free speech implicative case, *Murthy v. Missouri*, and while that decision wasn't returned at the time of this writing, their preliminary hearings on the case were frightening. The case is centered around whether the government could pressure social media companies to remove posts they deem harmful or misinformative. Ultimately, that power would mean the government could use the social platforms as their own dissent-quashing tools. Justice Ketanji Brown Jackson said, "Some might say that the government actually has a duty to take steps to protect the citizens of this country, and you seem to be suggesting that that duty cannot manifest itself in the government encouraging or even pressuring platforms to take down harmful information."⁴ Silencing in the name of protection is still their go-to argument. This is the same associate Supreme Court justice who was stumped when asked, "Can you provide a definition for the word 'woman'?" and famously answered with, "I'm not a biologist."⁵

As I write a conclusion to my first book, I'm struck by the events that are happening around the world. Freedom of speech is being attacked not just in America and in our own Supreme Court but throughout the world at large. As this book goes to print, Brazil has become a dictatorship, Scotland has enacted hate speech laws to attack comedians,⁶ while Ireland is debating passing its own versions.⁷ Are you paying attention yet?

After Hillary Clinton lost to Trump, I tweeted, "I haven't seen the Democrats this angry since we freed the slaves." Well, even though my sentiment was historically accurate, it didn't shield me from being attacked by a Hollywood that was still pretty sore because that "not-very-nice man" beat *their* "not-very-nice woman." But, like it or not, facts are facts and history is history, and the Democrats will always be known as the party of Stephen Douglas and slavery. I swear to you that, like the days of Stephen Douglas, today's Democrats will be forever shamed that they ever supported these misogynistic antiwomen initiatives (biological boys playing against biological girls in sports) and child surgical mutilation conversions (allowing minor children, mostly young impressionable girls, to decide to permanently damage their bodies and reproductive abilities, and giving young boys repurposed prison castration drugs nicely renamed "puberty blockers").

When you're attacked, it is scary at first. But our Founding Fathers never said this was going to be easy. They risked *everything*. Your courage is required now. This is not the time to rely on others to stand up. As we have painfully learned, a large percentage of the population will go along with whatever dictates the government gives them. But there is even more good news! We don't need everybody in this fight, we just need enough.

Mattias Desmet, an accomplished professor of clinical psychology and a psychotherapist, explained when he testified to the US Senate how stifled dissent through propaganda during COVID-19 was a slip into tyranny and a totalitarian system. He testified, "You need two things for a totalitarian system. On the one hand, you need an elite which excessively and relentlessly uses propaganda to keep control over the population. And then you need the part of the population, twenty to thirty percent, usually, to go along in that propaganda and to buy fanatically into the narrative. We've seen, I think, both components of a totalitarian system, in this [COVID-19] crisis."[8]

This is only possible with the right psychological manipulations on a society, and like Desmet also said in his testimony, COVID tyranny was possible *only* if "a society of the population should be isolated, should struggle with lack of meaning making, should be anxious, frustrated, and aggressive, and if under these circumstances, propaganda is used, then there is a good chance that propaganda...which offers a strategy to deal with the object of anxiety of virus and lockdowns, for instance, then...a major part of the population will be willing to participate in a strategy to deal with the object of anxiety, even if the strategy is utterly absurd."[9]

I know this doesn't sound like it, but it is good news! It's good news to know that they can only control us if they manage to isolate, confuse, frustrate, and worry us, all of which are just symptoms of fear. We have the control to not let them. Here's how: if someone in the government, the media, or a tech company says something or creates a situation to make you fearful, question it. Keep questioning it. What you will find is that you are being used again.

My friend Dr. David Martin, one of the most brilliant guys I know, has served as an advisor to "numerous Central Banks, global economic forums, the World Bank and International Finance Corporation, and national governments."[10] Dr. Martin recently gave a talk to the EU Parliament, which has, at the time of this writing, gotten over 3.2 billion views over its various online locations combined. That's billion with a *b*! Dr. Martin helped me with a chapter that didn't quite fit in this book, but if you want to read it, you can go to my website. I highly recommend you do.

On this note about what it will take to defeat the oncoming tide of tyranny, Dr. Martin says, "When it comes to the politicians, media, pharma, finance, and tech giants you realize we're dealing with people who are not smart. They're relying on the inertia of *fear*. While [fear] appeals to a certain amount of the audience — for example during Covid when we were all supposed to run to the savior of the needle — the great news is only a third of the population fell for it. Another third had to be coerced into it, whether it was for employment, travel, or access to family. But a final third of the population said *fuck off* and wouldn't stand for it. We are not alone when we look at it that way — those are nearly the same divisions our nation had during the revolutionary war, where one-third was for it, one-third was against it, and one-third was indifferent."

And we won that war.

I have faith in comedians because there are so many good ones. But we're all human beings, so we will make mistakes in our position as de facto intellectuals. There will be missteps, but hopefully they'll be funny enough to keep people entertained and powerful enough to help society question authority when necessary.

While I found what Jimmy Kimmel said was reprehensible by attacking people for making their own personal health choices, I genuinely know that Jimmy Kimmel has to be basically a good person. Adam Carolla is someone I greatly admire and look up to, and he wouldn't be friends with somebody if they didn't have admirable qualities. So Kimmel *must* be a good person.

At the same time, Colbert was uproariously funny as a correspondent on *The Daily Show* and I wish him all the best as well. Even John Oliver, I wish him well. And Howard Stern is one of the most incredible artists ever. Howard changed the radio industry all by himself! He's one of the greatest people I've ever met. I love Howard.

It should be of note that there is no forgiveness in woke ideology, unlike in my new Catholic religion. This is the sign there's something wrong with this woke religion. Christianity has forgiveness at its core — love thy neighbor, love your enemy, and love thy neighbor as thyself. While some other religions, like the woke movement, say hate your enemy or call them infidels. With hatred, there is no understanding, tolerance, or forgiveness.

Because of the lack of forgiveness, some of academia's most brilliant thinkers have been drummed out of their profession. They didn't succumb to the attacks and instead they have become today's greatest intellectuals — and academia is poorer for it. These courageous individuals not only didn't bow to the pressure, they got louder as they discussed and questioned the very quick and irrational turns society is making. James Lindsay, Andrew Doyle, Jordan

Peterson, Peter Boghossian, Helen Pluckrose, and Bret Weinstein, just to name a few.

Through every chapter of this book, and from every expert and every free speech hero we've highlighted from Mort Sahl and Lenny Bruce to Dr. Nikolov, Mr. Bystrianyk, and Mr. Lindsay, we've learned that fear is the only thing they have on us. I'm inspired by and indebted to other intellectuals that rebuked fear and didn't bow to today's cultural authoritarians like Jordan Peterson, Douglas Murray, and Thomas Sowell.

Only when we live a life without fear do we truly live.

Perhaps in my life I could've played the Hollywood game better. I could've not given a shit about free speech, the health of our children, capture of agencies, the liberal Marxist attack on society, but as John Philpot Curran said in 1790, "The condition upon which God hath given liberty to man is eternal vigilance..."[11]

We are in the situation we're in now because, over time, many Americans, either consciously or unconsciously, have gotten tired of that eternal vigilance. Millennials in the United States, for example, are "voting at lower rates than previous generations, they report low levels of trust in government and their fellow citizens, they are increasingly abandoning traditional political parties and identifying as political Independents."[12] Overall, they are tired of participating in their own democracy, and they would rather just elect somebody and let them make all the democratic decisions for them. The problem, we know, is that those making the democratic decisions don't have our best interests in mind.

An even worse problem is this evolution from *democracy* fatigue to *freedom* fatigue. American millennials have lost so much faith in the political system that while they think they're tired of democracy, they're really tired of freedom. "A number of millennials no longer find it essential to live in a democracy...view democracy in a negative light, and may even be more open to alternatives such as military rule."[13]

We got here after enduring generations of division, isolation, anxiety, and frustration. There are "the goods," and there are "the bads," and the only thing that changes is which group is wearing which label. So much of this division has led the younger generations to now not only rebuke the two-party system or crave an independent like my good friend Robert F. Kennedy Jr., but they are actually so disillusioned they think another form of government could somehow be *better*! Hey millennials, there's always China's one-party system!

I'd like to wind down our discussion with this statement from George Washington:

"Parties are likely... to become potent engines by which cunning, ambitious and unprincipled men will be enabled to subvert the power of the People and to usurp for themselves the reins of government, destroying afterwards the very engines which have lifted them to unjust dominion."[14]

Washington predicted this usurping we're experiencing today hundreds of years ago — yet history is short and only those who learn from it will be spared from reliving it.

I, for one, have my gas-powered car on and sitting in my driveway, packed and ready to drive to my off-the-grid farm, with my chickens and cows, where I'll grow my own vegetables and homeschool my kids to avoid the public elementary school porn. The kids are yelling, "Dad, hurry up!" while I finish typing this.

Whatever sacrifice I have made, however incredibly insignificant, meant that I couldn't stay silent and that's the reason I really wanted to write this book — to show that for those who try to attack freedom, we are not afraid of them, and to show you, dear reader, that we are not alone.

I am humbled by what our Founding Fathers who signed the Declaration of Independence sacrificed by putting their name on a piece of paper that threatened the greatest authority of its day — the Crown of England and its monarch, King George III.

Fifty-six men from thirteen different colonies bravely put their names down, and risked their lives, and their families lives, for something greater than themselves.

Here are some of the sacrifices these men made that we need to remember:

**Francis Lewis (New York):** Lewis had his home destroyed and his wife taken prisoner by British forces; she died shortly after being released.[15]

**Richard Stockton (New Jersey):** Stockton was captured and imprisoned by the British who devastated his estate and confined him in the inhumane prison Provost Jail in New York where he was starved and brutalized.[16]

**John Hart (New Jersey):** Hart was forced into hiding, during which his farm was destroyed, his wife died, and he never saw his children again.[17]

**Lewis Morris (New York):** Morris' entire estate was seized, and his family was homeless. His entire wealth was spent on the Revolution.[18]

**Philip Livingston (New York):** Livingston died before the end of the war due to the stress and strains of his work — not before he sold several properties to support the Revolution while losing others to the British.[19]

**Thomas Jefferson (Virginia):** Jefferson had to flee his home, Monticello, because of the British forces and as a repercussion of being the principal author of the Declaration.[20]

**John Hancock (Massachusetts):** The president of the Continental Congress at the time, Hancock spent much of his personal fortune to support the Revolution.[21]

**Samuel Adams (Massachusetts):** Adams was constantly evading arrest and lived much of his life in financial difficulty as a result of his insistence to build public support for independence.[22]

**John Adams (Massachusetts):** Became the second president despite the intense pressure and danger he faced as an independence leader. Notably, this danger forced him to endure long separations from his family through his life.[23]

**Benjamin Franklin (Pennsylvania):** His family properties were targeted by the British and he spent much of the Revolutionary War in France working to secure French support for the Americans.[24]

This list is just a small glimpse into the profound sacrifices made by our Founding Fathers.

Many of the others lost their fortunes, their families, and if they didn't lose their lives they certainly lost their health. They were all hunted down and their lives were ruined, but they don't talk about that in today's universities. I have learned that teaching cursive writing in elementary schools is to be curtailed in the United States. Is it because our educators no longer find it useful to students? Or, more deviously, so that one day today's children will no longer be able to read what the Constitution says? I'll leave that for you to decide.

The freedoms that we enjoy today were earned in blood, real blood — red, white, and blue blood. The freedoms were earned in the Revolutionary War, and on battlefields like Gettysburg, where thousands lie buried still. As a boy, I saw the carefully maintained graves of American WWII Marines, in the Philippines, where even in 1972 the bayonets were still stuck in the ground marking the spot where soldiers had died and were buried. The Filipinos were very grateful for their liberation from the Japanese and are still grateful to America to this day. The United States was, is, and with God's help, and with a conviction renewed by its people, will continue to be the beacon call of freedom to inspire the world.

I'd like to say thanks to my mother and father, who taught me never to shy away from what I know is right, and that to not listen to your own conscience will cost you more than any financial or career loss ever could.

Thanks to my sister April, my brother-in-law, Matt, my brothers, Stan and John, and my sister Linda.

I would like to say thank you to all the comedians and all the people in entertainment who have been so nice to me over the years. To Jay Leno, who taught me exactly what I needed to do to become a successful comedian. To Jerry Seinfeld, who laid out some very basic rules about what stand-up comedy is and what should be in your stand-up routine. I'm thankful for the generosity and humanity of Dana Carvey, who was kind enough to let me know that even for the super talented like Dana, show business is always going to be a struggle.

To Dennis Miller, not only a great comedian, he was ahead of his time when it came to conservatism. Like me, he's a traditional liberal. Miller's contribution to comedy would be large enough, just as a great comedian himself, but his contribution to comedy should also include the fact that if it weren't for Dennis Miller, you might not have had Adam Sandler, David Spade, and me on *Saturday Night Live.*

To the guys of *South Park*, one of the honors of my life was you skewering me. It was truly an honor. You have been brilliant for twenty-five years and are one of the few satiric voices that continue to illuminate what is really happening in society in animated form.

To the writers of *The Simpsons*, Matt Selman, Dan Greaney, Mike Reiss, and Ian Maxtone-Graham. These are people much funnier than me and who were kind enough to help me make my movies much funnier than they would have been.

To Lou Morton, the most talented young writer that I worked with on *Saturday Night Live.* Louis Morton is a brilliant young man with a great sense of humor. We wrote some funny pieces together, and he'll always have a career in the business of funny.

Thank you, Jimmy Dore, for being a powerful voice in the freedom movement, for not staying stuck in your foundational thinking, and for being a brave, terrific, and hilarious comedian.

I'd like to thank my publisher, Alex Pappas. I'm not sure this was the book you expected. Unfortunately for you, I had way too much time on my hands.

Thanks to Ian Kleinert and my manager, Michael McConnell.

Thank you, Forbes Shannon, for all your hours of work researching every last detail of this book so I don't lose my house.

Thank you to Jamie Lissow for not just being a great comic and cowriter, but for also being my great buddy.

The late Scott Wilson, an actor who exemplified that being an actor was a noble profession.

Drake Sather, my best buddy from my stand-up days, I miss you, pal.

My Canadian director and longtime friend, Boon Collins, for being a role model to remind me to never stop learning.

My best friend since grammar school, Rick Glosser, and my friend Nino.

My pal, Dr. Bas.

Thank you to Joe Rogan, who was able to really show how stand-up comics could be so much more than just comedians. They can affect the entire planet by increasing freedom of speech during such a dictatorial time. He was one of the few voices of reason that they tried to silence and couldn't because of his intellect, his bravery, and his balls.

To my comedic hero and dear friend John Cleese, who once told me, "The story of mankind is a story of crime." Monty Python was the high-water mark for comedy in the twentieth century. No one ever made me laugh harder than Cleese.

Thanks to Lorne Michaels, comedy kingmaker, for hiring me and all my friends for the funnest five years of my life.

Jim Downey, my professor of comedy who would be able to

explain why something was funny or why it wasn't and where it came from and what its comedic antecedents were. We are all humbled by how smart that guy was. But as brilliant as he was, a true comedic giant, he was the most generous and kind person at *Saturday Night Live*. He had the most generous laughter of anybody, and when you made him laugh, it really felt good.

To Chris Rock, thank you for talking me into doing stand-up when I was hesitating coming back. He said, "You know what I think? I think you don't like money!" Thank you for that, Chris, that was the push I needed because I *do* like money.

To the always hilarious David Spade for being my friend and colleague going into our fifth decade of friendship. Thank you, and thank you for helping me decide on my new favorite place and home, Arizona!

And to my brother Adam Sandler, who during all my trials and tribulations, never backed or shied away from hiring me, and more importantly, has always remained my friend. Adam, standing next to you in over twenty-seven films has been the honor of my career. Truthfully, no other man has ever been kinder and more generous, not just to me, but to so many people in our business it is impossible to count. In the history of show business, Adam Sandler has had and continues to have perhaps the greatest career of any entertainer.

Most importantly, it is the love of my life, Patricia, that I must forever give my undying love, gratitude, and devotion. Since I am no poet, I must borrow from F. Scott Fitzgerald, to truly express how I feel about my Patricia: "You are the finest, loveliest, tenderest, and most beautiful person I have ever known — and even that is an understatement." Thank you for standing by me when it seemed like the walls were caving in. I'm sorry you had to endure these attacks with me. Thank you for healing my heart by telling me that you finally understood that protecting our children *inside* the house could only do so much, and that you realized that I needed to protect them *outside*, in society as well, so they could enjoy the same freedoms that have been given me. Te amo, para siempre!

I think that's about it. I'm sure I'm forgetting others, too. If I have left you out and you were a significant part of my life, I apologize, but I must blame my publisher.

And lastly, I'd like to thank the people who have attacked me over the years. You've only made me stronger. If you thought you could knock me down or shut me up, guess what?!

You picked on the wrong Filipino.

Speak your mind, America. You can do it!

# NOTES

## CHAPTER ZERO

1. "History of the Philippines," Cal State University, Bakersfield, www.csub.edu /pacificrim/countryprospectus/history.htm. Accessed March 25, 2024.
2. "Spanish-American War and the Philippine-American War, 1898–1902," National Parks Service, US Department of the Interior, www.nps.gov/goga/learn /historyculture/spanish-american-war.htm#:~:text=On%20April%2021%2C %201898%2C%20the,Maine%20in%20Havana%20Harbor. Accessed March 25, 2024.
3. "The Spanish-American War, 1898," Office of the Historian, US Department of State, history.state.gov/milestones/1866-1898/spanish-american-war#:~:text=Spain %20also%20agreed%20to%20sell,the%20independent%20state%20of %20Hawaii. Accessed March 25, 2024.
4. Kyle Mizokami, "The American Pistol That's Served the US Military in Battle for More Than 100 Years," The National Interest, *Task & Purpose*, December 10, 2020, taskandpurpose.com/tech-tactics/1911-pistol-history-american-troops/#:~:text =The%20.,–1902)%20discovered%20the%20revolver's%20.
5. Rob Schneider, *Woke Up in America*, performed by Rob Schneider, June 2023, Tampa Theater, Tampa, Florida.
6. Henry Olsen, "How the Right Gets Reagan Wrong," *Politico*, June 26, 2017, www .politico.com/magazine/story/2017/06/26/how-the-right-gets-reagan-wrong -215306/. Accessed March 25, 2024.
7. Katie Yoder, "Rob Schneider Opens Up about His Catholic Conversion and the Life of Faith," Diocese of Gary, Indiana, n.d., https://dcgary.org/news/rob-schneider -opens-about-his-catholic-conversion-and-life-faith.

## CHAPTER ONE

1. "You Don't Find Out Who's Been Swimming Naked Until the Tide Goes Out," CNBC, April 25, 2018, buffett.cnbc.com/video/1994/04/25/buffett-you-dont -find-out-whos-been-swimming-naked-until-the-tide-goes-out.html.

2.  Jeremy W. Peters, "From Jerry Falwell Jr. to Dr. Drew: 5 Coronavirus Doubters," *New York Times*, March 18, 2020, www.nytimes.com/2020/03/18/us/politics /coronavirus-doubters-falwell-drew.html.

3.  "Editorial: ICUs Are Full and People Are Dying, but, Sure, Open the Strip Clubs," *Los Angeles Times*, December 18, 2020, www.latimes.com/opinion /story/2020-12-18/san-diego-strip-club-ruling?_amp=true.

4.  Jeffrey Kopstein and Mark Irving Lichbach, *Comparative Politics: Interests, Identities, and Institutions in a Changing Global Order* (Cambridge University Press, 2009).

5.  S. Osipov, G. Stenchikov, K. Tsigaridis et al., "The Toba Supervolcano Eruption Caused Severe Tropical Stratospheric Ozone Depletion," *Communications Earth & Environment* 2, no. 71 (April 12, 2021).

6.  Toshiko Kaneda and Carl Haub, "How Many People Have Ever Lived on Earth?," PRB, November 15, 2022, https://www.prb.org/articles/how-many-people-have -ever-lived-on-earth/.

7.  Katie Canales and Aaron Mok, "China's 'Social Credit' System Ranks Citizens and Punishes Them with Throttled Internet Speeds and Flight Bans If the Communist Party Deems Them Untrustworthy," Business Insider, November 28, 2022.

8.  Andrew Doyle, *Free Speech and Why It Matters* (Little Brown, 2022).

9.  *Manufacturing Consent: Noam Chomsky and the Media*, directed by Mark Achbar, performed by Noam Chomsky, 1992.

10. Sequoia Carillo, "U.S. Reading and Math Scores Drop to Lowest Level in Decades," NPR, June 21, 2023, https://www.npr.org/2023/06/21/1183445544/u-s-reading -and-math-scores-drop-to-lowest-level-in-decades.

11. "Al Capone," History.com, April 26, 2021, https://www.history.com/topics /crime/al-capone.

12. James Bikales, "Treasury Lays Out Rules for Instant EV Rebate," *Politico*, October 6, 2023, https://www.politico.com/news/2023/10/06/treasury-biden -electric-vehicle-rebate-00120253.

13. Steffanie Dupree, "Tesla Owners Run into Battery Charging Trouble in Chicago's Bitter Cold," CBS News, January 19, 2024, https://www.cbsnews.com/chicago /news/tesla-owners-run-into-trouble-amid-bitter-cold/#:~:text=Some%20 Tesla%20batteries%20died%20in,longer%20than%20usual%20to%20charge.

14. Hustler Magazine, Inc., v. Falwell, 485 US 46, No. 86-1278 (US Supreme Court, decided February 24, 1988).

15. Amanda Patterson, "Dario Fo," Writers Write, www.writerswrite.co.za/literary -birthday-24-march-dario-fo/. Accessed March 29, 2024.

16. Samuel J. Abrams, "Think Professors Are Liberal? Try School Administrators," *New York Times*, October 16, 2018, www.nytimes.com/2018/10/16/opinion /liberal-college-administrators.html.

17. "Thomas Kyd," *Encyclopaedia Britannica*, n.d.

18. "Federico García Lorca," *Encyclopaedia Britannica*, n.d.

19. "Mikhail Bulgakov," *Encyclopaedia Britannica*, n.d.

20. John Freedman, "Exile and Honor: Nikolai Erdman in Tomsk," *Moscow Times*, April 4, 2011, www.themoscowtimes.com/2011/04/04/exile-and-honor-nikolai -erdman-in-tomsk-6098-a6098.

21. Judith Yaross Lee, "Mark Twain as a Stand-up Comedian," *The Mark Twain Annual* no. 4 (2006): 3–23.

22. Miller v. California, 413 US 15, no. 70–73 (Supreme Court, decided June 21, 1973).

## CHAPTER TWO

1. James Curtis, *Last Man Standing: Mort Sahl and the Birth of Modern Comedy* (University Press of Mississippi, 2017).

2. Maria, "Michael Parenti: The JFK Assassination and the Gangster Nature of the State (One of Two)," TUC Radio, March 13, 2018, tucradio.org/catalog /newest-catalog-items/michael-parenti-the-jfk-assassination-and-the -gangster-nature-of-the-state-one-of-two-2/.

3. Harry Elmer Barnes, "Perpetual War for Perpetual Peace," Mises Institute, December 21, 2020, mises.org/mises-daily/perpetual-war-perpetual-peace#: ~:text=%5BIn%201947%2C%20historian%20Charles%20Beard,revisionist %20historians%20of%20the%20era.

4. Dwight Eisenhower, "President Dwight D. Eisenhower's Farewell Address (1961)," National Archives and Records Administration, www.archives.gov/ milestone-documents/president-dwight-d-eisenhowers-farewell-address. Accessed March 25, 2024.

5. Tom Wicker et al., "C.I.A.: Maker of Policy, or Tool?; Survey Finds Widely Feared Agency Is Tightly Controlled," *The New York Times*, April 25, 1966.

6. Maria, "Michael Parenti: The JFK Assassination and the Gangster Nature of the State (One of Two)," TUC Radio, March 13, 2018, tucradio.org/catalog /newest-catalog-items/michael-parenti-the-jfk-assassination-and-the-gangster -nature-of-the-state-one-of-two-2/.

7. "CIA DOC 1035 960: Countering Criticism of the Warren Report," Internet Archive, April 1, 1967, archive.org/details/CIADOC1035960/page/n1/mode /2up?view=theater.

8. Katherine Schaeffer, "A Look at the Americans Who Believe There Is Some Truth to the Conspiracy Theory That Covid-19 Was Planned," Pew Research Center, July 24, 2020, www.pewresearch.org/short-reads/2020/07/24/a-look -at-the-americans-who-believe-there-is-some-truth-to-the-conspiracy-theory -that-covid-19-was-planned/.

9. "CIA DOC 1035 960: Countering Criticism of the Warren Report," Internet Archive, April 1, 1967, archive.org/details/CIADOC1035960/page/n1/mode /2up?view=theater.

10. "CIA DOC 1035 960: Countering Criticism of the Warren Report," Internet Archive, April 1, 1967, archive.org/details/CIADOC1035960/page/n1/mode /2up?view=theater.

11. Natasha Bertrand, "Hunter Biden Story Is Russian Disinfo, Dozens of Former Intel..." *Politico*, October 19, 2020, www.politico.com/news/2020/10/19/hunter-biden-story-russian-disinfo-430276.

12. "CIA DOC 1035 960: Countering Criticism of the Warren Report," Internet Archive, April 1, 1967, archive.org/details/CIADOC1035960/page/n1/mode/2up?view=theater.

13. "CIA DOC 1035 960: Countering Criticism of the Warren Report," Internet Archive, April 1, 1967, archive.org/details/CIADOC1035960/page/n1/mode/2up?view=theater.

14. "The Twitter Files: The Censorship Industrial Complex with Matt Taibbi," YouTube, April 27, 2023, www.youtube.com/watch?v=cDVKR5uVPmM; John V. Walsh, "The Twitter Files Explained: Matt Taibbi on the Censorship Industrial Complex," Antiwar.Com Blog, May 8, 2023, www.antiwar.com/blog/2023/05/08/the-twitter-files-explained-matt-taibbi-on-the-censorship-industrial-complex/.

15. "Cognitive Dissonance," *Encyclopaedia Britannica*, March 4, 2024, www.britannica.com/science/cognitive-dissonance.

16. James Curtis, *Last Man Standing: Mort Sahl and the Birth of Modern Comedy* (University Press of Mississippi, 2017).

17. James Curtis, *Last Man Standing: Mort Sahl and the Birth of Modern Comedy* (University Press of Mississippi, 2017).

18. James Curtis, *Last Man Standing: Mort Sahl and the Birth of Modern Comedy* (University Press of Mississippi, 2017).

19. "Summary of Findings," National Archives and Records Administration, www.archives.gov/research/jfk/select-committee-report/summary.html. Accessed March 22, 2024.

20. Emily Hoeven, "What's Behind California's New Rules for Mass Events?," CalMatters, August 19, 2021, https://calmatters.org/newsletters/whatmatters/2021/08/california-vaccine/.

21. "Patton Oswalt Cancels Shows in Florida, Utah over Venues' Refusal of COVID-19 Protocols," FOX 29 News Philadelphia, September 10, 2021, https://www.fox29.com/news/patton-oswalt-cancels-shows-in-florida-utah-over-venues-refusal-of-covid-19-protocols.

22. Sarah Abraham, "Selma Blair Is 'Fine' with Rob Schneider Voicing His 'My Body My Choice' Stance on the COVID-19 Vaccine and 'Understands the Concern'... after Comedian Goes on Twitter Rant Urging People to 'Just Say No' to the Jab," Daily Mail Online, Associated Newspapers, July 11, 2021, www.dailymail.co.uk/tvshowbiz/article-9776865/Selma-Blair-fine-Rob-Schneider-voicing-anti-vax-stance-COVID-19-vaccine.html.

23. Sarah Abraham, "Selma Blair Is 'Fine' with Rob Schneider Voicing His 'My Body My Choice' Stance on the COVID-19 Vaccine and 'Understands the Concern'... after Comedian Goes on Twitter Rant Urging People to 'Just Say No' to the

Jab," Daily Mail Online, Associated Newspapers, July 11, 2021, www.dailymail
.co.uk/tvshowbiz/article-9776865/Selma-Blair-fine-Rob-Schneider-voicing
-anti-vax-stance-COVID-19-vaccine.html.

24. "AstraZeneca to Withdraw Covid Vaccine Globally as Demand Declines;
Faces Legal Challenges over Side Effects," Economic Times, May 9, 2024,
https://economictimes.indiatimes.com/news/international/business
/astrazeneca-says-it-will-withdraw-covid-19-vaccine-globally-as-demand-dips
/articleshow/109931803.cms?from=mdr#.

## CHAPTER THREE

1. Jonathan Day, "What Is Self-Censorship? How Does It Kill Media Freedom?,"
Liberties.Eu, European Liberties Platform, June 10, 2021, www.liberties.eu/en
/stories/self-censorship/43569.

2. "Ibram X. Kendi," www.bu.edu/antiracism-center/profile/ibram-x-kendi/.
Accessed March 22, 2024; Tyler Austin Harper, "Ibram X. Kendi's Fall Is a Cau-
tionary Tale—so Was His Rise," www.washingtonpost.com/books/2023/09/28
/ibram-kendi-stamped-center-antiracist-research/. Accessed March 22, 2024.

3. Douglas Murray, The War on the West (HarperCollins Publishers, 2023).

4. Jennifer Schuessler et al., "Harvard President Resigns after Mounting
Plagiarism Accusations," New York Times, January 2, 2024, www.nytimes
.com/2024/01/02/us/harvard-claudine-gay-resigns.html#:~:text=Harvard
%20President%20Resigns%20After%20Mounting,scrutiny%20of%20her
%20academic%20record; Sally E. Edwards and Asher J. Montgomery et al.,
"Harvard President Claudine Gay Plagued by Plagiarism Allegations in the
Tumultuous Final Weeks of Tenure: News: The Harvard Crimson," The Harvard
Crimson, www.thecrimson.com/article/2024/1/3/plagiarism-allegations-gay-re
signs/. Accessed March 22, 2024.

5. David Remnick, "Salman Rushdie on Surviving the Fatwa," The New Yorker,
February 6, 2023, www.newyorker.com/podcast/the-new-yorker-radio-hour
/salman-rushdie-on-surviving-the-fatwa#:~:text=Thirty%2Dfour%20years
%20ago%2C%20the,It%20caused%20a%20worldwide%20uproar.

6. Sarah Karp, "Chicago Could Move Away from School Choice. Here's What
That Means for Parents and Students," Chicago Sun-Times, December 27, 2023,
chicago.suntimes.com/education/2023/12/27/24012377/cps-school-choice
-education-chicago-mayor-brandon-johnson-magnet-hunger-games
-city-hall-downtown.

7. Denette Wilford, "Transgender Cyclists Take Gold, Silver Medals at Chicago
Women's Race," Toronto Sun, October 13, 2023, torontosun.com/news/world
/two-for-one-transgender-cyclists-take-gold-and-silver-medals-at-chicago
-womens-race.

8. "The $25 Billion Wizarding World of 'Harry Potter' by the Numbers—
Marketwatch," MarketWatch, www.marketwatch.com/story/the-25-billion

-wizarding-world-of-harry-potter-by-the-numbers-2018-08-30. Accessed April 16, 2024.

9. J. K. Rowling, "Not Safe, I'm Afraid...," Twitter, April 10, 2024, twitter.com /jk_rowling/status/17781244467027267804.

10. *The Dana Carvey Show*, IMDb, https://www.imdb.com/title/tt0115148 /episodes/?season=1&ref_=tt_eps_sn_1. Accessed May 2, 2024.

11. Julie Hinds, "Hulu Film Tells Story of How 'Dana Carvey Show' Became an Influential Disaster," *Detroit Free Press*, October 14, 2017, https: //www.freep.com/story/entertainment/2017/10/14/dana-carvey-show-hulu -documentary/758746001/.

## CHAPTER FOUR

1. Andrew Silow-Carroll et al., "Judd Apatow Gives Louis C.K. a Master Class on Comedy—and Being a Mensch," Jewish Telegraphic Agency, December 31, 2018, www.jta.org/2018/12/31/culture/judd-apatow-gives-louis-c-k-a-master-class -on-comedy-and-being-a-mensch.

## CHAPTER FIVE

1. Mike Sacks, "SNL's James Downey on Working with Norm Macdonald and Getting Fired for Making Fun of OJ Simpson," Vulture, June 24, 2014, www .vulture.com/2014/06/snls-james-downey-on-working-with-norm-macdonald -and-getting-fired-for-making-fun-of-oj-simpson.html.

2. Alexi Cohan, "'SNL' Poked Fun and Bush Enjoyed It," *Boston Herald*, December 3, 2018, www.bostonherald.com/2018/12/02/ae%CB%9Csnlae-poked-fun -and-bush-enjoyed-it/.

3. Alexi Cohan, "'SNL' Poked Fun and Bush Enjoyed It," *Boston Herald*, December 3, 2018, www.bostonherald.com/2018/12/02/ae%CB%9Csnlae-poked-fun-and -bush-enjoyed-it/; Jackie Bischof, "Five Times of Crisis When 'Saturday Night Live' Was Exactly What Americans Needed," Quartz, December 4, 2016, qz.com/852601/saturday-night-live-five-times-of-crisis-when-the-show-was -exactly-what-americans-needed.

4. Matthew Love, "50 Best Stand-up Comics of All Time," *Rolling Stone*, February 14, 2017, www.rollingstone.com/culture/culture-lists/50-best-stand-up-comics -of-all-time-126359/.

5. Ronald Collin and David M. Skover, *The Trials of Lenny Bruce: The Rise and Fall of an American Icon* (Sourcebooks, 2003); "How Lenny Bruce Started Trail Blazed Comedy Career in San Francisco," www.sfchronicle.com/oursf/article /Our-SF-Early-support-for-comedy-trailblazer-6290726.php. Accessed March 22, 2024; "Lenny Bruce: A Comedian so 'Obscene' He Was Kicked out of the U.K. Twice in One Month," CBCnews, CBC/Radio Canada, April 14, 2013, www.cbc.ca/strombo/news/lenny-bruce.html.

6.  Douglas O. Linder, "The Trials of Lenny Bruce: An Account," Famous Trials, UMKC School of Law, www.famous-trials.com/lennybruce/556-home. Accessed March 26, 2024.

7.  Linder, "The Trials of Lenny Bruce: An Account."

8.  Linder, "The Trials of Lenny Bruce: An Account."

9.  Ronald Collin and David M. Skover, *The Trials of Lenny Bruce: The Rise and Fall of an American Icon* (Sourcebooks, 2003).

10. Linder, "The Trials of Lenny Bruce: An Account."

11. Sharif Paget, "Bassem Youssef: The Wild Story of 'Egypt's Jon Stewart,'" BBC News, February 24, 2022, www.bbc.com/culture/article/20180110-bassem -youssef-the-wild-story-of-egypts-jon-stewart.

12. Sonia Faleiro, "Munawar Iqbal Faruqi Was Arrested for Joke He Didn't Tell," *Time*, February 10, 2021, time.com/5938047/munawar-iqbal-faruqi-comedian-india/.

13. "Man Guilty of Hate Crime for Filming Pug's 'Nazi Salutes,'" BBC News, March 20, 2018, www.bbc.com/news/uk-scotland-glasgow-west-43478925.

14. Lenny Bruce, *How to Talk Dirty and Influence People: An Autobiography* (Da Capo Press, 2016).

15. Chris Rock, *Chris Rock: Selective Outrage*, Netflix official site, March 5, 2023, https://www.netflix.com/title/80167499.

## CHAPTER SIX

1.  Owen Adams, "Never Let a Crisis Go to Waste," HealthcarePapers, US National Library of Medicine, April 20, 2022, pubmed.ncbi.nlm.nih.gov/36433903/.

2.  Richard Fisher, "The Fiasco of the 1976 'Swine Flu Affair,'" BBC News, February 24, 2022, www.bbc.com/future/article/20200918-the-fiasco-of-the -us-swine-flu-affair-of-1976.

3.  "The History of the Swastika," United States Holocaust Memorial Museum, encyclopedia.ushmm.org/content/en/gallery/history-of-the-swastika -photographs. Accessed March 26, 2024.

4.  Mathijs Binkhorst and Daniel J. Goldstein, "Athlete Deaths during the Covid-19 Vaccination Campaign: Contextualisation of Online Information," medRxiv, Cold Spring Harbor Laboratory Press, January 1, 2023, www.medrxiv.org /content/10.1101/2023.02.13.23285851v1.full.

5.  Jimmy Dore, "Jimmy Dore—Before COVID, Doing Your Own Research Used to Be Called Reading," YouTube, March 12, 2024, youtu.be /AwRQh1NZ4Sc?si=Bj2TK7FwWmDoiUUz.

6.  Anton Troianovski et al., "Tucker Carlson Says His Putin Interview Will Be Shown on Thursday," *New York Times*, February 6, 2024, www.nytimes .com/2024/02/06/world/europe/tucker-carlson-putin-interview.html.

7.  Peter Suciu, "Tucker Carlson's First 'Show' on Twitter Has Been Seen 35 Million Times—but Will the Audience Stick Around," *Forbes*, June 8, 2023, www

# NOTES

.forbes.com/sites/petersuciu/2023/06/07/tucker-carlsons-first-show-on-twitter
-has-been-seen-35-million-times--but-will-the-audience-stick-around/?sh
=3a4d1ef61f36.

8. Morgonn McMichael, "Report: Teen Dies from Sex Change Surgery Complications
during Dutch Study," TPUSA LIVE, April 25, 2023, www.tpusa.com/live/report
-teen-dies-from-sex-change-surgery-complications-during-dutch-study.

9. Caitlin O'Kane, "California Governor's Office Tells Diners to Wear Masks
'in Between Bites,'" CBS News, October 6, 2020, www.cbsnews.com/news
/gavin-newsom-california-face-mask-restaurant/#.

10. Jeremy White, "Newsom Faces Backlash after Attending French Laundry
Dinner Party," *Politico*, November 13, 2020, www.politico.com/states/california
/story/2020/11/13/newsom-faces-backlash-after-attending-french-laundry
-dinner-party-1336419.

11. Khaleda Rahman, "Gavin Newsom Slammed for Only Cleaning up San
Francisco 'for Xi Jinping,'" *Newsweek*, November 14, 2023, www.newsweek
.com/gavin-newsom-slammed-cleaning-san-francisco-1843412.

12. "Human Waste Map: DataSF: City and County of San Francisco," San Francisco
Data, City of San Francisco, data.sfgov.org/City-Infrastructure/Human
-Waste-Map/nxe9-9tyg. Accessed March 26, 2024.

13. Lucy Madison, "Fact-Checking Romney's '47 Percent' Comment," CBS News,
September 25, 2012, www.cbsnews.com/news/fact-checking-romneys-47
-percent-comment/.

14. "Households Paying No Income Tax by Income Level U.S. 2022," Statista,
November 23, 2023, www.statista.com/statistics/242138/percentages-of
-us-households-that-pay-no-income-tax-by-income-level/#:~:text=U.S
.%20households%20that%20paid%20no%20income%20tax%202022%2C
%20by%20income%20level&text=In%20total%2C%20about%2059.9
%20percent,paid%20no%20individual%20income%20tax.

15. Jack Nicas, "He Has 17,700 Bottles of Hand Sanitizer and Nowhere to Sell
Them," *New York Times*, March 14, 2020, www.nytimes.com/2020/03/14
/technology/coronavirus-purell-wipes-amazon-sellers.html.

16. Katie Peek, "Flu Has Disappeared for More Than a Year," *Scientific American*,
February 20, 2024, www.scientificamerican.com/article/flu-has-disappeared
-worldwide-during-the-covid-pandemic1/.

17. "Milgram Experiment," *Encyclopaedia Britannica*, www.britannica.com/sci
ence/Milgram-experiment. Accessed February 23, 2024.

18. Rachel Goldstein, "Three Things You Didn't Know about the American
Revolution," News Center, University of Rochester, December 15, 2023, www
.rochester.edu/newscenter/three-things-you-didnt-know-about-the-american
-revolution/#:~:text=At%20no%20time%20did%20more,colonists
%20fought%20for%20the%20British.

19. David Robson, "The '3.5% Rule': How a Small Minority Can Change the World," BBC News, March 3, 2023, www.bbc.com/future/article/20190513-it-only-takes-35-of-people-to-change-the-world.

20. "Operation MK Ultra," Central Intelligence Agency Freedom of Information Act Reading Room, Central Intelligence Agency, www.cia.gov/readingroom/document/06760269. Accessed March 26, 2024.

21. "Operation Paperclip," Central Intelligence Agency Freedom of Information Act Electronic Reading Room, Central Intelligence Agency, www.cia.gov/readingroom/document/cia-rdp88-01070r000100200004-9. Accessed March 26, 2024.

22. Michael Christopher Carroll, *Lab 257: The Disturbing Story of the Government's Secret Germ Laboratory* (HarperCollins Publishers, 2005).

23. "Public Health Service Study of Untreated Syphilis at Tuskegee Timeline," Centers for Disease Control and Prevention, December 5, 2022, www.cdc.gov/tuskegee/timeline.htm.

24. "Public Health Service Study of Untreated Syphilis at Tuskegee Timeline," Centers for Disease Control and Prevention, December 5, 2022, www.cdc.gov/tuskegee/timeline.htm.

25. "Project MKULTRA," *New York Times*, www.nytimes.com/packages/pdf/national/13inmate_ProjectMKULTRA.pdf. Accessed March 26, 2024.

26. "Serratia Has Dark History in Region/Army Test in 1950 May Have Changed Microbial Ecology," SF Gate, October 31, 2004, www.sfgate.com/health/article/Serratia-has-dark-history-in-region-Army-test-2677623.php.

## CHAPTER SEVEN

1. "Sunday Edition: Yeonmi Park," YouTube, February 11, 2024, www.youtube.com/watch?v=M60gTcKtQAs.

2. "Pravda," *Encyclopaedia Britannica*, February 8, 2024, www.britannica.com/topic/Pravda.

3. Robert Epstein et al., "Suppressing the Search Engine Manipulation Effect (SEME)," Proceedings of the ACM on Human-Computer Interaction 1, no. 42 (December 6, 2017), dl.acm.org/doi/10.1145/3134677.

4. "Farm Population Lowest Since 1850's," *New York Times*, July 20, 1988, www.nytimes.com/1988/07/20/us/farm-population-lowest-since-1850-s.html#:~:text=According%20to%20Agriculture%20Department%20estimates,the%20population%20of%20101.6%20million.

5. Saladin Ambar, "Woodrow Wilson: Campaigns and Elections," Miller Center, August 28, 2023, millercenter.org/president/wilson/campaigns-and-elections.

6. "Biden Promise Tracker," PolitiFact, www.politifact.com/truth-o-meter/promises/biden-promise-tracker/?ruling=true. Accessed March 26, 2024.

7. Christopher Daly, "How Woodrow Wilson's Propaganda Machine Changed American Journalism," Smithsonian Institution, Smithsonian.com, April 28, 2017, www.smithsonianmag.com/history/how-woodrow-wilsons-propaganda -machine-changed-american-journalism-180963082/.

8. "Sedition Act of 1918," Free Speech Center, Middle Tennessee State University, March 26, 2024, firstamendment.mtsu.edu/article/sedition-act -of-1918/#:~:text=The%20targets%20of%20prosecution%20under,and %20a%20fine%20of%20%2410%2C000.

9. "Underwood-Simmons Tariff Act," *Encyclopaedia Britannica*, www.britannica .com/event/Underwood-Simmons-Tariff-Act. Accessed March 26, 2024.

10. Kelsey Vlamis, "Bad Night for a Furious Biden," Business Insider, www .businessinsider.com/bad-night-furious-biden-press-conference-memory -classified-documents-2024-2. Accessed March 26, 2024.

## CHAPTER EIGHT

1. Norm Macdonald, Twitter post, April 10, 2019, 10:03 p.m., twitter.com /normmacdonald/status/1116159872393867265?lang=en.

2. Norm Macdonald, Twitter post, April 10, 2019, 10:03 p.m., twitter.com /normmacdonald/status/1116159872393867265?lang=en.

3. Joe Marino et al., "Police Believe Four of the Migrants Arrested in Cop Beatdown Near Times Square Fled on a Bus to California," *New York Post*, February 6, 2024, nypost.com/2024/02/01/metro/police-believe-4-of-the-migrants-arrested -in-nyc-cop-beatdown-fled-to-california/.

4. Audrey Conklin, "Where Are Noncitizens Allowed to Vote in the US?," Fox News, December 15, 2021, www.foxnews.com/politics/united-states-noncitizen -voting-cities.

5. "Does the Moon Have Air?" Union University, January 2002, www.uu.edu /dept/physics/scienceguys/2002Jan.cfm#:~:text=However%2C%20the %20field%20on%20the,sixth%20that%20of%20our%20Earth. Accessed March 26, 2024.

6. "Dick Gregory and Jack Paar's Couch," *American Masters*, PBS, September 14, 2017, www.pbs.org/video/dick-gregory-and-jack-paars-couch-p0jsad/.

7. "Read Martin Luther King Jr.'s 'I Have a Dream' Speech in Its Entirety," NPR, January 16, 2023, www.npr.org/2010/01/18/122701268/i-have-a -dream-speech-in-its-entirety.

8. Todd Spangler, "Joe Rogan's Spotify Deal Renewal Worth up to $250 Million, Podcast Will No Longer Be Exclusive to the Platform," *Variety*, February 3, 2024, variety.com/2024/digital/news/joe-rogan-renews-spotify-deal-not-exclusive -1235895424/.

9. United States Holocaust Memorial Museum, encyclopedia.ushmm.org/content /en/article/the-murder-of-people-with-disabilities. Accessed March 26, 2024.

10. Daniel Jonah Goldhagen, *Hitler's Willing Executioners* (Random House, 1997).

# NOTES

11. With an MBA from Berkeley and thirteen years of experience at Goldman Sachs and Credit Suisse, Financial Samurai Sam started Financial Samurai in 2009 to help make sense of financial chaos. Financial Samurai, "Income by Race: Why Is Asian Income So High?" January 20, 2024, www.financialsamurai.com /income-by-race-why-is-asian-income-so-high/.

## CHAPTER NINE

1. "Columbia Protestors Clarify They Only Want Death to America after America Is Done Paying Their Student Loans," *The Babylon Bee*, April 23, 2024, https: //babylonbee.com/news/columbia-protestors-clarify-they-only-want-death -to-america-after-america-is-done-paying-their-student-loans.

2. Alice Yin and Nell Salzman, "No Migrants Camped Out at O'Hare International Airport for First Time since Summer, Questions Loom over Dwindling City Funds," *Chicago Tribune*, February 9, 2024, www.chicagotribune.com /2024/02/08/no-migrants-at-ohare-airport/.

3. Jake Offenhartz, "New York City Turns to School Gyms to House New Migrants, Prompting Uproar," AP News, May 16, 2023, apnews.com/article/migrants -asylum-new-york-eric-adams-schools-2c61324054e55b0532c48996794cc30a.

4. "Fidel Castro Announces Mariel Boatlift, Allowing Cubans to Emigrate to U.S.," History.com, www.history.com/this-day-in-history/castro-announces -mariel-boatlift. Accessed March 26, 2024.

5. "The Chinese Revolution of 1949," US Department of State, history.state.gov /milestones/1945–1952/chinese-rev. Accessed March 26, 2024.

6. Mao Zedong and F. G. Hudson, *Let a Hundred Flowers Bloom: The Complete Text of "On the Correct Handling of Contradictions Among the People* (Tamiment Institute, 1957).

7. "Mao, Criticism, and Unity," New Discourses Bullets, ep. 43, March 30, 2023, YouTube video, 13:16, www.youtube.com/watch?v=VZ29kEPPakA&t=1s.

8. "Bitcoin Mining Could Use More Energy Than All of Italy by 2024," *VICE*, April 7, 2021, www.vice.com/en/article/dy8amw/bitcoin-mining -energy-consumption#.

9. Cindy Gordon, "AI Is Accelerating the Loss of Our Scarcest Natural Resource: Water," *Forbes*, March 7, 2024, www.forbes.com/sites/cindygordon /2024/02/25/ai-is-accelerating-the-loss-of-our-scarcest-natural-resource-water /?sh=7bcd63a47c06.

10. Laura Sullivan, "Recycling Plastic Is Practically Impossible—and the Problem Is Getting Worse," NPR, October 24, 2022, www.npr.org/2022/10 /24/1131131088/recycling-plastic-is-practically-impossible-and-the-problem-is -getting-worse.

11. Mao Zedong and F. G. Hudson, *Let a Hundred Flowers Bloom: The Complete Text of "On the Correct Handling of Contradictions Among the People* (Tamiment Institute, 1957).

12. "Antonio Gramsci, Cultural Marxism, Wokeness, and Leninism 4.0," New Discourses, ep. 16, January 21, 2021, YouTube video, 57:33, https://www.you tube.com/watch?v=VdsSIWh_VkQ.

13. "Obama Did Not Sign a Law Allowing Propaganda in the U.S.," AP News, November 17, 2023, apnews.com/article/archive-fact-checking-7064410002.

14. Isabel Vincent, "Inside BLM Co-Founder Patrisse Khan-Cullors' Million-Dollar Real Estate Buying Binge," *New York Post*, April 16, 2021, https://nypost.com/2021/04/10/inside-blm-co-founder-patrisse-khan-cullors -real-estate-buying-binge/.

15. Jamie Joseph, "Coca-Cola Quietly Deletes Language Supporting BLM After Ted Cruz Calls Out Pro-Hamas Post," Fox News, October 20, 2023, www .foxnews.com/politics/coca-cola-quietly-deletes-language-supporting-blm -ted-cruz-calls-out-pro-hamas-post.

16. "Open Letter from the National Security and Human Rights Campaign," Open Society Foundations, December 14, 2008, www.opensocietyfoundations.org /newsroom/open-letter-national-security-and-human-rights-campaign.

17. Howard Husock, "Bill Gates and the Common Core: Did He Really Do Anything Wrong?," *Forbes*, June 18, 2014, www.forbes.com/sites /howardhusock/2014/06/18/bill-gates-and-the-common-core-did-he-really -do-anything-wrong/?sh=5b09ef236faa.

18. Dan Byrne, "What Is the History of ESG?," The Corporate Governance Institute, June 12, 2023, www.thecorporategovernanceinstitute.com/insights /lexicon/what-is-the-history-of-esg/#:~:text=The%20UN%20makes%20it %20official,ESG%20in%20the%20modern%20context.

19. "2023 Corporate Equality Index Criteria," Human Rights Campaign, www.hrc .org/resources/corporate-equality-index-criteria. Accessed March 26, 2024.

20. Ross Kerber and Jin Hyunjoo, "Tesla Cut from S&P 500 ESG Index, and Elon Musk Tweets His Fury," Reuters, May 19, 2022, www.reuters.com/business /sustainable-business/tesla-removed-sp-500-esg-index-autopilot-discrimination -concerns-2022-05-18/.

21. "How Many Guns Does the Average American Own [2023 Edition]," Arms Directory, December 1, 2023, armsdirectory.com/how-many-guns-does -average-american-own/#:~:text=Currently%20the%20number%20of %20firearms,owning%20American%20has%205%20firearms%20.

22. "Dietrich von Choltitz," *Encyclopaedia Britannica*, www.britannica.com /biography/Dietrich-von-Choltitz. Accessed March 26, 2024.

## CHAPTER TEN

1. Melissa Rudy, "Face Masks Made 'Little to No Difference' in Preventing Spread of Covid: Study," *New York Post*, February 14, 2023, nypost.com/2023/02/14 /face-masks-made-little-to-no-difference-in-preventing-covid-study/.

# NOTES

2. Pascal Sabino, "Lightfoot on Telling West Side Teens to Go Home: 'I'm Not Going to Apologize for Caring About Black Chicago,'" Block Club Chicago, May 12, 2020, blockclubchicago.org/2020/05/12/lightfoot-on-telling-west-side-teens -to-go-home-im-not-going-to-apologize-for-caring-about-black-chicago/.

3. "Lori Lightfoot, Former Chicago Mayor, Named Senior Leadership Fellow for Fall 2023," Harvard T. H. Chan School of Public Health, June 7, 2023, www .hsph.harvard.edu/news/hsph-in-the-news/lori-lightfoot-former-chicago -mayor-named-senior-leadership-fellow-for-fall-2023/.

4. Chuck Goudie, "Chicago Looting Leaves Residents Feeling Unsafe, Ready to Leave City, Property Management Company Tells Mayor," ABC7 Chicago, August 13, 2020, abc7chicago.com/chicago-looting-sudler-propert y-management-lori-lightfoot/6367902/.

5. Kendall K. Morgan and Shawna Seed, "Covid Variants and Strains," WebMD, November 11, 2021, www.webmd.com/covid/coronavirus-strains.

6. C. Nicole Swiner, "Common Cold Causes: Coronavirus, RSV, Rhinovirus & More," WebMD, May 16, 2023, www.webmd.com/cold-and-flu/common _cold_causes.

7. Eric Schmitt, "Here Is the Full Transcript of the Anthony Fauci Deposition," Twitter, December 5, 2022, twitter.com/Eric_Schmitt/status /1599853022489718784; Editorial Board, "Anthony Fauci Fesses Up," *Wall Street Journal*, January 11, 2024, www.wsj.com/articles/anthony-fauci-covid-socia l-distancing-six-feet-rule-house-subcommittee-hearing-44289850; Michael Dorgan, "New Report Blasts Government's Covid Response, Warns of Repeating Same Mistakes," Fox News, March 16, 2024, www.foxnews.com/health/new -report-blasts-governments-response-covid-warns-repeating-mistakes.

8. Sara Auld et al., "ICU and Ventilator Mortality Among Critically Ill Adults with Covid-19," National Library of Medicine, April 26, 2020, https://www.ncbi .nlm.nih.gov/pmc/articles/PMC7276026/

9. "Infectious Diseases: a Scientist." Texas A&M University Veterinary Medicine & Biomedical Sciences, March 7, 2022, https://vetmed.tamu.edu /peer/infectious-diseases-meet-a-scientist/.

10. Suzanne Humphries and Roman Bystrianyk, *Dissolving Illusions: Disease, Vaccines, and the Forgotten History* (CreateSpace Publishing, 2013).

11. Humphries and Bystrianyk, *Dissolving Illusions*.

12. Nate Pedersen and Lydia Kang, "Mercury Was Considered a Cure— Until It Killed You," *Toronto Star*, October 22, 2017, www.thestar.com/news /insight/mercury-was-considered-a-cure-until-it-killed-you/article _e1b3e3a9-f0d1-573a-848c-4b3119b6426a.html.

13. Gerry Greenstone, "The History of Bloodletting," *British Columbia Medical Journal* 52, no. 1 (January-February 2010): 12–14, Premise, bcmj.org/premise /history-bloodletting. Accessed March 26, 2024.

14. "The Death of George Washington," George Washington's Mount Vernon, www.mountvernon.org/library/digitalhistory/digital-encyclopedia/article /the-death-of-george-washington/#:~:text=Washington%20was%20bled %20for%20the,vomiting%2C%20though%20without%20beneficial %20results. Accessed March 26, 2024.

15. Peter Poczai and Laszlo Z. Karvalics, "The Little Known History of Cleanliness and the Forgotten Pioneers of Handwashing," National Institute of Health, October 20, 2022, https://www.ncbi.nlm.nih.gov/pmc/articles/PMC9632745 /#:~:text=Doctors%20did%20not%20routinely%20wash,the%20spread %20of%20puerperal%20fever.

16. Ignaz Philipp Semmelweis, *The Etiology, Concept, and Prophylaxis of Childbed Fever* (University of Wisconsin Press, 1983).

17. "United Kingdom Vaccination Act 1853," Policy Navigator, navigator.health .org.uk/theme/united-kingdom-vaccination-act-1853#:~:text=The %20Vaccination%20Act%201853%20made,be%20subject%20to%20a %20fine. Accessed 26 March 2024.

18. "Victorian Health Reform," National Archives, November 25, 2022, www .nationalarchives.gov.uk/education/resources/victorian-health-reform/#:~:text =In%201867%2C%20the%20government%20increased,sake%20of %20improving%20public%20health.

19. Humphries and Bystrianyk, *Dissolving Illusions*.

20. Humphries and Bystrianyk, *Dissolving Illusions*.

21. Humphries and Bystrianyk, *Dissolving Illusions*.

22. "History of Measles," Centers for Disease Control and Prevention, November 5, 2020, www.cdc.gov/measles/about/history.html.

23. Melinda E. Wharton, "Measles Elimination in the United States," *Journal of Infectious Diseases* 189, issue supplement 1 (May 2004): S1–S3, https://academic .oup.com/jid/article/189/Supplement_1/S1/820569#.

24. "National Update on Measles Cases and Outbreaks—United States," Centers for Disease Control and Prevention, October 10, 2019, https://www.cdc.gov /mmwr/volumes/68/wr/mm6840e2.htm.

25. Katherine Drabiak, "During Measles Outbreaks, Fines and Public Bans Are Legal, but There Are Limits," PBS, April 12, 2019, www.pbs.org/newshour /health/during-measles-outbreaks-fines-and-public-bans-are-legal-but-there -are-limits.

26. Humphries and Bystrianyk, *Dissolving Illusions*.

27. Preeti Vankar, "U.S. Health Expenditure as GDP Share 1960-2022," Statista, February 16, 2024, www.statista.com/statistics/184968/us-health-expenditure -as-percent-of-gdp-since-1960/#:~:text=In%202022%2C%20U.S. %20national%20health,GDP%20share%20among%20developed%20countries.

28. Aaron O'Neill, "United States: Life Expectancy 1860-2020," Statista, February 2, 2024, www.statista.com/statistics/1040079/life-expectancy-united-states-all-time/.

29. David M. Morens et al. "Rethinking Next-Generation Vaccines for Coronaviruses, Influenzaviruses, and Other Respiratory Viruses," *Cell Host & Microbe* 31, no. 1 (2023): 146–157, doi:10.1016/j.chom.2022.11.016.

30. "Fauci: Recent Paper Doesn't Suggest COVID Vaccines Ineffective," AP News, February 10, 2023, https://apnews.com/article/fact-check-covid-mrna -vaccine-fauci-387418337013.

## CHAPTER ELEVEN

1. "'Era of Global Boiling Has Arrived,' Says UN Chief as July Set to Be Hottest Month on Record," *The Guardian*, July 27, 2023, www.theguardian .com/science/2023/jul/27/scientists-july-world-hottest-month-record -climate-temperatures#:~:text=The%20era%20of%20global%20warming ,It%20is%20terrifying.

2. "More Quotes about Uncertainty," Department of Mathematics, University of Texas at Austin, accessed May 7, 2024, https://web.ma.utexas.edu/users/mks /statmistakes/uncertaintyquotes.html; Richard P. Feynman, Jeffrey Robbins, and Freeman J. Dyson, *The Pleasure of Finding Things Out: The Best Short Works of Richard P. Feynman* (New York: Basic Books, 2021).

3. Bella Isaacs-Thomas, "When It Comes to Sucking Up Carbon Emissions, 'the Ocean Has Been Forgiving.' That Might Not Last," PBS, March 25, 2022, www.pbs.org/newshour/science/the-ocean-helps-absorb-our-carbon-emissions -we-may-be-pushing-it-too-far#:~:text=But%20as%20the%20ocean %20continues,more%20acidic%20its%20waters%20become.

4. "A Study of Climatological Research as It Pertains to Intelligence Problems," Central Intelligence Agency Climate Research Intel, www.governmentattic .org/18docs/CIAclimateResearchIntellProbs_1974.pdf. Accessed March 27, 2024.

5. "Climategate 10 Years on: What Lessons Have We Learned?," *The Guardian*, November 9, 2019, www.theguardian.com/theobserver/2019/nov/09 /climategate-10-years-on-what-lessons-have-we-learned.

6. "A Study of Climatological Research as It Pertains to Intelligence Problems," Central Intelligence Agency Climate Research Intel, www.governmentattic .org/18docs/CIAclimateResearchIntellProbs_1974.pdf. Accessed March 27, 2024.

7. M. D. H. Jones and A. Henderson-Sellers, "History of the Greenhouse Effect—CRC Research," www.crcresearch.org/sites/default/files/u11276 /historyofgreenhousegaseffect.pdf. Accessed March 27, 2024.

8. M. D. H. Jones and A. Henderson-Sellers, "History of the Greenhouse Effect—CRC Research," www.crcresearch.org/sites/default/files/u11276 /historyofgreenhousegaseffect.pdf. Accessed March 27, 2024.

9. Den Volokin and Lark ReLlez, "On the Average Temperature of Airless Spherical Bodies and the Magnitude of Earth's Atmospheric Thermal Effect,"

*SpringerPlus* 3, no. 723 (December 10, 2014), springerplus.springeropen.com/articles/10.1186/2193-1801-3-723; Ned Nikolov and Karl Zeller, "New Insights on the Physical Nature of the Atmospheric Greenhouse Effect Deduced from an Empirical Planetary Temperature Model," *Environment Pollution and Climate Change*, February 13, 2017, www.omicsonline.org/open-access/New-Insights-on-the-Physical-Nature-of-the-Atmospheric-Greenhouse-Effect-Deduced-from-an-Empirical-Planetary-Temperature-Model.pdf.

10. "What Is Albedo?," NASA, August 10, 2020, mynasadata.larc.nasa.gov/mini-lessonactivity/what-albedo#:~:text=Albedo%20is%20the%20fraction%20of,immediately%20reflected%20back%20to%20space.

11. Ned Nikolov and Karl Zeller, "New Insights on the Physical Nature of the Atmospheric Greenhouse Effect Deduced from an Empirical Planetary Temperature Model," *Environment Pollution and Climate Change*, February 13, 2017, www.omicsonline.org/open-access/New-Insights-on-the-Physical-Nature-of-the-Atmospheric-Greenhouse-Effect-Deduced-from-an-Empirical-Planetary-Temperature-Model.pdf.

## CHAPTER TWELVE

1. Robert Bryce, "Cheney's Multi-Million Dollar Revolving Door," *Mother Jones*, August 2, 2000, www.motherjones.com/politics/2000/08/cheneys-multi-million-dollar-revolving-door/.

2. "Private Military Security Services Market Size USD 446.81 Billion by 2030," Vantage Market Research, www.vantagemarketresearch.com/industry-report/private-military-security-services-market-1578. Accessed March 27, 2024.

3. Steven Nelson, "Lock Him Up? Lawmakers Renew Calls for James Clapper Perjury Charges," *US News and World Report*, November 17, 2016, https://www.usnews.com/news/articles/2016-11-17/lawmakers-resume-calls-for-james-clapper-perjury-charges.

4. Olga Craig, "From Tearaway to Terrorist—the Story of Richard Reid," *The Telegraph*, December 30, 2001, www.telegraph.co.uk/news/uknews/1366666/From-tearaway-to-terrorist-The-story-of-Richard-Reid.html.

5. Susan Stellin, "Are Scanners Worth the Risk?," *New York Times*, September 7, 2010, www.nytimes.com/2010/09/12/travel/12prac.html.

6. "Female Passengers Say They're Targeted by TSA," CBS News, February 13, 2012, www.cbsnews.com/texas/news/female-passengers-say-theyre-targeted-by-tsa/.

7. "Vaccine Injury Compensation Data," Health Resources & Services Administration, March 1, 2024, www.hrsa.gov/vaccine-compensation/data.

8. Paul Offit, "Vaccines and Autism Revisited—the Hannah Poling Case," New England Journal of Medicine 358, no. 20 (May 15, 2008), www.nejm.org/doi/full/10.1056/nejmp0802904.

9.  "Transcript: Donald Trump's Taped Comments about Women," *New York Times*, October 8, 2016, www.nytimes.com/2016/10/08/us/donald-trump-tape-transcript.html.

10. "Event 201," Johns Hopkins Center for Health Security, centerforhealthsecurity.org/our-work/tabletop-exercises/event-201-pandemic-tabletop-exercise. Accessed March 27, 2024.

11. "Ten Health Issues WHO Will Tackle This Year," World Health Organization, www.who.int/news-room/spotlight/ten-threats-to-global-health-in-2019. Accessed March 27, 2024.

12. "Measles Outbreak—California, December 2014–February 2015," Centers for Disease Control and Prevention, February 20, 2015, www.cdc.gov/mmwr/preview/mmwrhtml/mm6406a5.htm.

13. "Former CDC Head Lands Vaccine Job at Merck," Reuters, December 21, 2009, https://www.reuters.com/article/idUSTRE5BK2K5/.

14. John Pitcairn and Jay Frank Schamberg, *Both Sides of the Vaccine Question* (Anti-Vaccination League of America, 1911).

15. Christina D. Bethell et al., "A National and State Profile of Leading Health Problems and Health Care Quality for US Children: Key Insurance Disparities and Across-State Variations," *Academic Pediatrics* 11, no. 3 Suppl (2011): S22–33, doi:10.1016/j.acap.2010.08.011.

16. Christina Jewett, "F.D.A.'s Drug Industry Fees Fuel Concerns over Influence," *New York Times*, September 15, 2022, www.nytimes.com/2022/09/15/health/fda-drug-industry-fees.html#:~:text=The%20pharmaceutical%20industry%20funding%20alone,faces%20a%20deadline%20of%20Sept.

17. "Leading Lobbying Industries U.S. 2023," Statista, February 26, 2024, www.statista.com/statistics/257364/top-lobbying-industries-in-the-us/#:~:text=In%202023%2C%20the%20pharmaceuticals%20and,million%20U.S.%20dollars%20on%20lobbying.

18. Oliver J. Wouters, "Lobbying Expenditures and Campaign Contributions by the Drug Industry in the United States," *JAMA Internal Medicine* 180, no. 5 (May 2020), jamanetwork.com/journals/jamainternalmedicine/fullarticle/2762509.

19. Michele Majidi, "U.S. Pharma TV Ad Spend 2020," Statista, December 20, 2023, www.statista.com/statistics/953104/pharma-industry-tv-ad-spend-us/#:~:text=Pharmaceutical%20industry%20TV%20ad%20spend%20in%20the%20U.S%202016%2D2020&text=In%202020%20TV%20ad%20spending,of%20the%20total%20ad%20spend.

20. Gardiner Harris, "Pfizer Pays $2.3 Billion to Settle Marketing Case," *New York Times*, September 2, 2009, www.nytimes.com/2009/09/03/business/03health.html#:~:text=WASHINGTON%20%E2%80%94%20The%20pharmaceutical%20giant%20Pfizer,fine%20of%20any%20kind%20ever.

21. C. Lee Ventola, "Direct-to-Consumer Pharmaceutical Advertising: Therapeutic or Toxic?," *P T* 36, no. 10 (2011): 669–684.

22. *DPT: Vaccine Roulette*, WRC-TV, April 19, 1982.
23. Harris L. Coulter and Barbara Loe Fisher, *DPT: A shot in the dark* (San Diego: Harcourt Brace Jovanovich, 1985).
24. "NVIC Position Statement," National Vaccine Information Center (NVIC), February 2018, www.nvic.org/law-policy-federal/vaccine-injury-compensation /nvic-position-statement.
25. "NVIC Position Statement," National Vaccine Information Center (NVIC), February 2018, www.nvic.org/law-policy-federal/vaccine-injury-compensation /nvic-position-statement.
26. Barbara Loe Fisher et al., "National Vaccine Information Center (NVIC) Letter to Carolyn Garvey," National Vaccine Information Center (NIVC), July 11, 2014, www.nvic.org/.
27. "NVIC Position Statement," National Vaccine Information Center (NVIC), February 2018, www.nvic.org/law-policy-federal/vaccine-injury-compensation /nvic-position-statement.
28. Brent Kendall, "Supreme Court Clears Way for Seat-Belt Lawsuits," *Wall Street Journal*, February 23, 2011, www.wsj.com/articles/SB100014240527487037757 04576162273193408118.
29. "House Judiciary Committee Advances Domestic Terrorism Legislation, Minus Safeguards—Congressman Steube," Congressman Greg Steube, April 6, 2022, steube.house.gov/in-the-news/house-judiciary-committee-advances -domestic-terrorism-legislation-minus-safeguards/.
30. Todd Rokita, "DOJ Letter Based on NSBA Apology...," Texas Attorney General, State of Indiana Office of the Attorney General, October 26, 2021, www .texasattorneygeneral.gov/sites/default/files/global/images/DOJ Letter based on NSBA Apology Letter 10.26.21 final.pdf.

## CHAPTER THIRTEEN

1. Mary Chao, "Andrew Cuomo Crosses Another Line, Blaming His Heritage for Harassment: Mary Chao," North Jersey Media Group, NorthJersey.com, August 11, 2021, www.northjersey.com/story/news/2021/08/10/andrew-cuomo -harassment-allegations-blamed-italian-heritage/5557308001/.
2. Cynthia Littleton, "Jay Leno on Bill Cosby: 'I Don't Know Why It's So Hard to Believe Women,'" *Variety*, January 21, 2015, variety.com/2015/tv/news/jay-leno -on-bill-cosby-i-dont-know-why-its-so-hard-to-believe-women-1201411051/.
3. "Alec Baldwin Says Rob Schneider 'Has a Point' in Criticism of 'SNL' Trump Impersonation," Fox News, April 30, 2018, https://www.foxnews.com /entertainment/alec-baldwin-says-rob-schneider-has-a-point-in-criticism-of-snl -trump-impersonation.
4. "Record Audience Tunes in to Carson's Final 'Tonight Show'—Upi Archives." UPI, May 23, 1992, www.upi.com/Archives/1992/05/23/Record-audience -tunes-in-to-Carsons-final-Tonight-Show/6045706593600/.

5. Mark Joyella, "With 2.5 Million Viewers, Fox News Channel's 'Gutfeld!' Beats Every Show in Late Night TV," *Forbes*, September 12, 2023, www .forbes.com/sites/markjoyella/2022/10/27/fox-news-channels-gutfeld-hits -25-million-viewers-highest-rated-night-in-shows-history/?sh=28ea2dc462aa.

6. Nick Burns, "Glenn Greenwald: The Greatest Journalist of All Time?" *New Statesman*, October 20, 2022, www.newstatesman.com/politics/2021/08 /glenn-greenwald-greatest-journalist-all-time.

7. "A Talk with Lowell Bergman | Smoke in the Eye," *Frontline*, PBS, www.pbs.org /wgbh/pages/frontline/smoke/bergman.html. Accessed March 27, 2024.

8. Michael Mann, dir., *The Insider*, film (Buena Vista Pictures, 1999).

9. Stuart N. Brotman, "90 Years Later, the Broadcast Public Interest Standard Remains Ill-Defined," Brookings, March 9, 2022, www.brookings.edu/articles /90-years-later-the-broadcast-public-interest-standard-remains-ill-defined/.

10. David Browne, "Eric Clapton Isn't Just Spouting Vaccine Nonsense—He's Bankrolling It," *Rolling Stone*, November 3, 2021, www.rollingstone.com/music /music-features/eric-clapton-vaccine-lockdown-racist-comments-1239027/; "Eric Clapton Feared He Would 'Never Play Again' after 'Disastrous' Time with Vaccine," *Los Angeles Times*, May 17, 2021, www.latimes.com /entertainment-arts/music/story/2021-05-17/eric-clapton-astrazeneca-vaccine.

11. "Noam Chomsky Says the Unvaccinated Should Just Remove Themselves from Society," *National Post*, October 27, 2021, nationalpost.com/news/world/noam -chomsky-says-the-unvaccinated-should-just-remove-themselves-from-society.

12. "Reimagining the Project of Persuasion with Sam Harris—Ep 1," Uniting America with John Wood, Jr., January 13, 2023, YouTube video, 2:06:00, www .youtube.com/watch?v=yVnc4YZc9hQ&t=5900s.

13. "Sean Penn Compares Being Unvaccinated to 'Pointing a Gun in Somebody's Face,'" *The Independent*, August 23, 2021, www.independent.co.uk/arts-enter tainment/films/news/sean-penn-vaccine-covid-gun-b1907011.html.

14. Jamie Burton, "George Clooney: 'I Support Mandatory Vaccines. Period,'" *Newsweek*, October 12, 2021, www.newsweek.com/george-clooney-interview -mandatory-covid-vaccines-1637506.

15. Harry Brent, "Piers Morgan Sparks Furious Backlash After Saying Those Who Don't Take Vaccine Should Be Refused Health Care If They Catch Covid," *The Irish Post*, July 30, 2021, www.irishpost.com/news/piers-morgan-sparks-furious -backlash-after-saying-those-who-dont-take-vaccine-should-be-refused-health -care-if-they-catch-covid-217173.

16. Daniel Kreps, "Howard Stern to 'Imbecile' Anti-Vaxxers: 'Go F-K Yourself,'" *Rolling Stone*, September 9, 2021, https://www.rollingstone.com/culture /culture-news/howard-stern-anti-vaxxers-go-fuck-yourself-1222672/.

17. "'Screw Your Freedom': Schwarzenegger Calls out Anti-Vaxxers," CNN, August 13, 2021, https://www.cnn.com/videos/health/2021/08/13/arnold -schwarzenegger-screw-your-freedom-anti-vax-mask-orig-kj.cnn.

18. Jude Dry, "John Oliver Calls out Anti-Vaxxers on 'Last Week Tonight,' Including Rob Schneider and His Hat—Watch," IndieWire, June 26, 2017, www.indiewire.com/features/general/john-oliver-anti-vaccination-rob-schneider-last-week-tonight-watch-1201847093/.

19. "The VAX-Scene—the Box Set," The Late Show with Stephen Colbert, June 20, 2021, YouTube video, 10:49, www.youtube.com/watch?v=sSkFyNVtNh8.

20. Zoe Christen Jones, "Jimmy Kimmel Jokes Hospitals Shouldn't Treat Patients Who Used Ivermectin for COVID-19 Treatment," CBS News, September 9, 2021, www.cbsnews.com/news/jimmy-kimmel-ivermectin-covid-19-pandemic-hospitals/.

21. Cecile Starr, "Ideas on Film: Edinburgh's Documentary Festival," *The Saturday Review*, October 13, 1951, 60.

22. Michael Shapiro, "Kings Announcer Loses Job after 'All Lives Matter' Tweet," Sports Illustrated, June 2, 2020, https://www.si.com/nba/2020/06/02/kings-announcer-grant-napear-leave-all-lives-matter-tweet.

23. Noam Chomsky, "On Fake News and Other Societal Woes," Noam Chomsky interviewed by Irene, December 7, 2005, chomsky.info/20051207/.

24. Uri Berliner, "I've Been at NPR for 25 Years. Here's How We Lost America's Trust," The Free Press, April 9, 2024, www.thefp.com/p/npr-editor-how-npr-lost-americas-trust?utm_source=tfptwitter.

25. Berliner, "I've Been at NPR for 25 Years."

## CHAPTER FOURTEEN

1. Michael Shellenberger, "Elon Musk Is All That Stands in the Way of Totalitarianism," Twitter, April 8, 2024, twitter.com/shellenberger/status/17773214202 77628968?s=42&t=Yxm5L0fcoNAdqMCeBY3_mA.

2. Elon Musk, "We Are Lifting All Restrictions," Twitter, April 6, 2024, twitter.com/elonmusk/status/1776739518240170254?ref_src=twsrc%5Etfw%7Ctw camp%5Etweetembed%7Ctwterm%5E1776739518240170254%7Ctwgr%5E3 d11224da1a156673025e7e2659e69753d4d8f9a%7Ctwcon%5Es1_&ref _url=https%3A%2F%2Fembedly.forbes.com%2Fwidgets%2Fmedia .html%3Ftype%3Dtext2Fhtmlkey%3D3ce26dc7e3454db5820ba084d28b 4935schema%3Dtwitterurl%3Dhttps3A%2F%2Ftwitter.com%2Felon musk%2Fstatus%2F1776739518240170254image%3D.

3. Robert Hart, "Elon Musk's Feud with Brazil Escalates as Billionaire Promises 'Data Dump' Once Employees Are 'Safe' from Authorities," *Forbes*, April 9, 2024, www.forbes.com/sites/roberthart/2024/04/09/elon-musks-feud-with-bra zil-escalates-as-billionaire-promises-data-dump-once-employees-are-safe -from-authorities/?sh=718d978b4cf4.

4. Melissa Quinn, "Supreme Court Wary of Restricting Government Contact with Social Media Platforms in Free Speech Case," CBS News, CBS Interactive, March 18, 2024, www.cbsnews.com/news/supreme-court-government-pressure-social -media-free-speech/.

5. Alia E. Dastagir, "Marsha Blackburn Asked Ketanji Brown Jackson to Define 'Woman.' Science Says There's No Simple Answer," *USA Today*, Gannett Satellite Information Network, March 28, 2022, www.usatoday.com/story/life /health-wellness/2022/03/24/marsha-blackburn-asked-ketanji-jackson -define-woman-science/7152439001/.

6. "More than 7,000 Hate Crime Reports in First Week of New Law," BBC News, April 10, 2024, www.bbc.com/news/articles/c2x3ljydn67o.

7. Jennifer Bray, "What Are the Proposed New Hate Crime Laws and Why the Delay?" *Irish Times*, December 5, 2023, www.irishtimes.com/politics/2023/12 /05/qa-what-are-the-proposed-new-hate-crime-laws-and-why-the-delay/.

8. Mattias Desmet, "My Speech at the U.S. Senate," February 28, 2024, mattiasdesmet.org/p/my-speech-at-the-us-senate.

9. Desmet, "My Speech at the U.S. Senate."

10. Kaleb Nation, "Dr. David Martin: The Pandemic Was a 'Biological Weapon of Genocide' w/ Dr. Kelly Victory—Ask Dr. Drew," Dr. Drew official website, August 21, 2023, drdrew.com/2023/dr-david-martin-the-pandemic-was-a -biological-weapon-of-genocide-w-dr-kelly-victory-ask-dr-drew/.

11. "Eternal Vigilance Is the Price of Liberty (Spurious Quotation)," Monticello, www .monticello.org/research-education/thomas-jefferson-encyclopedia/eternal-vigilance -price-liberty-spurious-quotation/#:~:text=It%20can%20be%20traced %20back,directly%20quoted%20(more%20or%20less. Accessed March 27, 2024.

12. Wesley Menard Chaput, "Democratic Apathy: Exploring the Roots of Millennial Democratic Fatigue," master's thesis, Harvard Extension School, 2020.

13. Chaput, "Democratic Apathy."

14. Holden Culotta, "George Washington, Our First and Only Independent President, Left Future Generations with Two Warnings in His 1796 Farewell Speech," Twitter, March 12, 2024, twitter.com/holden_culotta /status/1767383549286494662?s=42&t=Yxm5L0fcoNAdqMCeBY3_mA.

15. "Francis Lewis," Descendants of the Signers of the Declaration of Independence, www.dsdi1776.com/signer/francis-lewis/. Accessed March 27, 2024.

16. "Signers of the Declaration of Independence: Richard Stockton," UShistory .org, Independence Hall Association, www.ushistory.org/declaration/signers /stockton.html#:~:text=Originally%2C%20he%20was%20taken%20to,parole %2C%20his%20health%20was%20battered. Accessed March 27, 2024.

17. "Signers of the Declaration of Independence: John Hart," UShistory.org, Independence Hall Association, www.ushistory.org/declaration/signers/hart .html. Accessed March 27, 2024.

18. "Lewis Morris," Descendants of the Signers of the Declaration of Independence, www.dsdi1776.com/signer/lewis-morris/. Accessed March 27, 2024.

19. "Philip Livingston," New York State Museum, web.archive.org/web /20160303173845/www.nysm.nysed.gov/albany/bios/l/phlivingston86.html. Accessed March 27, 2024.

20. "1774 to 1783: The Thomas Jefferson Papers Timeline: 1743 to 1827: Articles and Essays: Thomas Jefferson Papers, 1606–1827: Digital Collections: Library of Congress," The Library of Congress. Accessed June 28, 2024, https://www .loc.gov/collections/thomas-jefferson-papers/articles-and-essays/the-thomas -jefferson-papers-timeline-1743-to-1827/1774-to-1783/#:~:text=June%202 %2C%201781,flee%20Monticello%2C%20barely%20escaping%20capture.

21. "5 Founding Fathers Whose Finances Shaped the American Revolution," History.com. Accessed June 28, 2024, https://www.history.com/news/founding -fathers-finances-american-revolution.

22. "Samuel Adams," Descendants of the Signers of the Declaration of Independence. Accessed June 28, 2024, https://www.dsdi1776.com/signer/samuel-adams /#:~:text=He%20was%20poor%20while%20he,been%20buried%20at %20public%20expense.

23. C. James Taylor, "John Adams: Family Life," Miller Center, August 28, 2023, https://millercenter.org/president/adams/family-life.

24. "5 Founding Fathers Whose Finances Shaped the American Revolution," History.com. Accessed June 28, 2024, https://www.history.com/news/founding -fathers-finances-american-revolution.

# ABOUT THE AUTHOR

Rob Schneider is an accomplished actor, comedian, screenwriter, and director. A stand-up comic and veteran of the award-winning NBC sketch comedy series *Saturday Night Live*, Schneider has gone on to a successful career in films and television and continues his worldwide stand-up tour.

He was most recently seen in the Netflix animated feature *Leo* with Bill Burr and Adam Sandler; the independent feature *Dead Wrong* from director Rick Bieber; and *Daddy Daughter Trip*, which he directed, starred in, and produced. It also stars his daughters Miranda Scarlett Schneider and Elle King as well as Jackie Sandler, Mónica Huarte, Miguel Ángel Muñoz, and John Cleese. He also released a comedy special, *Rob Schneider: Woke Up in America*, which premiered on Fox Nation last year. The one-hour special featured Schneider's signature comedic take on a variety of topics, including culture wars, living in a woke world, and navigating the nuanced times of identity politics.

Schneider has just finished directing and costarring in the Spanish-language film *Amor es Amor* for Paramount Plus.

Born in San Francisco, Schneider's mixed background has been a common theme in his comedy acts. Schneider joined *SNL* as a writer during the 1989–1990 season. He swiftly moved from a writer and featured player to a full cast member with a cast that included Adam Sandler, Chris Rock, David Spade, and the late Chris Farley.

After leaving *SNL* in 1994, Schneider went to roles in film and television, including a starring role in the NBC sitcom *Men Behaving Badly* and starring roles in the feature films *Deuce Bigalow: Male Gigolo, The Animal, The Hot Chick, Deuce Bigalow: European Gigolo*, and *The Benchwarmers*. Schneider has appeared in more Adam Sandler movies than anyone else, all of which were some of the biggest films in the past twenty years, including *Grown Ups, The Waterboy, Little Nicky, The Longest Yard, 50 First Dates, I Now Pronounce You Chuck and Larry, You Don't Mess with the Zohan,* and he narrated the animated film *Eight Crazy Nights*. He also recently appeared in Netflix's *The Wrong Missy, Hubie Halloween,* and *Home Team*.

On television Schneider starred in the CBS comedy *Rob* and *Real Rob*. He released his first comedy album, *Registered Offender*, in 2010, and Schneider's Netflix comedy special, *Asian Momma, Mexican Kids*, premiered globally in 2020.